AYAHUASCA

AYAHUASCA

THE VISIONARY AND HEALING POWERS OF THE VINE OF THE SOUL

JOAN PARISI WILCOX

Park Street Press

Rochester, Vermont

Park Street Press
One Park Street
Rochester, Vermont 05767
www.InnerTraditions.com

Park Street Press is a division of Inner Traditions International

Library of Congress Cataloging-in-Publication Data
Wilcox, Joan Parisi.
  Ayahuasca : the visionary and healing powers of the vine of the soul /
Joan Parisi Wilcox.
    p. cm.
  ISBN 0-89281-131-5 (pbk.)
  1. Indians of South America—Peru—Drug use. 2. Ayahuasca
ceremony—Peru. 3. Ayahuasca—Psychotropic effects. 4. Hallucinogenic
drugs and religious experience—Peru. 5. Women shamans—United
States—Biography. 6. Women shamans—Peru—Biography. I. Title.
  F3429.3.D79 W55 2003
  299'.84—dc21
                    2003010986

Printed and bound in the United States at Lake Book Manufacturing, Inc.

10 9 8 7 6 5 4 3 2 1

Text design and layout by Priscilla Baker
This book was typeset in Sabon, with Kabel as the display typeface

Selections of the Wallace Stevens poetry are from *The Collected Poems of Wallace
Stevens* by Wallace Stevens, copyright 1954 by Wallace Stevens and renewed 1982
by Holly Stevens. Used by permission of Alfred A. Knopf, a division of Random
House, Inc.

*To my mother, Victoria, for her indomitable spirit;
and to my husband, John, who brings such magic to my life*

Contents

Part One:
THE BEAUTIFUL STRANGENESS BEGINS

Part Two:
THE MOTHER OF THE VOICE IN THE EAR

Acknowledgments

The personal journey that I share in this book would not have been possible without the support of and inspiration provided by several people, all of whom I would like to thank publicly. Because of the nature of the subject matter, however, most of these people prefer to remain anonymous. So I will call them by the pseudonyms I use for them in the book.

To "Michelle" and "Andrew," thank you for the sincerity of your friendship. To my husband, John, as always, thank you for loving me so well and for supporting my individual path while together we explore a joint one.

To "Jack," my heartfelt appreciation for bearing with me and for providing me with bearings when I most needed them. Thank you, as well, for serving as an expert reader for large portions of this manuscript. To "don Luis," thank you for guiding the journey so well and for your healing songs, which my cells and spirit now sing. To "don Emilio," please accept my gratitude for your generous giving of yourself and for opening my heart so unexpectedly during one of the healing sessions. To "Chico" and "Mateo," and to the others at camp whose names I never learned, thank you for your service.

I would like to honor psychonauts past and present who broke trail through unknown terrain and then boldly showed us the way. Their names are too numerous to list, but I would like to publicly acknowledge at least a few: Carlos Castaneda, Walter Pahnke, Huston Smith, Aldous Huxley, Albert Hofmann, Jonathan Ott, Ralph Meztner, R. Gordon Wasson, Stanislav Grof, Michael Harner, Dennis McKenna, Terence McKenna, Jeremy Narby, Luis Eduardo Luna, and Pablo Amaringo.

Finally, I would like to thank two other "beings": the Mother of All Plants, ayahuasca, for reasons only she knows; and the Amazon jungle, for all of its green gifts to humanity.

Author's Note

Readers should be aware that it is illegal in the United States and many other countries to ingest or in some cases even to possess *ayahuasca*, the psychedelic Amazonian "tea" that is the subject of this book.* My writing about ayahuasca, and my personal experiences with it, are not endorsements for the unsupervised or recreational use of it or any other consciousness-altering substance. Although research has suggested that ayahuasca is biologically safe, especially if one follows traditional dietary restrictions, it can cause psychological and even physical harm if not used properly and with spiritual sobriety. I have experienced ayahuasca only in its sacramental and ceremonial context, under the guidance of a trained Peruvian *ayahuasquero*. I consider my work with ayahuasca to be part of my continuing training in the spiritual arts of Peru and of my personal spiritual journey.

It has only been recently, in the past two decades, that the U.S. government has allowed researchers to once again begin clinical studies with psychedelics such as DMT (dimethyltryptamine) and MDMA, more commonly known as Ecstasy. Indiscriminate and uninformed use of these substances by individuals interested in exploring states of

---

* Actually, the legal status of ayahuasca use in the United States is hard to pin down. DMT (dimethyltryptamine), a component of ayahuasca tea, is a Schedule 1 substance and hence illegal, but the status of the ayahuasca liana is somewhat murky. Since the ayahuasca vine *(Banisteriopsis caapi)* doesn't contain DMT, it is not illegal. But because the tea is brewed with chacruna or other DMT-containing plants, it is illegal. Of late the Federal Drug Administration has been cracking down on shipments of ayahuasca vine, often imported as an herb into the United States, and there are legal challenges here and abroad that should soon define the situation more clearly. As someone speaking and writing publicly about this visionary plant, I choose to take a conservative stance in this issue as a matter of propriety.

consciousness* could jeopardize this opportunity for our society to open a considered, mature debate about the beneficial uses of consciousness-altering substances and to overcome the media-induced myths about their perceived dangers. I urge young psychonauts, whose presence is most evident on the plethora of Internet sites dealing with ayahuasca and other psychoactives, to not repeat the mistakes of their compatriots from the sixties and seventies whose abuse of such substances contributed to the government's decision to criminalize them.

It is my hope that vicariously sharing my experiences with ayahuasca —from the most terrifying to the most sublime—will allow readers to develop respect for the sacramental use of this powerful "plant teacher" in the context of its ancient tradition. Ayahuasca has been in use in the Amazonian regions of South America for thousands of years. Ayahuasqueros passed on, from generation to generation, fairly uniform ways of using this and other plant teachers. There are reasons for the diet retreat, for the darkened conditions, for the sacred songs—for almost every aspect of an ayahuasca ceremony. I believe that we have nothing new to invent or discover about how to use ayahuasca in the most beneficial ways. Both individual psychonauts and medical researchers cast off what they may view as the ritual "trappings" of the ayahuasca ceremony to their own detriment.

---

* Hereafter I use the term "psychonauts" to describe people who are serious explorers of the realms of consciousness through the use of psychoactives.

INTRODUCTION

Exploring Ayahuasca

"I was the world in which I walked, and what I saw / Or heard or felt came not from but myself; / And there I found myself more truly and more strange."[1] These lines from Wallace Stevens's "Tea at the Palaz of Hoon" speak to what I feel as I attempt to write about ayahuasca, the consciousness-altering plant brew of the South American Amazon. Through partaking of ayahuasca, I did indeed find myself "more truly" than ever before and yet "more strange" than I anticipated. So when trying to explain to people what my experiences with ayahuasca were like, I become strangely inarticulate for one who is a writer and editor. At such times I feel tempted to quote Wallace Stevens. For me, many of his lines and stanzas strike to the bone of the ayahuasca experience. Stevens was writing about aesthetics and poetry, language and meaning—subjects that are not entirely foreign to the ayahuasca experience. *Is there any area of inquiry foreign to the ayahuasca experience?* I doubt it. Ayahuasca is not only an experience of body, mind, and spirit but also one of meaning, both epistemological and ontological. It is an experience that transcends its botany and pharmacology, its medicinal and curative tradition, and its Amazonian roots.

Ayahuasca expertly "debones" the mind, perhaps even the spirit, and certainly consensual reality and the contexts of meaning. This bitter jungle brew can saw through the gristle and tendons that hold the meat of who we are—or who we think we are—to the bone of body. It frees us in ways inexplicable to those who have not experienced it. This millennia-old sacrament can expose the marrow of our delusions and

1

our desires, sucking out the stem cells of the I for infusion into a more cosmic Self. It can wickedly trim the fat of our sureties and fillet our beliefs, plopping them matter-of-factly under the see-through wrapping of the Styrofoam tray of our cultural traditions.

But my prose, purple as it is, pales next to Stevens's superbly hued words, which, for me, articulate why it is impossible, really, to describe the ayahuasca experience:

> *Description is revelation. It is not*
> *The thing described, nor false facsimile.*
>
> *It is an artificial thing that exists*
> *In its own seeming, plainly visible,*
>
> *Yet not too closely the double of our lives,*
> *Intenser than any actual life could be*[2]

That last line, "Intenser than any actual life could be," actually does describe ayahuasca. Drinking the brew can blast you off the scale of intensity, which is why it is so important to have an experienced guide nearby.

I emphasize the difficulty of describing the experience of ayahuasca because it is largely beyond the scope of language and needs to be experienced directly for full understanding. The allure of ayahuasca—and perhaps one of the reasons it and synthetic DMT* are growing in popularity—is precisely that it can take you to such intensely strange places within and without, places you ultimately have to go yourself if you want to truly understand what others who have been to similar places are talking about. The descriptions of people's journeys are so incredible that if you have even the slightest tendency toward traveling the inner realms, toward being a psychonaut, you will probably feel compelled to take the trip yourself.

Since it is so difficult to describe the experience of ayahuasca, why

---

* I will discuss DMT, both the natural psychoactive ingredient in the ayahuasca admixture and the synthetic version of it, in more detail in chapter 2.

write a book about it at all? There are already several good compilations of people's ayahuasca journeys from which those who do not plan to take the trip themselves can catch a glimpse of the landscape or which those who are about to head out can use as a guidebook that at least highlights the attractions. There are also many books that serve as educational background reading and that orient us in the ancient traditions of the ayahuasqueros, the healer-shamans of the jungle who are masters of preparing and using ayahuasca. These types of books teach the pharmacology of ayahuasca and its ethnobotanical history. They orient us to the difference between doing psychedelics recreationally and partaking of entheogens (literally, "manifesting the divine within") for spiritual awareness and personal growth.* They raise serious issues about the psychological conditions that affect our experience, especially the importance of "set" and "setting" (personal intention and the environment in which you take the substance, respectively).

This book intends neither of those objectives. If there is an objective beyond being a personal chronicle of my own journey toward, through, and out the other side of ayahuasca, it is this: to instill a respect for using ayahuasca in the way that indigenous peoples have done for millennia. There is a purpose for every aspect of the traditional ayahuasca session, and we would do well to know that tradition and to follow it whenever we can. The problem is that many of the people who log on to chat rooms, post messages to boards on Internet ayahuasca sites, or seek ayahuasca experiences by joining tour groups to South America haven't got a clue that there is a protocol for taking ayahuasca. If they are aware of the procedures, they often do not follow them. Many of the inner explorers who do understand the context of indigenous ritual express the opinion that as ayahuasca use finds its way out of the indigenous Amazonian cultures and into modern Western cultures, we are free to adapt its use in our own way. I take issue with this opinion, for what gets lost in the translation is the reality that for

---

*The term *entheogen* was coined in the 1970s to describe the use of psychedelic substances as a way to access the sacredness of inner realms and to differentiate the recreational or therapeutic uses of such substances from their sacramental use. I briefly discuss these distinctions, and the panoply of terminology for psychedelics, in chapter 2.

indigenous users, ayahuasca, the Mother of All Plants, is a *sentient being* and not just a visionary plant substance. According to ayahuasqueros and indigenous ayahuasca-using cultures, the preparations for undertaking an ayahuasca journey were given to them by the spirit of the plant itself. This kind of at-face-value acceptance of the reality that plants have spirits—and that those spirits can communicate with humans—is foreign to our culture, and yet who are we to think we know better? Our Western hubris, our seeing the world through the lens of our own material-realist belief structure, has been a problem across the board—from missionaries to anthropologists to ethnobotanists—when it comes to our relationship of inquiry to indigenous, and especially shamanic, cultures. And so I urge caution to psychonauts who think they know better than the people who first developed a relationship with this potent visionary plant, this plant *spirit*.

Despite the impressive level of knowledge about the chemistry and preparation of ayahuasca and its analogs by participants on Internet sites and the sincerity of their intent in their use of entheogens, there remains a worrisome level of ignorance about its traditional use. Some of the questions I have seen repeated over and over on Internet sites include the following: What is a typical ayahuasca diet and why should we follow it, whether we are taking ayahuasca in the jungle or in a darkened living room? What is the role of music, especially the sacred *icaros*, in an ayahuasca session? And why won't Enya or Pink Floyd serve as a substitute? More philosophical questions I have extrapolated from my Internet browsing include the following: When does an ayahuasca journey begin—with the swallowing of the brew, or with the personal preparation for the journey (which can start days or even weeks before the actual ingestion of the entheogen)? Where does it end? What can we learn about ourselves, our community or world, and our reality by altering our consciousness? How does ayahuasca reverberate through our lives? Should we even expect it to? Can we trust the visions and insights—or the nightmares—ayahuasca shows us?

Why is it important to offer possible answers to these questions? Because ayahuasca and synthetic DMT—the active ingredient in the ayahuasca brew—are fast becoming the psychedelics of choice for the "underground." Which means they are about to burst through to the surface of our culture. I would hate to see our ignorance about ayahuasca make a fiasco of the use of this soul-inspiring substance, as has happened with other hallucinogenics in the United States. The popular emergence of psychedelics during the 1960s and 1970s resulted in a political backlash and the prohibition of LSD and other substances. Most hallucinogens were banned during this era as Schedule 1 drugs. Consequently, the therapeutic or spiritual use of LSD and other psychedelics was and continues to be lost to the vast majority of citizens and their supporting medical institutions.

I am encouraged that current underground ayahuasca and synthetic-DMT users seem not to be recreational drug users but sincere seekers of the inner spiritual realms. Dr. Rick Strassman, the psychiatrist and clinical researcher who in the early 1990s led the first FDA-approved study of synthetic DMT, calls it the "spirit molecule."[3] I have many reservations about the set and setting of Dr. Strassman's study and his conclusions about the value of entheogens. Nonetheless, it is heartening that there is a revitalization, as lethargic as it is, of research into the possible benefits of consciousness-altering substances. Even more heartening is the resacralization of the Western world by the throngs of spiritual seekers who are dawning a "new old age" through their study of shamanism and other nature-based spiritual pursuits.

I see evidence of a new intensity in the search for meaning, especially in the form of a reaching back to retrieve knowledge from shamanic cultures. More and more of us are abandoning the existentialism of our immediate forebears, rejecting the determinism of evolutionary biology and genetics as they are espoused by mainstream science, and becoming ever more disgusted with the environmentally destructive and soul-deadening effects of our consumer-driven materialism. We are forming an ever more vocal and visible countermovement to the reentrenchment of fundamentalism in its many forms, religious to political. I refer readers to Daniel Pinchbeck's splendid autobiographical book, *Breaking Open the Head: A Psychedelic Journey into the Heart of Contemporary Shamanism,* for a considered account of how psychoactives are playing a part in this re-visioning of who we are and who we want to become. Aspects of my own journey from a skeptical, intellectual rationalist to a spiritual curiosity seeker to an inhabitant of a shamanized universe are mirrored in Pinchbeck's journey. Now that I have had my own head broken open by the Mother of All Plants, I have to admit that all my years of shamanic journeying did not really prepare me for the bizarreness of the other realities I touched through ayahuasca. Like Pinchbeck, now that my head has been sundered, my sureties about who I am and what "it" all means are slipping out like so much gray matter. In the final chapter of this book I attempt a summation of what "it" all means to me, but I must warn readers that my summation is little more than a suturing together of many lines of inquiry and displays no surgical precision of thought.

It is my hope that we can, as a society, grow up enough to treat ayahuasca, synthetic DMT, and other entheogens as doorways to spirit. There seems to be a slow-growing consensus that labeling all psychedelic substances as dangerous is a myopic view that is at the very least naive. Perhaps we as a society are ready to mature in our view of how natural, or synthetic, entheogenic substances might be beneficial in the medical and psychotherapeutic arenas and to our evolution as individuals and societies. But perhaps I am being overly optimistic. In any case, after experiencing ayahuasca myself, reading dozens of books and articles, and browsing on ayahuasca Web sites, I have reached the conclusion that it is time for a nonscientist who has used ayahuasca in the traditional way to describe what it was like and why the rigors of partaking of ayahuasca this way were worth it.

This book is a chronicle of my experience with ayahuasca, supplemented by my subsequent readings in the ayahuasca literature and the input of a few others who consented to share their experiences and insights. In part 1 I describe my introduction to ayahuasca and my subjective reaction to it. I also briefly cover the factual, objective aspects of ayahuasca. I relate my preparation for heading into the jungle to partake of ayahuasca in the traditional way, and some of the strange, even inexplicable events that preceded my journey. In part 2 I discuss the jungle experience itself, covering the diet retreat, my four jungle ayahuasca sessions, and the use of other plant teachers. I have reproduced conversations from my memory, journal notes, and tape recordings. This book is a personal chronicle of what it was like for me to travel deep into the Amazon jungle to meet Mother Ayahuasca on her turf and on her terms. This is what she showed me, and how. This is what I make of it all.

A few final notes before I begin my story: As I have already pointed out, the DMT in the ayahuasca brew is a Schedule 1 substance in the United States—it is illegal to ingest it. Ayahuasca, the vine and the tea, are not illegal in Peru. Still, at the request of my fellow journeyers, I have used pseudonyms for everyone who was on this trip (except for my husband, John), as well as for all the participants I mention (except for my sister-in-law Karla) from other ayahuasca sessions in which I participated. I have also protected their privacy by changing the specifics of their places of residence, professions, and the like. In addition, the names and identifying characteristics of the ayahuasquero with whom I work and his assistant, who is from the United States, have been changed. I call this ayahuasquero don Luis. Don Luis is very private in his work because he does not want his jungle retreat to be inundated with spiritual seekers hunting the ayahuasca experience. As you will read in this book, he believes ayahuasca is for everyone, but he is not in the ayahuasca tourism business. He is a healer foremost, and he wants to keep it that way. For that reason, I have agreed not to reveal any geographical details that could lead someone to his jungle camp. I trust that these omissions will not detract from the tale.

Finally, although I conducted months of research before writing this book, I certainly am no expert on either ayahuasca or the Amazon. As a former academic and a professional writer, I have tried to be a careful researcher and a truthful chronicler of my experience, and I take full responsibility for any factual errors or misinterpretations that may occur in this book.

PART ONE

The Beautiful
Strangeness Begins

1

Meeting Ayahuasca

. . . Beauty is nothing
but the beginning of terror, which we still are just able to endure,
and we are so awed because it serenely disdains
to annihilate us.

—RILKE, *DUINO ELEGIES*

I never thought I would drink ayahuasca. Although I was a teenager during the late 1960s and came of age in the 1970s, I had not participated in the drug culture of that time. Sure, I had tried marijuana a few times while in high school, but I didn't like it. It only put me to sleep, and I never saw its attractions. As for other drugs, especially psychedelics, I simply had no interest in messing with my brain cells. My metaphysical curiosity was well satisfied by my practice of mantra meditation. By the early 1980s I was already married, a four-year veteran of the air force, and immersed in school, having attended college under the old G.I. Bill. I excelled in school and received a master's degree in English from Purdue University in 1986; then I began work on my Ph.D. in modern literature. I completed doctoral course work, but in 1988 I decided to leave academia without that final degree, disillusioned by the academy's publish-or-perish mind-set and disgusted with the state of literary criticism at that time, which was ensnared in the circular reasoning and logical absurdities of deconstruction and other such postmodern philosophies. My husband and I moved back to my home state of Massachusetts, where I worked for two years as a librarian and then left the nine-to-five world to earn my keep as a free-lance writer and editor. By 1993 my husband and I had become immersed in the study of shamanism, especially the Andean spiritual arts. My many trips to Peru and my work with the Q'ero Indians led to the publication of my book *Keepers of the Ancient Knowledge*. Since the mountain spiritual tradition of Peru does not involve the use of consciousness-altering substances, I had no compulsion to experiment with them.

But I had several offers over the years. Peru is a country of spiritual contrasts, and the indigenous spiritual tradition of the Andes region is markedly different from that of the San Pedro-using northern tradi-tion* and the ayahuasca-using Amazonian tradition. Several of my friends from the States had gone into the jungle to experience ayahuasca, and they brought back alluring tales. One told me that everyone had to try ayahuasca at least once in order to get his or her "life message." But I didn't bite.

Interestingly, I was even encouraged—well, "encouraged" may be too emphatic a term—to try ayahuasca by the man who is most respon-sible for making its botanical secrets known to the West, the late Dr. Richard Evans Schultes. I was recently rereading Wade Davis—a former student of Dr. Schultes at Harvard and a terrific writer—and his reminis-cence of a conversation he had with Dr. Schultes about ayahuasca, and it called to mind my own conversation with Dr. Schultes. In his book *One River*, Davis writes that when he went to see Dr. Schultes for advice before his own first, yearlong trip to South America, Schultes told Davis not to return from Colombia without having sampled the Vine of the Soul, which is a literal translation of the Quechua word *ayahuasca*.[1] Davis reports that Dr. Schultes claimed "a power lay within this plant."[2]

Dr. Schultes once made the same suggestion to me. He and I lived in the same town, Melrose, Massachusetts, and he was among the most emi-nent of Melrosians.† I knew of him but had never met him, until one

---

* The San Pedro cactus *(Trichocereus pachanoi)* contains mescaline. It is used especially in the coastal regions of Peru during curing and divination ceremonies.

† Dr. Richard Evans Schultes, known as the father of American ethnobotany, died in 2001.

morning in early 1994. As a freelance writer and editor, I would often walk down the street from where I lived to the Green Street Pharmacy, a tiny nook of a store, where I could make copies cheaply. The copy machine was stationed by the front door, near the pharmacy counter and across from the three rows of shelves that were crammed with everything from zinc throat tablets to crutches to inexpensive, and often yellowing, greeting cards, and I would shoot the breeze with the pharmacist as I ran the pages, one by one, through the copier. One day Dr. Schultes walked in to fill a prescription. The pharmacist knew of my interest in the Andes, that I was soon leaving for my first trip to Peru to walk the Inca Trail into Machu Picchu, and that I studied the spiritual arts of the Q'ero Indians of central Peru, so he introduced me to Dr. Schultes.

I remember Dr. Schultes as tall and lanky, with close-cropped hair, glasses, and the frail look of aging about him. He seemed genuinely interested in my upcoming journey. We talked for the few minutes it took for his prescription to be filled. Mostly he asked me questions, and as he was leaving, he asked if I would have the chance to try ayahuasca while I was in Peru. "No," I replied, "the Q'ero are from the mountains, and they don't work with those kinds of substances." He smiled and said something like, "Well, if you ever get the chance, you should try it. You might find it interesting."

From what I have since read about Professor Schultes from people who knew him well, that kind of understatement was characteristic. And understatement it was. Ayahuasca is certainly "interesting."

Finally, in 2000, I felt ready to take the plunge. I had been doing intense spiritual and energetic work for more than a decade, and I was steadfastly getting to know myself from the inside out. I had lived through adventures in the Andes that were both immeasurably uplifting and downright perilous. While most of my trips there were in some way or another physically and emotionally daunting, one trip in particular had tested the limits of my fear, or perhaps the threshold of my foolhardiness. While on the way to Q'ollorit'i, a sacred Andean festival held at the base of a more than sixteen-thousand-foot-high glacial mountain, my horse slipped into a crevasse. Miraculously, I escaped unharmed, as did the horse. So, although earlier in my life I had been relatively timid, Peru had turned me stouthearted, at least in terms of my physical self.

The decision to finally try ayahuasca, however, raised all kinds of other fears. I had never taken a psychedelic,* so how could I even think of drinking the brew known as "green magic," one of the most potently psychoactive brews known? Would I be able to handle the experience mentally and emotionally? What happened if I had a bad trip? Although at that time I had read only slightly in the literature, I knew that a "good" ayahuasca trip could be excruciatingly intense, so I could not even fathom what a "bad" trip might be like. I was more than a little nervous.

My husband, John, and I had previously received invitations to experience ayahuasca in the United States with people whom we trusted implicitly and under the guidance of a Peruvian ayahuasquero. We were delighted and thought we were ready. My attitude toward consciousness-altering substances had changed over the years, and I could now understand how they could be used to open the inner realms in a sacramental way. Drinking ayahuasca would be another way for me to live the Peruvian spiritual arts, a new way for me to express my spiritual practice. However, John and I apparently had unconscious reservations about actually undergoing the experience, for we found an excuse not to accept the invitation two years in a row.

In 2000 we finally followed through. Why? I cannot explain it, except to note that I had just come through the most emotionally tumultuous three years of my life, a period that I can describe only as a shamanic test or initiation. I had not only survived it but also gone

---

* To be accurate, while I had never taken consciousness-altering substances recreationally, I had taken them three times ceremonially during the course of my shamanic studies. I had partaken of San Pedro during a ceremony in Peru, and I had drunk peyote tea during two different sweat lodge ceremonies with a Diné (Navajo) teacher and friend. With San Pedro I had experienced only the most minor of visual effects, mostly the "energy grid" one sees in the air, and curiously, I had, for the first and only time of my life, incredibly acute night vision. With the peyote tea, I had only felt nauseated and not in the least bit "altered." So I should say that I had never experienced the *effects* of psychedelics before.

deeper than ever before into my interior spaces, and I had learned many useful lessons as a result—especially to trust my knowledge of and capacity to work with energy and to relax into the uncertainties and strangeness of life. I finally felt mature enough, and psychologically and spiritually integrated enough, to peek into the deepest recesses of my being with the help of ayahuasca. Of course, ayahuasca is not about "peeking" at anything, as I would soon discover.

So off we went. The session was held at a remote and verdant rural location in a southeastern state. It felt as if we were in the jungle, far from civilization and completely safe from prying eyes. So, the "setting" was perfect. As for the "set," our personal intentions, John seemed to know what he wanted from the experience—unity consciousness, that is, to see, feel, and connect with the underlying oneness of cosmic consciousness. But I was still unclear about mine. Intentions drifted through my awareness like dust motes, flitting here and there, becoming momentarily framed in the light of knowing and then drifting out of sight. These intentions ranged from the vague (to simply observe my own psyche while under the influence of an entheogen) to the more concrete (to expose and heal any fear I still held or to break through the stubborn barrier of my intellect or to enhance my creativity, especially my writing) to the outright transpersonal (to touch the face of God or to explore my own divinity as part of the interconnected whole).

Physically, we had prepared for the Saturday-night session for days, eliminating meat, fats, sugar, salt, most dairy products, and alcohol from our diets and abstaining from sex. We fasted for most of the day of the session itself. I will talk in part 2 about the ayahuasca diet, but for now all I will say is that this was the protocol required by the ayahuasquero, don Luis, and his U.S. assistant, whom I shall call Jack, and we didn't question it.

On Friday evening, twenty or so invited guests gathered for the talk don Luis gave about ayahuasca, although only nine of us would actually be working with ayahuasca the next night. I was attentive as don Luis performed a healing on one of the women in the audience. I took notes during the talk and paid close attention to don Luis's technique during the healing. Engaging my intellect helped mask my fear about what I might experience the next night during the actual session. But soon my response shifted, from my head to my heart. Don Luis's healing songs—a mix of Spanish and Quechua words and vocables—mesmerized me, moving me into a dreamy sort of state. The sounds and rhythms, complemented by the steady swishing of his *schacapa*-leaf rattle, were sonorous and undulating, and they lulled me to a place within that was unfocused, malleable, less defined by ego. If I had experienced nothing else that weekend, sitting there in the candlelight allowing the flow of don Luis's sounds to wash through me would have been enough. The woman undergoing the healing also seemed entranced by the songs, and she was trembling and clearly moved emotionally as the healing ended.

Saturday we had a light breakfast, then fasted for the rest of the day. John and I were staying in a small guest house on the property, and we spent most of the day alone or visiting with our hosts, a delightful older couple, and with the two friends who had invited us to the session, Michelle and Andrew. By nightfall, nine of us had gathered to participate in the ayahuasca session. It was time. Despite my intention for using ayahuasca sacramentally, I was about to mess with my brain cells. Still, I felt safe. I had connected almost immediately with don Luis and Jack, and all the good things I had heard about them seemed to be evident in our brief initial interactions. My comfort level had risen during the previous night's healing session, which had confirmed for me that don Luis is a man of power, someone I could trust to be my guide during whatever was about to happen.

Don Luis does not speak much English, so Jack translated for him as he talked for a short time about ayahuasca—what it is, how it works, how it is used in the Amazon, and what we could expect during the session and after. I will never forget Jack's explanation that "ayahuasca finds where you are crooked and straightens you." I laughed to myself as the phrase "scared straight" came to mind. As the time to drink approached, however, my apprehension increased, threatening to overtake my newfound confidence.

In addition to don Luis, Jack, and the nine of us who would drink the brew, there were two people who would serve as "sitters." They would stay straight* and help us with anything we needed during the night, such as getting to the bathroom. We each had a small plastic bucket next to us in case we needed to vomit. Ayahuasca is a powerful purgative and is notorious for causing vomiting and diarrhea. It was also reputed to taste nasty. It definitely is not a recreational pursuit.†

The small building we were in had nearly floor-to-ceiling windows on three sides, and the landscape around us was truly breathtaking—a barely pruned tangle of green that was deliciously junglelike, with a wide river behind us. In the large, central room we each nestled into our places, forming a circle on the floor. We had piled mats, sleeping bags, and pillows on the carpet to make reclining beds for ourselves. Jack cautioned us that we should not lie flat but stay in a relatively upright or reclined position. He preferred we keep our spines straight, but he also urged us to be comfortable. We covered ourselves with light blankets. The darkness of the room was punctuated by the wavering glow of a lone candle, which was placed in a brass holder on the floor at the center of the room. The ceremony began about nine o'clock.

Don Luis put on a ceremonial poncho, as did Jack. Then he sat back on his haunches behind his *mesa,* a colorful, handwoven Peruvian cloth on which he had placed the plastic liter bottle of the reddish black ayahuasca brew, his schacapa-leaf rattle, and a few instruments, including a panpipe and a Native American flute.

Don Luis is of the short and stocky stature so typical of indigenous Peruvians, although he is mestizo (of Spanish and Indian descent). He has been working as an ayahuasquero for nearly twenty years. His full-

---

* "Straight" is slang in drug culture and refers to the state of "normal" consciousness as opposed to consciousness that is altered by one's having taken a psychoactive substance.

† As testimony to how unpleasant the taste and the physical experience of ayahuasca are, I offer two comments from the literature, both quoted in Wade Davis's *One River.* William Burroughs wrote that as he swallowed the ayahuasca brew, it had the "bitter foretaste of nausea" (Davis, 155, quoting from *The Yage Letters*). And Tim Plowman, the late ethnobotanist, said about *yagé* (another name for ayahuasca): "*Yagé* is many things, but pleasant isn't one of them" (Davis, 158).

moon shaped face is boyish, and when he smiles, which is often, he appears hardly old enough to be out of college, never mind an experienced healer. Jack, don Luis's assistant and friend, in contrast, is a well-educated American who speaks fluent Spanish. He had been traveling to Peru and studying with healers there for fifteen years. He is a tall man, with a quiet, dignified presence, although his humor is robust and can be disarming. He delivers his usually perceptive, and more often than not ironic, quips with the same quiet, measured cadence as he does all his sentences, and so his humor can catch you off guard. You are expecting another considered remark, and instead your brain finally registers the joke. I came to deeply appreciate Jack's sense of humor during my time in the jungle. And his intellect. He is an experienced psychonaut—a traveler of the inner realms through the use of psychoactive substances—and a gentle, if demanding, guide. He is selective about whom he invites to work with him and don Luis, especially about their psychological stability, and he can be a taskmaster about personal issues and behaviors, particularly integrity, responsibility, and maturity.

Before we drank, we went around the circle speaking our intention for the ayahuasca session. I still had not settled upon a specific intention, and when it was my turn to speak, I spontaneously chose one. "I struggle with getting past my intellect," I said. "So my intention, as a Tibetan friend of mine is always advising me, is to 'drop the mind.'"

After the others had shared their intentions, don Luis began the ceremony proper. He uncapped the bottle of ayahuasca and blew gently across its narrow opening. The soft whistling sounded surreal, both in its pitch and cadence. Don Luis was whistling to ayahuasca, communicating with the spirits of the two main plants in the brew—ayahuasca and *chacruna*—in a low, quiet tune that had an odd staccato edge to it. The series of modulating and soft whistles suddenly dropped an octave and repeated, then raised up half an octave and repeated. Now that I am so familiar with this breathy benediction to ayahuasca, I often find myself whistling it under my breath, and whenever I do, it is almost as if I can taste ayahuasca, which inevitably causes my body to involuntarily shudder in revulsion.

Don Luis then began to sing in barely audible vocables. It was a song of seemingly meaningless sounds and syllables, but it evoked a visceral response in me, drawing me into it physically, emotionally, energetically. He raised the bottle of ayahuasca up and offered it to the four directions. Then he readied the cup to pour. My pulse quickened. It was now or never. I thought for a moment about refusing to partake, but I rejected that thought almost immediately. I was the fourth person to drink.

I went over to don Luis, who was almost directly across the room from me in the circle, and squatted on the carpet before him while he filled a white mug, slightly smaller than a standard coffee mug, about half full with ayahuasca. The pungent, earthy smell assaulted my nostrils as I raised the cup in front of me and connected my energy with the brew by gently blowing on the cup three times, following the tradition of my Q'ero and Andean teachers.* I quickly tipped the cup to my lips and swallowed once, twice. Ugh! I shiver now as I write this. My throat literally contracts at only the memory of that taste. It was vaguely like molasses, only earthier and vegetative. It was sludgy and coated my tongue and throat. I physically shuddered as I returned to my place and quickly sipped some water.

Then I sat back, covered myself with the blanket, pulled my vomit bucket and water bottle close to me, and waited. I closed my eyes and silently repeated a mantra, *Om mani padme hum.* By focusing on the mantra, I was trying to avoid thinking about, or rather feeling, my stomach, which was recoiling from the ayahuasca. I did not want to regurgitate the brew, which would mean I would have to drink again. The objective is to keep ayahuasca down for at least thirty minutes, so it has time to get into your bloodstream and wend its way to your brain. When I was fairly certain I was not going to vomit, I began to

---

* In Andean ceremony, one blows one's finest energies into a sacred object through breath. One does so three times to represent the three worlds (upper world, middle world, and lower world) and the three ways of knowing and being: *llank'ay,* which is the capacity to work and is physical power; *yachay,* which is the intellect and ability to reason; and *munay,* which is love and empathy grounded through will and experience.

silently chant to myself, "I am an open and receptive vessel. Ayahuasca, teach me." Over and over I repeated these lines, this time in an effort to dampen my apprehension. I looked over at John, who was reclining to my right, his eyes closed. I wondered how he was doing. He has a sensitive stomach, and I prayed for him, that he not feel sick and would be able to keep the brew down. By this time, everyone had drunk and returned to his or her place, and the candle flame was extinguished. I closed my eyes and waited, repeating to myself, "I am an open and receptive vessel. I am an open and receptive vessel. Ayahuasca, teach me."

Jack had told us it might take thirty to sixty minutes for us to feel any effects, and though it was difficult to judge time and too dark to see my watch, I sensed that nearly an hour had passed. I was not feeling anything, except the still-bitter aftertaste of the brew. Would the onset of the altered state happen slowly, a lazy transition from this world to whatever realms awaited me? Or would it happen quickly? I didn't know.

Then it happened—with no warning. *Bam!* Reality shifted as if someone had dropped a slide into a projector, and the dark, blank wall of my consciousness suddenly lit up with a scene beyond belief. I was thrust into a reality that was stranger to me than anything I could have imagined. I was overcome with its suddenness, its vividness, its utter alienness. One moment there was darkness, punctuated with the pleasant, flitting colors of the phosphenes one normally sees with closed eyes, and the next was an eruption of carnivalesque color and pattern so intense as to be almost dizzying. I was assaulted with geometry. Looming before me were huge spheres, dense and darkly hued. They formed complex patterns, spinning in ways so intricate I could barely fathom their movements. Their immensity was overwhelming, shocking, even terrifying.

I bolted upright from my reclining position. The eruption of color and movement was so volcanic that a fight-or-flight response gripped me. I could feel my eyes straining behind my closed lids, as if I were trying to open my inner eyes wider to determine if I was really seeing what I was seeing. I actually opened my eyes briefly. The normal world was almost gone, but not quite. What I was seeing behind closed eyelids was what I saw with my eyes open, only it seemed superimposed over the "real" world. Despite being in the grip of total shock and intensifying fear, I was able to grapple intellectually with this split vision. I was not lost to myself. There was some "I" who was perfectly straight and able to observe and reason. This was not a hallucination, which is a mind-created image that completely transfigures and replaces reality. Instead, I felt as if I were seeing two different worlds, both existing independently of me—the normal world of nine people reclining in a darkened room through whose huge windows I could see the palm trees outside, and this weird, almost macabre world of architectonic spheres. I strained to see only one or the other, but my stereoscopic vision refused to coalesce into one, more-sensible world. I was fighting hard to manipulate my vision, straining to gain a measure of control. Fear gripped me more tightly as I closed my eyes again and burrowed back into the cushions. I was more frightened than I had ever been, and although I knew that I would be better off to simply surrender to the ayahuasca-induced reality that dominated both my inner and outer vision, I could not manage to do so.*

The dimensionality of these huge spheres was beyond my comprehension. It is impossible, we are told by scientists and topologists, to truly visualize more than three dimensions, yet the spheres that were rotating before me seemed to be infinitely dimensional. They are simply impossible to describe except in the most anemic of ways. They were nearly monochromatic, and yet were shimmering with color. Browns, olive greens, taupes, blacks, ochers, brick reds, burnt oranges. The color pallet seemed subdued and brilliant at the same time. I have read of others' frustrations at attempting to describe the paradoxes that confront them during a psychedelic experience, and I feel that frustration

---

* Professor Benny Shanon speaks eloquently to the subject of how one must approach fear during an ayahuasca session, especially for those new to the experience. Part of the mastery of ayahuasca, he says, is learning how to control fear. He goes on to outline how fear can be instructive and helpful for working with the visions, aiding the skeptical mind to accept the visions as real and so engage them more deeply. See Benny Shanon, *The Antipodes of the Mind* (Oxford: Oxford University Press, 2002), especially pages 352–53.

now as I write. How can a color be dull and shimmering at the same time? How can a solid be so multidimensional as to be nearly unfathomable and yet be so perfectly comprehensible? How can the same object be so terrifying and yet so sublimely beautiful? There are answers to these questions, but they are beyond the scope of words. They just are, and no amount of linguistic puffery can capture their essences.

What stood out most about the spheres, and what was pushing me into an abyss of awe—and I use the word *awe* in its archaic sense, as a fusion of both beauty and fear—was that they were intensely architectonic and mechanical, and yet they seemed inherently organic and *alive*. I thought they might be the machines of life. I thought of molecules, atoms, and DNA, although the spheres were too close in my field of vision for me to ascertain a laddered spiral pattern. I somehow knew these spheres were at least partly responsible for life, for all that is alive on Earth. I also somehow knew that they were cosmic in scope and origin. They felt intensely alien. Yet I knew they were me, actually *in* me or *of* me at some fundamental level. They were at their core personal and impersonal simultaneously. I was ecstatic and repulsed at the same time, for the spheres' awareness of me was as undeniable as their profound indifference to me. They had no personality, just purpose—some indefinably awesome purpose. That there was no discernable benevolence behind that purpose profoundly distressed me. My ego self wanted more than anything at that moment to feel emotionally connected to them, to know that they cared for me somehow or in some measure. But they did not. Their detachment was absolute. I felt no relief that they—and the spheres were definitely *theys,* not *its*—also exuded no malevolence.

One sphere moved closer into my field of view, dominating it. It was huge beyond imagining, yet I could intuit its entire complex structure: it was made up of thousands, perhaps millions, of tiny rectangles, each connected yet each in individual movement. Each rectangle was at least three-dimensional, and they formed rows and columns that curved around to form the sphere. Each rectangle rotated, some clockwise and some counterclockwise, on the horizontal axis; others flipped end over end on the vertical axis. But each moved in perfect unison with those contiguous to it, so that each column or row was moving harmoniously, effortlessly coordinated into some impossibly intricate organic system.

In addition to the individual rotations of the rectangles and of their unified revolutions as columns and rows around the circumference of the sphere, there was an infinite interaction of the layers. Each sphere comprised layer upon layer upon layer of these rotating, revolving spherical sheets, yet each layer was three-dimensional, or more, and in perfectly coordinated countermotion to all the others.

To confuse and fascinate me even more, each individual rectangle was inscribed on each side with symbols: hieroglyphic-like patterns—of a language just beyond my capacity to understand—entirely covered each side of each rectangle in an orderly, nearly comprehensible way. Each symbol itself was in motion, and each column and row of symbols was in motion on each of the six faces (or more than six faces?) of every rectangle. I felt that I was immersed in this "reality" only a tiny bit, and that to allow myself to dive fully into the experience would be to face death. I thought of a puddle, of dipping the tip of my baby finger into a puddle, barely breaking its surface. If I pushed that finger in any deeper, I would be sucked body and soul into the puddle, never to emerge—at least not sane. Yet, I *wanted* to plunge in. I felt a longing, a compulsion even, to merge with the sphere. I felt that if I could only let go in a deeper way I would understand the symbols. I knew that as organically mechanistic and impersonal as this entire structure was—and as were the uncountable numbers of other spherical constructions that filled my view almost holographically—it was also throbbing with life, with consciousness, but with a profoundly impersonal consciousness. I was aware of what it is like to be nonhuman and yet conscious. The feeling of nonhuman, impersonal sentience was so foreign as to be terrifying, too terrifying for me to take the plunge, and so I resisted allowing myself to merge with it. I willed myself to maintain my separateness from it.

I was awestruck. Overwhelmed. In utter distress as to where from within myself, or from without myself, these structures (beings?) had emerged. They could not possibly have arisen from my own imagination, of that I was sure. If there is one intellectual or perceptual area where I lack talent, it is in spatial reasoning and imagination. My husband has always kidded me about how poorly I visualize spatial relationships and how I have next to no sense of direction. And what I was experiencing—not just seeing—now was not about spatiality or even dimensionality at all. It was about beingness. As the reality of the spheres' deeply mechanistic makeup and their simultaneously profoundly impersonal consciousness swept through every fiber of my being, I panicked and began to bargain with God.

"Oh, please, let this be over. I know it's only the plant, and it will wear off, but *please* let this stop *now*. I promise I will never drink ayahuasca again. *Please make this stop!* I'll never do this again. Please. Please. *Please!*"

But it did not stop. My fear was not lifted from me. Instead, the experience became increasingly unfathomable—and yet perfectly comprehensible. I had no concept of time. Ten minutes could have passed or ten hours. Although I remember the spheres in intimate detail, the rest of my experience is a blur punctuated with periods of intense memory and gaps where I was beyond myself to the point of no-self.*

Vaguely, through the engulfing fog of my fear, I became aware of song. It was don Luis, singing an icaro, a sacred song that ayahuasqueros uniformly claim is taught to them by the spirits of the plants themselves. The song seemed to be probing into the darkness of my fear like a comforting beam of light, offering me hope of rescue, or at least of respite.

---

* Some people have asked me how I remember my ayahuasca journeys so vividly. My reply is twofold: (1) what I remember was so vivid and surprising and alien to me that I think I will never forget it, and (2) I don't actually remember much. What I have managed to record in this book are only snippets of journeys that each lasted from three to four hours on average. Most of the content of these journeys is lost to my conscious memory. Even within journeys, there were stretches where I seemed to be nonconscious. That is, I only knew I had been "somewhere else" when I "came back," such as one might feel when one has been in the "gap" in meditation and then returns to the observing mind. What I have been able to reproduce for you here are the portions of the journeys I remember and that I recorded in my journal or into a tape recorder soon after regaining "normal" consciousness.

Don Luis sings in a mixture of Spanish and Quechua, and this song was mostly Quechua. I recognized some of the words, which helped pull me back into myself and away from the alien spheres. Each word became a stepping-stone along which I could negotiate myself back across the river of unreality toward the safe shores of the known: *Mamacuna,* a Quechua word meaning something like "honored mother," and historically the name for the female Inca elders who supervised the virgins of the Temple of the Sun. *Chuya,* a Quechua word meaning "clean," or, as the Q'ero use it in their spiritual lexicon, to be spiritually and energetically cleansed. *Sachamama* and *Yacumama,* respectively the sacred serpent of the forest (literally, "Forest Mother") and the sacred anaconda of the jungle (literally, "River Mother").

As the icaro suffused my being, I watched the alien, organic, mechanistic spheres morph into abstract shapes and then become identifiable images. The colors brightened into luminescent pinks, blues, greens, and golds. Intricate geometric patterns, Byzantine in nature, undulated across a field of glowing blackness until a temple appeared to my inner eyes—an ancient stepped pyramid that seemed, for some reason, Indonesian. It looked Mayan or Aztec, but it *felt* Indonesian. Soon the figure of a woman seeped into being, a blur of color that took human form. She, too, seemed Indonesian, with a figure like a prehistoric goddess totem, rotund at the top and tapering down to pointed legs and feet. She climbed the steps of the tiered temple and danced on its uppermost platform in a gorgeous shimmering of silver. She moved sensuously yet determinedly, in an odd blending of spontaneous abandon and ritualistic choreography. She was completely immersed in her dance, seemingly unaware of me, or at least indifferent to me, although I was sure that she was aware that I was watching her. There was something severe in the intensity and seriousness with which she moved; her hands and fingers especially moved in fluid but taut arcs as she spiraled her arms around her head and body in serpentine fashion.

She captivated my vision, but my hearing was engrossed in an entirely different and totally autonomous activity. While I watched the dancer, I was also hearing—and participating in—multiple narratives: I was listening to myself talk to myself, and talk to the universe, which was talking to me while I talked to myself and to it, while I talked with ayahuasca, who was talking to the universe and to me while I was talking to myself and to the universe and to ayahuasca. I don't remember the content of the conversations; some rational "I" was more an eavesdropper, marveling at myself as I participated in multiple simultaneous conversations.

The visuals melted again, seeping away and re-forming into almost pure feeling. I was suddenly overcome by the urge to yawn, and I did repeatedly—long, deep, nearly jaw-unhinging yawns. (I noticed throughout the night that others did the same, and I have since learned that ayahuasca can stimulate the yawning reflex.) I became aware again of sound. Jack was standing in the middle of the room using a bull-roarer to make a low-pitched, humming, windlike noise. A red haze began to fill my inner vision, and I felt my attention focus in sharply, on high alert. I felt something ominous arising, like a storm brewing at a distance, and I instinctively knew I needed to take shelter. But where? How? I could not stop the spreading redness, which was backlighting my consciousness like a red sun shining through black tissue paper. My fear heightened, and it was attached to the expanding and deepening red glow. I was afraid I was going to be smothered by the redness. Instinctively, I sought out don Luis and Jack, who was still spinning the bullroarer in the center of the room. I could see their dark silhouettes, and I suddenly noticed a glowing, white-light cord stretched between me and don Luis, a luminescent lifeline of sorts, or an energetic umbilical cord. I grabbed hold and hoisted myself up it, hand over hand, one agonizing pull at a time. Soon I was close to don Luis, and I felt safe. I stayed there for some time, trying to get my bearings. I realized I was holding my breath, and I consciously willed myself to breathe. Soon I felt calmer, and I knew I had to make the most of this opportunity—I had to engage the experience and not flee from it. I had to observe but not become attached. I forced myself to begin backtracking down the energetic lifeline, reeling myself back out into the ayahuasca journey.

The red glow remained, blanketing me. Suddenly I had the mental image of the basement of my childhood home. Something awful was lurking there. In actuality, there is nothing menacing about this basement: it is large and completely finished, with four rooms, the central one fully furnished. But now it felt menacing. I sensed myself as a child and I also sensed a male presence, which I vaguely identified with my father, who died more than a dozen years ago. Suddenly I felt nauseated. I needed the bucket in case I vomited, but I could not move. My attention was riveted to the image of the basement and the uncertain sense of my deceased father, and a growing dread. "What is this?" I heard my inner voice pleading for answers. "What are you trying to show me? Show me! I can take it. I want to see!"

I sensed that ayahuasca was hinting at some repressed memory, but it was also toying with me, teasing me with feelings of unnameable dread, guilt, and pain. Curiously, I was aware that I was totally okay, that I was completely rational and all my logical faculties were functioning even though I was heavily "dreaming."* A struggle ensued between the straight me and the altered me. The straight me began to follow the thread of reason while the altered me urged my intellect to mind its own business and let the vision coalesce. The straight me won out, and I began an attempt to trace a series of logical connections between my feelings and the images. Because there was a vague sexual feeling around the image of the basement and the sense of my father's presence, I immediately thought *incest*. But as soon as that thought arose, I realized how preposterous it was. My father did not molest me. But I could not shake that thought free. What else made sense of the terms: father, sexuality, basement, fear, pain, guilt? The red glow intensified, as did my feeling of nausea. I pleaded silently with ayahuasca: "Please, I'm ready. I'm willing. Whatever memory it is I am resisting,

---

* Various terms are used to describe the state one is in while working with ayahuasca, including dreaming, tripping, journeying, flying, shining. In some parts of the Amazon, ayahuasqueros are deemed "bird shamans" because of their ability to take spirit flights while under the influence of ayahuasca.

help me to overcome that resistance and see. I'd rather know than not know." The wave of nausea rose full bore, and I erratically reached for the bucket—coordination can be a problem under ayahuasca—and purged into it in gut-wrenching releases. I felt the dread washing out of me, although because I had fasted there was not much of anything material to be expelled. Spent, I laid back on the cushions, confused and embarrassed. I was the first person in the group to purge. I looked around, but I could barely see the group through the vibrating grid of luminescent colors that overlaid the room. I thought, "This is how the world looks as pure energy."

The red glow had diminished, although it was not gone. I allowed myself to become more aware of it, to be attentive to it. I thought of the parable of Plato's Cave, how all we can see of reality is the shadow cast by the fire onto the cave wall. I also understood the red light as a male manifestation of ayahuasca. I knew this was "Red Ayahuasca" and that it was an unsympathetic taskmaster, perhaps even a trickster. I asked again, this time feebly but still sincerely, "*Please,* show me what this is about. What is frightening me so?" But the red continued to fade, and a riot of color replaced it. I surrendered, allowing a kaleidoscope of color and imagery to blot out my thoughts and feelings. A huge snake appeared, dark but vibrant blue, almost indigo. It seemed much larger than I, although I could see it in its entirety. It undulated up out of the darkness, arching toward me, facing me head-on. Intricate patterns cascaded down its back in shimmering pink, green, yellow, and sky blue. The patterns were three-dimensional, and they brought to mind curving ropes of frosting that ornament large, chocolate Easter eggs. The snake just stared, alive and conscious but not wanting anything from me. There was just pure "snakeness" hovering before me. I cannot remember exactly what happened next, but at some point the snake, at least energetically, entered my mouth and slid down my throat. I vaguely remember the odd sensation of its slithering along my spine.

The next thing I knew I was zooming out into the cosmos, into an infinite black expanse alive with dots of golden-white energy, which I took to be distant stars. I turned, looked down, and was startled to see the sphere of Earth hanging below me in the heavens. It was small and lovely, and it seemed to be breathing. I was enveloped in a surge of electric awe and incredulity at the authenticity of my perspective. I turned back toward the dazzlingly dark expanse behind and above me and suddenly I was swept out into it, moving at a tremendous speed. The exhilarating freedom, the raw power of unrestricted motion, was overwhelming. It was all so *real*.

However, this magnificent vision was about to become a cartoon.

I slowed and then stopped next to a swirling spiral galaxy, its arms of stars bright fire in the cold expanse of the vacuum. Suddenly "God" appeared to my left. Only it was not the God of my childhood Catholic Sunday school classes. This was a huge, potbellied man, of unidentifiable race, naked except for a Speedo swimsuit. He was sitting in a wood-and-canvas director's chair, floating in the chair in the middle of the cosmos, with a beer in his right hand. It is an understatement to say I was startled. But he was so real. He was flesh and blood. I could see the pores of his skin. I could see the condensation on the beer bottle (which, being dark brown, reminded me of a tall Budweiser!). He laughed a deep, baritone laugh and pointed to a spiraling galaxy. *Play!* he bellowed, laughing once again. *Play!* I could only look at him dumbfounded, in disbelief. *I have been creating for aeons,* he bellowed. *Go ahead and play! Create! It is all yours! Play! Play! Play!* I knew at that instant that I could dive into the matter, information, and energy of the cosmos and begin creating anything I wanted. But I couldn't move. I was paralyzed, stupefied. I don't remember what happened next.

The next thing I knew, I was lying back on my mat, nestled into the cushions and tugging the blanket up over me, the command "Play!" reverberating through my being. My straight self was shaking its head, exclaiming, "God, sitting at the edge of the cosmos! Like a day at the beach, creating the world. In that ridiculous swimsuit, and with a beer in his hand no less!" My altered self was giddy with delight, certain that it had just been given a chance to be the cocreator it obviously is, but only slightly disappointed that it had declined the offer.

Don Luis's music pulled me back into pure color and pattern. He was playing the panpipes, and the notes seemed to attach themselves to me, briefly ground me, and then pull me toward him and Jack. I drew closer and closer, and suddenly there was no boundary between us. I was don Luis and he was me. I was playing that flute, leading the session, at one with Mother Ayahuasca and at one with everyone. The connection was exquisite, and I remained there completely content at the same time that I was me, separate and in awe of the me that had coalesced into don Luis. Then slowly, gently, the music drew me back out of the oneness and into my personal journey again. I became aware for the first time of how integral the icaros—and sound in general—are to the unfolding of an ayahuasca journey.

As I listened, my mood changed, abruptly. Something, I'm not sure what, was uproariously funny. I laughed, almost in spite of myself. Then again. I became aware that someone else was laughing—my friend Michelle, who was lying two places down to my left. I heard her girlish giggle, then a hearty, full-throated laugh. Suddenly I was somewhere in the ether with her, hovering in the air above the others in the circle, and we were sharing a hilarious cosmic secret. We two knew that "it" was all a grand joke, and that we are all fools for taking "it" so seriously. I could not put a name to the pronoun, but "it" was all so obvious "it" needed no explaining. We laughed aloud together, unselfconsciously, not caring if we were disturbing anyone in the room. "It" was all way too funny for us to try to suppress our laughter. And then, almost as suddenly as our shared mirth had started, it was over. Michelle stopped laughing simultaneously with me, on cue, as if our emotional circuits had been synchronized.

I was reclining into the cushions with a smile on my face when the red glow reappeared, creeping in from the "lower left" of my being. The color seemed situated spatially within me, and the feeling of dread grew as the color intensified. Red Ayahuasca was back. The basement, the male figure (my father? I couldn't quite pin down who this person was), the sexual undertones, the fear, a sinking feeling of hopelessness, a suffocating dread. I pleaded with Mother Ayahuasca: "Show me what this means. Help me understand. I can take it. What could have been so terrible that I've completely repressed it? Help me to know. *I'm ready.* I don't want to keep this hidden. *Help me!*"

I heard a voice. Not my own inner voice, but a voice attached to an intelligence separate from myself, autonomous and unemotional. *This is yours and not yours.*

What did that mean?

I heard it again, this time more emphatically. *This is yours and not yours.* Abruptly it occurred to me that I might be psychically picking up an energy or memory from someone else in the group. I pounced on this idea, relief flooding through me, momentarily replacing my fear. "Maybe whatever it is, it didn't happen to me! It happened to someone else here!" Energetically, I began to go around the circle, connecting myself psychically with each person. When I got around to a man sitting on the other side of the room to my left, I felt it—an attachment. "This is his! It isn't mine! *It's his!*" I was flooded with relief, feeling like an animal who had narrowly escaped a hunter's trap. But my relief was short-lived.

The disembodied voice asserted itself. *Not so easy!*

What was that supposed to mean? But I knew what it meant. I was not going to be allowed to give this away, whatever "this" was. Yet, I was now sure that whatever this vision meant, whatever the feelings were intimating, they were not entirely personal.

The voice confirmed this: *This is yours and not yours.*

The fear was back full bore as the redness engulfed me. A wave of nausea arose. I reached for the bucket and purged.

Events become confused again. I remember taking a sip of water, and opening my eyes wide, as if to ground myself, as if to prove to myself in my growing panic that the "real" world existed. I could see the darkened room and make out the people in it, but everything was pulsating with a colorful grid of energy. Everything was vibrating, and I heard a voice, different from the previous one, say something like, *Why are you opening your eyes? The world you see with your eyes open is the illusion. Close your eyes and see the world that* really *is.*

I closed my eyes, and the redness was still there but began dissipating again, being slowly replaced by a soft, glowing whiteness. Not light, but color. A kind of white energy. I saw an old woman, and I instantly understood that this was "White Ayahuasca," and she was female— Grandmother Ayahuasca. The white field of vibrating color emitted a calming sweetness, a feeling that quickly formed itself into myriad white flowers, tiny calla lilies. Like a watermark, the image of the ancient, humpbacked indigenous woman, Grandmother Ayahuasca/ White Ayahuasca, was visible just beneath the overspreading blanket of lilies. She and I spent time together; she talked with me, but I do not remember our conversation.

Soon the redness returned. I cringed and swore. "Shit! Red Ayahuasca is back!" This time I felt up for a fight. The by now familiar inner scenario unfolded—the basement, a male presence, sexual feelings, guilt, shame, fear, despair. I heard the disembodied voice again, *This is yours and not yours.* I was getting angry: "Show me!" I demanded. "If this is something I need to retrieve and cleanse within myself, then let's do it! *Let's do it now!*"

Almost at once, I was drawn up into the cosmos. This startled me. Why wasn't I headed down into that basement? Unexpectedly, I was flying upward, higher and higher, the sensation of acceleration making me almost breathless. Then I slowed, and stopped. My eyes were drawn downward, and I once again saw the earth spinning slowly below me. My vision became telescopic. A beam of energy drew my attention down toward the surface of Earth, zeroing in first at one place, then at another on the other side of the globe, here, then there. What I saw were prison cells, darkened subterranean rooms, tiny closetlike cement spaces, thick plank doors with metal latches and locks. All the cells or rooms were empty. But echoing within each one was a ghostly moaning, a soul-sinking anguish. I understood at once: it was the resonance of the wound of womanhood. It was as if an archetypal force, or memory, were releasing itself like steam escaping from vents scattered around the world, each discharging the despair and suffering of women who had been abused for nothing more than their gender or their beliefs, or who had been made to suffer because of their "place"—their perceived lack of value—within the patriarchy. An empathetic, agonized, energetic wail poured forth from every cell of my being and reverberated throughout the cosmos. I vomited, for the third and final time.

I have no idea how long I suffered in the red-hued vision; how far my inner wail echoed through time; how long my head hung limp over the bucket, my mouth open and my eyes closed. But at some point I "woke up" to find myself sitting up, my back straight, my legs crossed, my hands resting on my knees with my palms facing upward—the classic posture of receiving. Don Luis was standing over me playing the Native American flute. I raised my face toward him and let the sound sweep over and through me. The tremulous notes of the flute were soft, womanly, almost motherly. As a honey-colored stream, they flowed into me through the crown of my head and drifted purposefully through spaces within me too small to be perceived but of sufficient quantity to be acknowledged. I felt cleansed, renewed. Mentally and energetically I thanked don Luis for being there for me at precisely the right moment. He played for a few minutes more, then moved on to another person, and once more I relaxed back into the cushions.

I remember only one more vision from this long night. At one point my inner vision was filled abruptly by a hawk. It was so close I could see each reddish feather individually. It seemed to be tightly encased in a wooden box, and it began thrashing wildly, its wings striking the confining sides of the box. It dawned on me that this was my mother! This was a symbolic image of my mother! She had survived an inordinately cruel and abusive childhood and had grown into a remarkable woman who embraces the world with love. She is an exceptional nurturer to me and my six brothers and sisters, and I consider her not only my beloved parent but also one of my closest friends. Yet now I was seeing the anger, the rage she had perhaps unconsciously thrust deep down into the recesses of her being in order to survive. I immediately reached out in love and began to "heal" her. Despite my long shamanic practice, I have never considered myself a healer in the traditional sense of healing physical or psychological illness. But now I knew I was not only capable of healing but also obligated to. So I began to soothe her energetically, to comfort her, to "digest" her heavy energy, as I have been taught to do in my Andean spiritual practice. Just as I began the healing, don Luis began to make bird calls from across the room. They were trills, chirrups, and whistles of pure innocence. Overwhelmed with gratitude, I allowed the bird calls to permeate every pore of my being as I continued working on my mother in the guise of this hawk. Then I "saw" don Luis there with me, assisting. He was sweeping his schacapa-leaf rattle over the hawk's body as I worked energetically. The hawk became quieter, more trusting, allowing us to work. I do not know how long the healing went on, but when I felt done, I stopped, and at precisely that moment, the image of don Luis disappeared and the bird calls ceased.

The bird calls were not part of my vision; don Luis actually had been making them, and I still marvel at the synchronicity of it all. Now that I have participated in six ayahuasca sessions with don Luis, I know that he is "there" for everyone individually, somehow in each person's trip simultaneously, guiding each of us as we need to be guided, assisting each of us as we need to be assisted. That night, during my first ayahuasca session, I had opened my eyes once to see him as the vine. He *physically* was the ayahuasca liana, a thick, twisting rope of vine somehow made human. Later, when I talked with others who had participated in the session that night, a few reported the same vision upon opening their eyes and looking at don Luis. That night I learned to trust don Luis implicitly.

The session ended approximately four hours after it started, the closing marked by the lighting of the candle. Most of us remained in our places, groggy and still deep into our own interior spaces. But I was awake, mentally energized, and I wanted to talk! My body was another story. I could not move with any measure of real coordination. I stumbled to the bathroom, and when I reentered the main room, the candle had gone out. I have poor night vision, and I could not orient myself to my place in the circle. I stumbled across the room, crashing into the brass candleholder (the only object in the circle, which proves, once again, the truth of Murphy's Law), and finally got down on all fours and crawled toward what I thought was my place. I worried I was going to end up in the lap of the man who had been lying to my left. I softly called out for John, who had been immediately to my right in the circle, but he did not hear me. So I steered across the circle roughly toward where I thought I should be, and I ended up grabbing someone's feet. Thankfully, they were John's.

He was stilled zoned out, but he asked me how it went. "It was terrifying. It was so alien. I promise to God I'll never do that again! It was *overwhelming*. It scared the shit out of me! I'll *never* do it again!" John sort of laughed as I continued my hyperbolic banter. Finally, I asked how his journey had gone. The candle had been lit again, so I could see his face. He smiled a dreamy, rather goofy-looking smile, and sighed. "It was blissful. I felt unconditional love. I was connected to the universe in every way. It was beautiful."

We talked for a while longer, but I could tell he wanted to sleep, or simply be left alone. Almost everyone in the room was curled up in place, sleeping. But I was wired. Jack came over. He was making a quiet circuit of the room, checking in on whoever was still awake. He asked me how it went.

"It was *overwhelming! Unbelievable!*" I said, as melodramatic as ever, although I was speaking exactly what I felt. "I was *so* scared at points. So much of it was so, so—" I struggled to find the word. "*Alien*. It wasn't me. I don't know what it was, or where some of it came from. All I know is I'll never do this again. *Ever!*" Jack graciously listened until I was spent of words.

"It sounds like you had an unusually intense experience for the first time," he replied in his characteristic matter-of-fact, soft-spoken way. "You never know. Some people get really high, and others don't feel a thing." He mentioned the name of the man who had been lying next to me in the circle but was now gone. Jack had apparently already checked in with him. "It was his first time, too," he said, "but he didn't feel or see much of anything. A few initial fireworks, some colors, and then nothing."

I could not believe that. We had all taken pretty much the same dose. I could not fathom how anyone could have had a wimpy experience, even factoring in how the amount of brew we each had drunk could have been affected by our body mass.

"You seem completely sober now," Jack remarked. "You're all right?"

"Yes," I replied. "But I'll *never* do this again." I paused. Then I expelled another rush of words. "Of course, in time, as the experience fades and as I have time to process, I *might* want to try it again. In fact, I probably *will* do it again, because I know I'll have to have a comparative experience. I'll *need* a comparative experience—to see if this session was an anomaly for me, or if they'll *all* be like this for me."

Jack laughed. "Joan," he said, "you just set a record. Usually people who have such an intense first experience say just the same thing, 'I'll never do this again.' Then, months later, or maybe even years later, they decide, 'Well, okay, maybe I'll consider it.' And then, eventually, some decide that they will do it again. You just went through that process in fifteen seconds. That's a record!"

I did drink ayahuasca again—the first chance I had to do so with don Luis and Jack, which was a little more than a year later.

2

Greater Than the Sum of the Parts

Things are not only truly real, or only mere illusions. There are many categories in between, where things exist: many categories of the real, simultaneously and in different times.

—César Calvo, *The Three Halves of Ino Moxo*

Having just read a subjective account of the effects of ayahuasca, you are no doubt curious about the specifics of the brew that precipitated such a wild trip. But before I discuss the ayahuasca liana or the tea that is made from it and other admixture plants, and before I provide an overview of its pharmacology, I feel it is wise for us to consider some larger, more philosophical issues. First, neither our experience of ayahuasca nor our exhaustive cataloging of knowledge about it qualifies us to enter the "world of ayahuasca." Ayahuasca is utterly foreign to our culture. No matter how untainted by Western influence or modern adaptation our ceremonial experience of ayahuasca might be, we can never really know it in the same way that a native of an ayahuasca-using culture does. There is simply no way for us to fully enter into the language, thought processes, and ways of knowing and being of these cultures, so our experience of ayahuasca must always be fundamentally different. If you will not grant me that our *experience* must of necessity be different—for it is true that many of the visuals people report while under the influence of ayahuasca are consistent across cultures—then surely you will allow that our *understanding* is different.

My point is beautifully articulated in a conversation reported between two ethnobotanists. Wade Davis, in his book *One River,* relates an exchange between him and Tim Plowman, the late ethnobotanist, that gets to the heart of the dilemma of cross-cultural experience. As Davis and Plowman finalized their preparations to journey to the villages of the Elder Brothers, the Kogi of Colombia, they surveyed the rundown mestizo village before them and marveled at the obstacles that awaited them (the "I" of the first speaker is Davis).

"It's hard to believe the Tairona were once here," I said.

"I know," Tim replied. "You think of this town and then try to imagine priests in cloaks woven with gold and jewels, feathered headdresses. Beautiful fields of plants." He stopped eating, looked to the sea, and then turned back to me. "I'd like to know more about them—how they lived, what they thought. Have you ever paid attention to language?"

"In what way?" I asked.

"The choice of words. What they mean. There's a tribe in Uruguay, one of the Guaraní groups, whose word for soul was 'the sun that lies within.' They called a friend 'one's other heart.' To forgive was the same word as to forget. They had no writing, and when they first saw paper, they called it the skin of God—just because you could send messages."

"Like magic."

"It was magic," Tim said. "Did Schultes ever tell you about the Indians in the Amazon who couldn't tell blue from green? I forget the tribe. I asked him whether they saw the same color or whether they considered the two colors to be one."

"What did he say?" I asked.

"He didn't know. I don't think he every really thought about it."

"But you have," I said. Tim laughed.

"Reichel talks about all this. In one of his books he says the

Tairona believed that gold was the blood of the Great Mother. He says the Kogi word for vagina is the word for dawn. Can you imagine what it means for a people to have such thoughts?"

"No," I said.

"I can't, either."[1]

Like Davis and Plowman struggling to find a linguistic, and ultimately an epistemological, toehold in an unfamiliar culture, we also struggle with our language choices when discussing ayahuasca and other consciousness-altering substances. Almost every researcher and writer on the subject has had to clearly define his or her terms, because the terms define that researcher's or writer's bias toward the subject. Ram Dass, the former academic and consciousness researcher turned spiritual teacher, has written of this dilemma:

The Mexican Curanderos labeled it [the psilocybin mushrooms they use in ceremony] *Teonanactyl* [*sic*]—the flesh of the Gods—useful for divinatory and mystical experience. Humphrey [*sic*] Osmond made the labeling a little more palatable for the Western mind by inventing the word *psychedelic,* meaning "mind manifesting." The psychiatric community's label of the same mushroom was "a psychotomimetic tryptomine [*sic*] derivative," of interest only for the experimental induction of pseudoschizophrenic states. Using one labeling system, we were explorers into the mystical realms tried by Moses, Mohammed, Christ and Buddha. According to the other, we were damned fools, driving ourselves insane.[2]

When dealing with psychoactive substances, language reveals one's ideological bent toward their use and purpose. A most blatant example is the difference between lumping all natural psychoactives into a category called "drugs" or allowing that some may be "plant teachers." Our language choices are numerous, but some of the most commonly used terms within the literature include *hallucinogen* (producing hallucinations or vision inducing, and implying that what is seen is not real), *psychedelic* (mind, soul, or psyche manifesting), *psychotomimetic* (mimicking psychosis), and *entheogen* (manifesting the divine within or generating the god within). I use several of these terms throughout this book, choosing according to the context within which the term is used. However, the term *entheogen* best expresses my belief that such substances, under the proper set and setting, help us to reach beyond the boundaries of body-mind to touch the numinous, the sacred, the interconnectedness of life. (And, since there is an inherent ambiguity, I believe that in the use of psychoactives we are also likely to touch the underbelly of the sacred, which is chthonic, dark, entropic, sinister, and destructive.)

I have so far outlined only the linguistic dilemma for Westerners. We must now factor in the nuances of the names indigenous peoples give to such plants and substances. We can glimpse some of ayahuasca's "secrets" by pondering the translation (which itself adds to the problem) of several of the evocative names it has been given by the more than seventy tribes where its use has been documented: Vine of the Soul, Rope of the Soul, Vine of the Dead, the Little Death, Vine of the Spirits, Vine of Gold, Vision Vine, Vine of Lightness, Green Magic, Mother of the Voice in the Ear.* To an Amazonian ayahuasquero—who may partake of the brew to heal psychological or physical illness, protect the village from enemies, predict the outcome of a battle, counter acts of sorcery, call in needed rain, or accomplish other mundane or metaphysical goals—to partake of ayahuasca may be a "jaguar-becoming" or a journey into the "shining."[3]

These journeys to alternative realities are both risky and revelatory, and one must be carefully trained to undertake them. In these cultures, which we deem "primitive" (meaning unscientific at best and downright backward and savage at worst), nearly everything in nature is

---

* A sampling of some of the more than forty names for ayahuasca, in the languages of different indigenous groups, follows: *yagé* (especially in Colombia), *datém* (Cayapa), *natema* (Jivaro), *caapi* (especially in Brazil), *inde huasca* (Ingano), *kamalampi* (Piro), *nixi* (Makuna), *mi-hi* (Kubeo), *nepi* (Colorado).

alive and conscious, and nature and other spirit beings can both help and harm humankind. In these cultures, humans for the most part are not outside the great Web of Being but are inextricably part of it. Nature has provided these cultures "plant teachers" who share information and energy with them, usually on behalf of their general well-being. Moreover, indigenous peoples generally do not seek philosophical answers in the same way that we do. Ayahuasca works for them—it helps them solve problems, restore health, foster greater social cohesion—and they are not interested in deciphering its metaphysical mysteries.

> Ayawaskha, for us, is not fugitive pleasure, venture, or seedless adventure, as it is for the virakocha [whites]. Ayawaskha is a gateway—not for escape but for eternity. It allows us to enter those worlds, to live at the same time in this and in other realities, to traverse the endless, unmeasurable provinces of the night.
>
> That is why the light of oni xuma [ayahuasca] is black. It doesn't explain. It doesn't reveal. Instead of uncovering mysteries, it respects them. It makes them more and more mysterious, more fertile and prodigal. Oni xuma irrigates the unknown territory: that is its way of shedding light.[4]

Our culture has a difficult, if not impossible, time accepting that indigenous peoples are not talking about ayahuasca in metaphor. Without getting into a structuralist debate, it is fair to say, I believe, that for indigenous people there is no subject-object dichotomy, no distinction between the name of the object and the object itself. Carol Cumes says of the Quechua language, the major indigenous language of Peru, especially of the Andean region, that it "implies an understanding of the deep texture of things. In [Quechua] there are no words that imply doubt such as 'perhaps' or 'maybe.' Each word expresses a definitive vision of reality."[5]

This is the epistemological, and even ontological, conundrum anthropologist Jeremy Narby overcame in his own immersion into an ayahuasca-using culture. He, like many other anthropologists and scholars, could not understand how the indigenous tribe he was living with and observing (the Ashaninca of Peru) could have arrived at their extensive knowledge of plant chemistry and healing through trial and error. When I discuss the pharmacology of the ayahuasca brew later in this chapter, you may feel something of the same wonder that Narby and others have felt when confronted with the natives' sophisticated plant knowledge. Narby finally realized that the only way he could make sense of his data was to take the natives at their literal word when they told him that the plants themselves were teaching them. As he doggedly followed the implications of this hypothesis, he came to believe that ayahuasca, and DMT in particular, may be working at the quantum level of our brains, allowing us to access information coded at the level of DNA.[6]

These ideas are difficult for us to even entertain, never mind accept. Our culture vilifies animistic beliefs and historically has deemed mentally ill anyone who claims to access other realms of reality. We cannot even resist labeling those who practice nature-based religions, calling them witches or, more insidious still, Satanists. Our Judeo-Christian heritage has instilled in us not only the fear of God but also the fear of anything metaphysical. In the sixteenth century, clerics and conquistadors, encountering South American shamans and their use of consciousness-altering substances such as ayahuasca for the first time, condemned such practices as the work of the devil. In more modern times, academics deemed such shamans schizophrenic or psychotic. Our culture's name for the strange and unknown changes with the times and according to the parameters of our consensual reality.* Today we have grown so averse to exploring the content of our own minds, let alone the vastness of consciousness, that we have declared illegal natural substances that help us to do so, even those, such as DMT, that our own bodies manufacture.

---

* For a succinct but coherent historical overview of the changing attitudes toward shamans, see Jeremy Narby and Francis Huxley, eds., *Shamans Through Time: Five Hundred Years on the Path to Knowledge* (New York: Jeremy P. Tarcher, 2001).

The problem certainly has been compounded by the materialist beliefs perpetuated by our current system of science, and to a large extent even by psychology. Our science is akin to religion in that its process of inquiry emerges from underlying belief structures. Although the processes of science may be different from those of religion, as are its requirements of proof, its foundational framework is, like religion, subject to the vagaries of consensus reality and personal biases (which is why some say, perhaps not so cynically, that science advances funeral by funeral). Although this opinion is controversial, I will not belabor the point by quoting from the scores of twentieth-century scientists, especially physicists, who have admitted publicly that, at the quantum level anyway, objectivism is dead. Consciousness is an inherent aspect of the natural world—an admission that, at a minimum, destabilizes the materialist underpinnings of modern Western science. Western scientists, for the most part, would still have us believe that consciousness is localized in and is an emergent property of our brains and that any worlds we may visit or entities we may encounter under the influence of consciousness-altering substances are hallucinations. For us to believe otherwise, or even to *entertain* the possibility of the reality of our visions, calls into question our mental health and betrays our magico-religious naïveté.

There are signs that we are evolving in our opinions about and reactions to the metaphysical. For instance, in psychology there is a relatively new field of inquiry called the "transpersonal," a paradigm within which psychologists can more legitimately study altered states of consciousness. In the first issue of the *Journal of Transpersonal Psychology,* the field's scope was defined:

Transpersonal Psychology is the title given to an emerging force in the psychology field by a group . . . who are interested in those ultimate human capacities and potentialities that have no systematic place in . . . behavioristic theory ["first force"], classical psychoanalytic theory ["second force"], or Humanistic psychology ["third force"]. The emerging Transpersonal Psychology ["fourth force"] is concerned specifically with . . . ultimate values, unitive consciousness, peak experiences, ecstasy, mystical experiences, awe, being, self-actualization, essence, bliss, wonder, ultimate meaning, transcendence of the self, spirit, oneness, cosmic aware- ness . . . and related concepts, experiences, and activities.[7]

Benny Shanon, a psychology professor at the Hebrew University of Jerusalem who embraces a radical phenomenological stance within his academic discipline of cognitive psychology, has written a ground- breaking study of ayahuasca in relation to the expression of conscious- ness. In his book *Antipodes of the Mind: Charting the Phenomenology of the Ayahuasca Experience,* he offers an exhaustive cataloging of the phenomenology of ayahuasca visions and a theoretical exegesis of what these visions might reveal about human consciousness. He rejects as reductionist the prevailing view that the visions and states of mind induced by the use of psychoactive substances can be fully explained by mapping correlative brain states. Struggling to determine how the visions induced by ayahuasca can best be explained by the current the- ories of psychology, and in particular cognitive psychology, he admits: "How they are produced is, I find, a veritable puzzle. . . . Whatever the mechanism at hand, the experience is that the images are created, or come into view, in ways that seem to transcend cognition as psycholo- gists normally conceive it to be."[8]

Shanon concludes that ayahuasca induces extremely enhanced states of awareness, perception, and cognition that result in "cre- ational" acts from which the ayahuasca drinker derives meaning that is implicitly invested with heightened significance. That significance can run the gamut from the personal to the noetic to the spiritual. He views the ontological status of ayahuasca-generated visions as arising neither from independent mind states, such as that of the Platonic realm, nor from the hidden depths of the ayahuasca drinker's mind, but rather from personal creational acts that reveal the human mind as more wondrous and fantastic than psychologists allow.[9] He deduces, from his more than one hundred ayahuasca experiences and his interviews with dozens of other experiencers, that ayahuasca provides fertile and provocative ground from which to study the scope of our own mind and our perceptual relationship to the world. Ultimately, he concludes: "The cross-cultural commonalities exhibited in Ayahuasca visions, the wondrous scenarios revealed by them, and the insights gained through them are perhaps neither just psychological, not just reflective of other realms, nor are they 'merely' a creation of the human mind. Rather they might be psychological *and* creative *and* real. But when we appreciate this, so much of the fundamental notions by which we view both the mind and world have to be considerably altered."[10] How much will that view have to be altered? According to Shanon, the field of psychology needs a radical revisioning in light of what ayahuasca reveals about human consciousness. Under the influence of ayahuasca, he reports, "the mind's ability to create surpasses anything we cognitive psychologists ever think of."[11] This is an opinion he repeats throughout his book, underscoring the need for scientists to actually experience these states of consciousness themselves before they attempt to fashion theoretical frameworks by which to explain them.

This brief but freewheeling discussion is crucial, I believe, to remind us to be wary of our reliance on our "superior" intellectual knowledge when it comes to ayahuasca. The fact that researchers and academics now understand something of the pharmacology of the plant tea and the brain states it induces should in no way delude us into thinking any of us understand anything really important about ayahuasca or its use as a healing agent or a stimulator of personal and/or spiritual growth. The truth is that we are only now just beginning to understand what *kind of questions* we should be asking in our investigations of this and other natural psychedelics.

What we do know factually about ayahuasca is not a lot, and we have only come to know the little we do know in the last few decades. Moreover, the types of knowledge we have accumulated are mostly botanical and chemical, and so provide a very different understanding of ayahuasca than does the more phenomenological knowledge acquired by ayahuasqueros over their millennia of accumulated experience. Ayahuasqueros claim they received their knowledge about ayahuasca, and other visionary and healing plants, from the plants themselves. The chemistry of the ayahuasca tea is so complex that one is hard-pressed not to believe ayahuasqueros might be speaking literally, for it was not until only a few decades ago that Western scientists figured out that chemistry. Although the active ingredient in the ayahuasca brew, N,N-dimethyltryptamine (DMT), was first synthesized in the laboratory in 1931, it took more than two decades for scientists to realize that this was the active compound in many of the teas and snuffs used by Amazonian healers.[12] J. C. Callaway, a chemistry professor who has published extensively on ayahuasca and the chemistry of other psychoactive plants, calls ayahuasca "without a doubt, one of the most sophisticated and complex drug delivery systems in existence."[13]

The word *ayahuasca* refers both to the plant species, *Banisteriopsis caapi,* and to the tea, which is a mixture of the ayahuasca vine and other plants, most usually chacruna, of the genus *Psychotria* (usually *Psychotria viridis*). However, the available admixture plants are many and are chosen by the ayahuasquero for a variety of reasons, including to effect a particular type of healing, to produce a specific quality of vision, and according to an ayahuasquero's personal preference (his "recipe," so to speak). *Banisteriopsis caapi* by itself is not particularly psychoactive, although it contains the alkaloids harmine, tetrahydroharmine, and harmaline, which are beta-carboline derivatives. Scientists at first thought these were new compounds, and even named one of them telepathine because of its alleged effect of heightening clairvoyance, but they soon realized that these alkaloids had been previously identified during studies of the psychoactive Syrian rue *(Peganum harmala).*

Chacruna contains a single major alkaloid, N,N-dimethyltryptamine, better known as DMT. DMT is broken down by an enzyme—monoamine oxidase (MAO)—in the stomach, so it is not orally active (which is why the smokable version of DMT, which is usually synthetic, is often preferred by recreational users).* The beta-carbolines in the ayahuasca vine act as MAO-inhibitors, so that the DMT in the chacruna can be absorbed into the bloodstream.

Many of the compounds found in ayahuasca are chemically similar to neurotransmitters, such as serotonin, that are made naturally in the body and that affect the central nervous system. Compounds molecularly similar to serotonin and other neurotransmitters occur profusely in nature. Callaway writes, "It is truly a wonder why so many different forms of life produce and conserve these unique patterns of atoms like serotonin, which is found in all animals and some plants. The mystery is only deepened by the fact that substantially similar molecules do impart such profound effects on the human mind."[14]

Surely the ancient shamans of western Amazonia had no understanding of ayahuasca's pharmacology, but still they figured out that boiling the macerated bark of the ayahuasca liana with chacruna leaves produced a visionary potion of unparalleled potency. Jeremy Narby, already mentioned as the investigator who took modern Amazonian shamans at their word when they told him that the plants themselves imparted this knowledge, has offered the hypothesis that ayahuasca actually activates a kind of molecular vision and memory and that the biosphere, at the level of DNA, is the source of ayahuasca images and visions. Simply put, he believes that ayahuasqueros are actually extracting information from the environment. In ayahuasca visions, snakes, ropes, and lattice structures are common images, and Narby equates these with the double helix of DNA. He writes:

---

* The effects of smoking DMT are qualitatively and quantitatively different from ingesting the ayahuasca tea (or so I am told and have read, since I have never smoked DMT). When one smokes DMT (which is usually a synthetic preparation rather than a natural substance), one has none or little of the physical discomfort, such as nausea, that one does when drinking the plant brew. Most noticeably, however, the visions are said to be more powerful but more short-lived. Experiencers report a blast of color and image within fifteen to thirty seconds of inhaling the DMT smoke, and the experience has a duration of only approximately ten to fifteen minutes. In contrast, the effects of the tea often take thirty minutes or more to be felt and the visionary experience can last up to four hours.

In their visions, shamans take their consciousness down to the molecular level and gain access to information related to DNA, which they call "animate essences" or "spirits." This is where they see double helixes, twisted ladders, and chromosome shapes. This is how shamanic cultures have known for millennia that the vital principle is the same for all living beings and is shaped like two entwined serpents (or a vine, a rope, a ladder . . .). DNA is the source of their astonishing botanical and medicinal knowledge, which can be attained only in defocalized and "nonrational" states of consciousness, though its results are empirically verifiable. The myths of these cultures are filled with biological imagery. And the shamans' metaphoric explanations correspond quite precisely to the descriptions that biologists are starting to provide.[15]

Narby's frustration with mainstream scientists' inability to even entertain the notion that shamanic knowledge has a verifiable base in nature arises from what he sees as their entrenched epistemology, and hence methodology:

The microscopic world of DNA and its proteins and enzymes is teeming inside of us and is enough to make us marvel. Yet rational discourse, which holds a monopoly on the subject, denies itself a sense of wonder. Current biologists condemn themselves, through their beliefs, to describe DNA and the cell-based life for which it codes as if they were blind people discussing movies or objective anthropologists explaining the hallucinatory sphere of which they have no experience: They oblige themselves to consider an animate reality as if it were inanimate.

By ignoring this obligation, and by considering shamanism and biology at the same time, stereoscopically, I saw DNA snakes. They were alive.[16]

Writer Paul Devereux also speaks eloquently to the matter:

> It is a remarkable fact that plant hallucinogens are hallucinogenic
> precisely because they contain the same, or effectively the same,
> chemicals as are found in the human brain, and so act on us as if
> we were indeed engaged in an interspecies communication. . . .
> This challenges the view held by many people that taking a plant
> hallucinogen is somehow "unnatural." Certainly, it takes the
> brain-mind to states that are not "normal" by the standards of our
> culture, but the "normal" state of Western consciousness cannot
> claim to be the one and only "true" state of consciousness.[17]

So we come full circle, moving from epistemology to chemistry and
back to epistemology again. Perhaps it is only my personal quirk that I
find these questions of "knowing" so important to any discussion of
ayahuasca. I will raise them again elsewhere in this book, and I am only
a little sorry that my intent to overview the history of ayahuasca got
pushed to the wayside as the subject of this chapter took on a life of its
own. I trust that readers can research that history themselves, as there
are many resources for doing so. The brief discussion in this chapter of
the ayahuasca brew's complex chemistry and the plant's reception
within the framework of Western epistemology has served only to whet
our appetite for the meaty questions concerning its proper use and its
benefits, if any, to humankind. Certainly they lead us, willingly or
unwillingly, as the case may be, into the thicket of meaning, for what
meaning are we to ascribe to our experiences of ayahuasca? I will
address some of these questions later in this book.

For now, I would like to end this chapter by raising one linguistic
question that intrigued me from my first introduction to ayahuasca:
Why is this magical brew called "ayahuasca," when it is the chacruna,
or some other DMT-containing admixture plant, that primarily causes
the visionary experience? Remember, in the brew, the ayahuasca vine's
main function is to suppress a stomach enzyme so that the DMT-
containing chacruna can set ablaze the dark skies of the mind. I asked

don Luis and Jack this question when we were in the jungle, and they answered as follows: Shamans claim that ayahuasca contains the "power," whereas chacruna contains the "light." This is an explanation I have since come across while reading about ayahuasca-using churches, such as the Santo Daime and União do Vegetal. *Ayahuasca contains the power and chacruna contains the light.* I was intrigued, but still unsatisfied. Jack also explained that because in the Amazon ayahuasca is seen as the Mother of All Plants, the supreme progenitor, it is valorized to the extent that the brew takes its name. After all, in the psychoactive tea, the admixture plants may vary, but the tea always contains the ayahuasca plant.

These facts gave me pause for thought, and I began to explore the etymology of these words, simply as a matter of curiosity. I found that the roots of the words *power* and *light* themselves are fairly self-evident. But the word *stomach,* the place where the power and light come together, held a surprise. The Latin, Old French, and Old English roots of the word *power* mean "to possess," "to have the ability to do something," "to achieve mastery." *Light* in its Old English root means "to illuminate." Interestingly, when I got to the word *stomach,* I came upon the fact that body parts were named for their shape or function. The stomach is named for its function as gatekeeper, from the two cognates for "gate" and "watcher." It also finds a root in an Old Germanic word meaning "mouth."

My idle inquiry afforded me a new understanding of ayahuasca as a sacrament: in the stomach, the power of ayahuasca and the light of chacruna merge and coalesce into a sum that is greater than the parts. Through this transubstantiation, the gate of the body opens, and consciousness is loosed.

3

Prelude to the Amazon

Listen, said the voice
This is your dream

I'm only stopping here for a little while.
Don't be afraid.

—MARY OLIVER, "BANYAN"

A little more than a year after my first ayahuasca experience, I had the opportunity to partake of the plant sacrament again. My husband and I traveled to another state, where we met Jack, don Luis, and eight others for the ceremony, which was scheduled for a Saturday evening. We fasted most of that day, and we had also followed the dietary and other restrictions for slightly more than a week before we arrived: no red meat or pork, salt, sugar, spices, dairy, fats, alcohol, or sex.

I was a walking contradiction, eager to be taught by Mother Ayahuasca once again, but anxious and unsure if I was ready for the lesson. My first experience had been frightening and disorienting, the worlds in which I had traveled alien and forbidding and at the same time enticing and beckoning. I was both enamored and repulsed. I was also intensely curious, driven almost, to keep exploring the inner and outer realms that I now realized I knew next to nothing about, despite my years of shamanic training. John and I had committed to traveling to the Amazon with Jack and don Luis three months hence to undergo an ayahuasca retreat, imbibing the green magic in the ancient way. Full immersion. When thinking about that upcoming trip, I vacillated between feelings of dread and exhilaration. Only one thing was clear: my intention for this session, which was to ask Mother Ayahuasca to prepare me in whatever way was necessary to meet her in her own territory.

The setting of this session, like that of the first session, was verdant and junglelike, with a wide, lazy river backing the property. We were blessed with warm, clear weather and a comfortable site remote enough to afford us privacy. We would again have two sitters, "Diane" and "Peter," the owners of the property. As with the first session, Jack and don Luis spent about an hour before the ceremony talking about ayahuasca and answering our questions. In response to a question about the icaros, the sacred songs that don Luis would be singing during the ceremony, Jack explained that taking ayahuasca is like setting out in a canoe on a river but not having any oars. You are at the mercy of the currents. The icaros, he explained, are oars by which the ayahuasquero helps you navigate the river. They provide direction. Jack also told us that the brew we would be taking this night had two additive plants in it in addition to chacruna: *bobinsana,* a plant with red flowers and very deep roots that grows by rivers, its arching branches reaching up and out over the water. Energetically, it grounds your lower chakras while opening your upper chakras. It also imparts water energy. And *brugmansia,* a plant with a trumpetlike flower from the datura family. I noticed that the brew was more red than the previous one; this time it was the dark reddish brown of a red velvet cake. Too bad it wouldn't taste like cake.

When don Luis and Jack donned their ceremonial ponchos, it was time to begin the ceremony. Don Luis had his cloth mesa laid out. On it were several musical instruments, such as flutes, a small guitar, and an ocarina; his schacapa-leaf rattle; a plastic liter bottle of the dark red brew; and a small cup. I was sitting second to the left of don Luis. Immediately to my left was Diane, one of the sitters, who would not imbibe and would be available to help us during the night. My husband, John, was halfway around the circle to my left, sitting next to his sister, Karla, who had decided to join us. Although Karla had taken hallucinogens before, this was her first experience with ayahuasca. Our friends Michelle and Andrew were also present. In addition to Jack and don Luis and those I have already named, five other people had gathered with us. Of the ten of us who had been invited to the session (not counting Jack and don Luis, who always ingest ayahuasca while leading a ceremony), six had never taken ayahuasca before.

I was sitting in a chair for this session. It was not as comfortable as the bed of cushions of my first experience, but it was not uncomfortable either. I propped my feet up on some cushions so I could more or less recline. It was fairly warm, so I was wearing a pair of denim shorts and a spaghetti-strap tank top. Because body temperature can fluctuate while under the influence of ayahuasca, I also had over my shoulders a lightweight denim shirt. Before I settled back into the chair, I made sure my water bottle was within reach and my vomit bucket handy. When everyone was settled, the lights were turned off, a candle was lit, and the ceremony began.

Don Luis began his honoring song, a soft stream of vocables that he whisper-sang into the bottle of ayahuasca. Soon he switched to the whistling song, each note of which rippled through me like a ghost. Just the sound of that whistling altered my consciousness. Don Luis took some florida water *(agua de florida)** in his mouth and *camay*ed his mesa, spraying a mist of the florida water through his pursed lips over it. Then he did the same to each of the four directions. He poured some of the perfume into his palms and washed his face, moving his hands back over his head and down his neck and back. He passed the bottle, and we each followed suit. I tried to go very easy with the florida water, as I am sensitive to scents and I did not want to provoke this allergy now.

Finally it was time to drink. I was the second to receive the partially filled cup of foul-tasting brew. I blew my breath through it three times, in the tradition of my Andean teachers, and drank. My portion was

---

* *Agua de florida* means "flower water." This perfumelike liquid is used widely in the Andes during ceremony to cleanse and purify both the body and ceremonial space.

only about two ounces, but the thick liquid filled my mouth as if I had guzzled the liter bottle. Ugh! Nasty! I sat back in my place, closed my eyes, and concentrated on keeping the brew down.

We had started at about nine o'clock, and when I next glanced at my watch, it was nearly ten. I was not feeling any effect. I had been sitting with my eyes closed, silently invoking Mother Ayahuasca. "Mother," I prayed, "I am soon going to your home, the jungle. Please prepare me to work with you there. Introduce yourself to me once again, and prepare me in whatever way is necessary." I had been repeating variations of this prayer for more than an hour, waiting for the ayahuasca blastoff, but it never came. So, at about ten o'clock, when Jack asked if anyone needed more, I went forward, as did several others. Don Luis poured the thick tea into the cup and I drank again. I returned to my seat and once again quietly appealed to Mother Ayahuasca. Within half an hour I was flying.

The black expanse before my inner eyes became an aurora borealis. The colors and patterns erupted unexpectedly, abruptly, just as they had during my first session. But this time they were a neon rainbow, electric colors in undulating sheets and fractal shapes—no monochromatic, mechanistic objects anywhere in sight. Don Luis was playing a small guitar-type instrument that sounded like a mandolin. I found its music sweet and the swathes of colors seductive. Each note was a color, and the melody sent bands of color shifting and swirling across the expanse of my inner vision. The notes/colors were lovers stroking my beingness, irresistibly beckoning me somewhere. The enticement was not to a place but to a state of being. I surrendered to the movement of the colors, entering their dance. I surrendered to the vibration of the music. I opened myself cellularly, a willing partner in the coitus of form and movement and vibration. At the moment of consummation, I was transported to the jungle—although I traversed no distance. It might be more accurate to say that in the moment of vibrational climax, I birthed a jungle.

There was Mother Ayahuasca, a thick double loop of vine twisting up a tree trunk—high, higher, so high I could see only where she entered the thick, tangled green canopy and no more. I was leaning against the tree trunk, stroking the Vine of the Soul, and she was responding to my touch by changing color with my every stroke. Each color had a sound, so that through my stroking, with each color shift, I was (she was) causing a symphony of sound almost too beautiful to bear. I was consumed.

Then, suddenly, a voice. A female voice. Not angry, but commanding: *Stop doing!* I flinched, pulled back from the vine, dropped my hands by my sides like a repentant child.

Stop doing! Only be receptive. You are in my home now. Open yourself to receive. I will "do," not you.

It was Mother Ayahuasca. I was momentarily confused. Wasn't I being receptive? To her colors, her sounds, her vibrations? An answer seemed to reverberate through my head. The stroking. That was "doing." I needed to not do but just be.

I accepted the message and focused my intention on being nothing more than an open vessel, as I had prayed so hard to be during my first experience of the vine: "I am an open and receptive vessel. Mother Ayahuasca teach me." Suddenly the entire jungle came alive. What had been only dark green-black background, a tangle of vines, bushes, and trees, now came alive in carnivalesque colors—a neon rush of life. Greens. Yellows. Blues. Purples. Each bush shimmering in its own eerily electric hum of color, each leaf distinct and seeming to glow from the inside out. This is what the phrase "alive with light" looked like. And felt like, for there was an ozonelike intensity, a heightened, almost static-electric sense of the juices of life pumping, cascading, flowing every which way, in an orderly disorder. Then I noticed the insects. Millions, billions, trillions of them. Dark gray masses, shining, glowing in feeler-feathery or exoskeletal or flitting-winged ways. Everywhere they were crawling, slithering, fluttering, flying, spawning, molting. I thought of Dylan Thomas's lines "The force that through the green fuse drives the flower / Drives my green age; that blasts the roots of trees / Is my destroyer." My view was panoramic; I could see almost 180 degrees, and the colors and movement, the throbbing organicity of the jungle, were too much to absorb. As beautiful as it was, I couldn't stand it. I felt as if I were going to implode from the sheer fecundity of it all.

I suddenly felt overcome with what I (now) call "the ayahuasca feeling." There's really no way to describe it, but it is a distinctly anxious body sensation, one that lets me know unequivocally that ayahuasca is in me and I am in it. It is the visceral message that the fusion has taken place and that at some level it is forever. It is an intensity of identification, an immensity of fullness that threatens to fry my circuits. I loathe the feeling, and it always brings me to something akin to despair, for with it comes the realization that I haven't got a clue— about myself, about the world, about reality, about anything. It's not an existential feeling, although it is. It's not one of helplessness, although it is. It's not even one of fear, although it is. It's not really an emotional feeling at all. It's a texture. In my mind, in my body, in my cells, in my being. And when I feel this texture, or when I *become* this texture, I feel as if I am about to be sucked into a black hole, the attracting force of which harbingers no escape.

I moaned inwardly as the thought crossed my mind that I was, in "real" life, soon to enter the jungle for ten days. I would never survive it, I was sure. I had no business going. I had no business thinking I was capable of handling whatever the jungle is.

I don't remember what happened next, but at some point a huge snake appeared—very nearly the same snake I had seen in my first session. It was royal blue with ribbons of stunningly bright colors down its back; the designs reminded me of the looping ropes of icing on a store-bought confectionary. Once again, the snake entered me, only this time, somehow, it entered through both my mouth and my vagina. I felt it slithering through me, and the kundalini rush took my breath away.

Suddenly I felt very frightened. I felt as if I were about to be shown something dark and forbidding that lived inside me. I saw insects scurrying at the corners of my mind—a few small reddish cockroaches, which have for decades been a dream image of mine, symbolizing doubt, fear, worry. I had just seen millions of darkly luminescent insects wriggling in every nook and cranny of the jungle, and they had not frightened me. But these few creepy-crawlies at the edges of my mind were *mine*. And they frightened me to my core. I felt my mind take hold, my ego, my rationality, and I heard myself say, "No! I am not going there. I won't go there!" I was simply too afraid to have this darkness revealed to me. And so it passed.

Suddenly, Mother Ayahuasca shook me, took me, hooked me—lifting me up, up, up, high into the canopy of a tree. I was breathless from the view. I was only forty, maybe fifty, feet up in this tree, in a canopy that was a biosphere unto itself, but as I looked down, following the twiggy finger of Mother Ayahuasca, I saw the world—humanity en masse. We swarmed like insects, covering the globe, talking, walking, building, destroying, suffering, laughing, loving, hating, eating, shitting, fucking, birthing, dying.

Mother Ayahuasca spoke, gently, her vegetal finger pointing down at the hordes below us. *See,* she said to me, still pointing. *I am receptive. I am so receptive that when a person drinks me I can be whatever that person needs me to be. At that time, in that moment, I am as that person is. At that time, in that moment, that person is as I am.*

I caught my breath at the implications of such an alchemy. Suddenly, within the mass of humanity, I could discern each person individually, and I understood that we are as fragile as blown glass, so delicate that a tremulous breath could shatter us into a thousand pieces. Our illusions about ourselves are like glass. Our self-identity is like glass. Our conception of ourselves is as fragile as glass. The least little stress, the tiniest crack, and we shatter. Our illusions, our identity, our self-image, all shatter around us in pieces. I wanted to cry at our fragility.

But at the same time I could feel our indestructibility. Our illusions, identities, perceptions, patterns, behaviors, neuroses are stubborn nearly beyond belief. We cling to them so tightly that our grip is nearly unbreakable. We even die for them. Our spirits are also indestructible. The glory of our spirits! We can take so much. We can endure so much. We can be wounded so deeply, but we can heal, we can grow, we can rise again from the ashes of who we thought we were. Our ability to take all the shattered shards of ourselves, grind them together, and remake ourselves was beyond astounding—it was miraculous.

I understood that Mother Ayahuasca makes it easier for us to see our paradoxical natures—and to eventually accept ourselves in all our glory and all our darkness. She makes it easier to integrate the many aspects of ourselves. She does so by helping us release the illusion that we are only one thing, that we can be only one way, that there is only one truth.

The scene shifted again. Now Mother Ayahuasca moved my attention to a lone tree, far down below, off to the left of us. Dancing beneath it was a woman; for some reason I thought she was Sri Lankan. She was pivoting around a point, her arms moving in sinuous rhythms, very much like the dancer I had seen in my first session. Like that first dancer, this one, too, was indifferent to our observing her. She was intent on her dance, and I realized that she was dancing in a strangely disconnected way, with no ego involved whatsoever. She was not interested in herself as dancer. She had no sense of her performance. She was just "dance." I thought of Yeats's famous line, "How can we know the dancer from the dance?"

I realized that I could see her from two perspectives simultaneously: from this height, it was like looking down on a point, a still point, as she revolved on the tips of her toes. But I could also view her from ground level, although I could not make out her features well. She wore some kind of elaborate dress and a headdress with multiple peaks to it, all royal blue and iridescent silver. I sensed she was emblematic of something too large for me to grasp, a force of nature of some kind. The thought "This is humanity, minus the flux" wafted its way through my awareness. Then I saw huge words flash across the screen of my inner eyes, and I thought of Plato and first causes: TRUTH. BEAUTY. VIRTUE. She was, and is, each of these and more. Or rather, in some unfathomable way, her dance was each of these.

Mother Ayahuasca pulled my awareness back up to the treetop, and she pointed out Jack and don Luis working far down below, leading our session. I thought of her earlier words, of how she is so receptive that she can be whatever a person needs her to be. She is the perfect mirror, an optical surface finely polished by the sands of time and being. I sensed, in a rush of knowing that caught me physically, that as her representatives, Jack and don Luis are impeccable. That she needs impeccable accomplices to work her magic. Through them she can be whatever she needs to be for a person because she trusts them implicitly to monitor the person's journey and channel any healing. No, I had misunderstood, gotten it backward. The process was dependent on *their* trust of *her*. They have to so trust her that they can stay focused in the midst of the potential chaos of the visions. It is their strength that allows her to work through them.

I also understood that she was showing me Jack's and don Luis's impeccability as her accomplices to make a comparison between their state—their experience and centeredness—and my own lack of those things. I was drifting in the river with little control over my journey. Jack and don Luis, by virtue of their trust in her, were able to connect with her and stay focused enough in the swirl of their own consciousnesses to channel her energy for others. Trust was the key, not experience. Total trust. I was also mesmerized by the strength Jack and don Luis seemed to be emitting, by their emotional will. I understood that I, too, could one day achieve this level of trust, but it would come only after a long and arduous training. I also heard Mother Ayahuasca counsel me, ever the Mother of the Voice in the Ear, to remember this feeling, for if I could achieve this kind of trust in the jungle, things would go much easier for me there. I understood that one of the reasons I tend to vomit is not only to cleanse myself energetically but also because I lose my center and my trust of the experience—and of myself. I allow myself to become attached to the visions and overwhelmed by them. I had to learn to release my fear but not my skepticism of the visions. This sounded like wise counsel, and I did remember it later in the jungle.

I was truly elsewhere at this point, completely unaware of the room and the people I was in session with, even of my own body—until I heard someone call my name, whispering it repeatedly, "Joan. Joan. Come. Joan, come." I felt myself rejoining "reality," being pulled back

ever so slowly, as if through a glass darkly. I was totally disequilibri-
ated. Someone was crouched in front of me, and it took a few seconds
for my eyes to focus in the darkness and see that it was don Luis.
"Come!" he whispered, motioning me toward his chair. He was calling
me for a healing. I groaned. I didn't think I could move at all. I realized
at that moment that I was having a wonderful trip, and that I had not
vomited. So far this journey was far different from my first session, and
I did not want to do anything to change my "head space." But I knew
I needed to follow don Luis's instructions, so I awkwardly slipped to the
floor on my knees and half crawled, half duckwalked the few feet to his
chair. I sat on the floor, my legs tucked under me, my backside resting
on my upturned heels. I had just had a vision of how implicitly don Luis
trusted Mother Ayahuasca and how exquisitely he served as her con-
duit. Now I had to trust whatever was to come, although I sensed that
it was not going to be pleasant.

I pushed my hair back from my face, raised my face toward don
Luis, who was standing over me, and allowed him to sing into the
crown of my head. I heard and felt the swish of the schacapa rattle, and
then I felt him dab a liquid onto my temples, but I didn't smell the
strong scent of flowers, so I don't think it was florida water. I tried
to focus my intention. I opened myself, trying to remain receptive to
whatever was to come, allowing the energy to flow through me to
heal whatever in me needed to be healed. The energy flow was intense,
mostly flowing through me via the icaro. Each note swept through me
viscerally, nudging its way through my cells, rearranging something
inside me. Within moments, I knew I was going to vomit. I reached out
in the darkness, feeling for a bucket. I could not find one. I felt panic
rising. If I didn't find a bucket soon, I was going to throw up all over
the floor, or worse yet all over myself or don Luis. As the bile rose in
my throat, at the last possible second, don Luis shoved a bucket into
my hands and I heaved so deeply that the force surprised me. Once,
twice, three times I felt myself release all that was inside me. With the
last heave, I felt myself pass gas, and I was mortified. I couldn't be sure
I hadn't just soiled myself. But I couldn't worry about it. I was so intent

on expelling what needed to be expelled, and I felt so awful while doing it, that I just could not care. Don Luis continued singing, fanning me with the schacapa-leaf rattle, and Jack reached over and handed me a wad of Kleenex. I put the bucket down and sat back on my legs, resting once again on my heels. That's when I heard Mother Ayahuasca's voice, this time commanding me: *Receive! Receive!*

I was exhausted and sick to my stomach. Although the healing had seemingly just started, I wasn't sure I could take any more—the energy rush was that intense. But I knew I had to. With deliberation, I turned my face back up to don Luis. "More," I heard my inner voice urge him as I closed my eyes. "There's more to be done." I squared my shoulders and opened my heart chakra to the energy flow. As sick as I was, I felt invincible, although totally vulnerable. Ayahuasca for me is all about paradoxes and simultaneity of feelings and senses. It was rarely a single clear feeling or understanding. Don Luis continued working on me. He crouched over me, bathed my temples once again, and lowered his mouth very close to my scalp, singing. Then he began to suck energy from the crown of my head. I couldn't really feel anything, but I heard the effort he was putting into it. Soon he stood up and worked the leafy fan over my heart. Again I felt the bile rise, I grabbed the bucket, and heaved, although this time not as forcefully.

Once again I raised my face, squared my shoulders, and offered my heart chakra. I was drenched with perspiration and feared I might faint. I felt deeply nauseated, even though I had expelled anything that could still have been in my stomach after a day of fasting and the last round of gut-wrenching vomiting. But I was conscious that I was marshalling my will to follow Mother Ayahuasca's counsel. I had to receive whatever she wanted to give me.

Don Luis reached down and took hold of the palms of my hands. He pushed them together and then separated them at the top, so they were in an open prayer position. He washed them with florida water, cleansing both the palms and the backs, and stroking liquid down each finger. He took a swig of florida water in his mouth and sprayed it over my head, on each temple, and over both my shoulders. The heavily rose-infused scent was making me sicker than I already felt, but the liquid felt wonderfully cool and soothing. I don't remember if I vomited again.

I also don't know how long I squatted there, receiving the ministering energy of don Luis, but it seemed like an eternity. When I finally turned to go back to my chair, I felt spent, but cleansed. Washed from the inside out. As tired as if I had just performed hard physical labor, and yet rejuvenated. But I could just barely crawl on hands and knees back to my chair. I struggled to get out of my denim shirt. I had started the evening with it over my shoulders, and I have no idea when I actually put it on. Now, however, it was taking a Herculean effort to get out of it. But I had to—I was burning up. I had never felt so hot. All I remember of the next block of time is fearing that I might faint from the heat. I had a wad of Kleenex in a pocket of my shirt, and I found it and mopped my brow, chest, and arms. I had nothing to tie my hair up with, but I twisted it up and off my shoulders. I was on fire! I weakly called out for Diane, who had been sitting right beside me, but she was gone, apparently assisting someone else. I felt desperate. Someone had to help me. I was going to faint. But there was no one to assist. So I mopped myself until the Kleenexes were sodden and shredded. I fumbled for my water bottle and doused myself with water. Then I don't remember anything—I was completely outside myself, although I did not realize it until I "came back" to find myself high in the tree canopy once again with Mother Ayahuasca.

We observed what was going on in the session. I again felt the implicit impeccability of don Luis as he worked on behalf of Mother Ayahuasca. I marveled at his control, his knowing, his sensitivity. I realized that he was doing a healing on everyone, going around the room and calling us to him one by one. Then, an odd and rather embarrassing thing happened. As one man was being healed, I felt myself pass gas, a small, silent release. With this release I heard a disembodied voice say, *Illusion detached!* Almost simultaneously with these words, the man being healed by don Luis vomited. I realized that I could see the scintillating grid of his energy body. As the illusion detached, a dark whiff of energy was released from his energy grid, dissipating into the air. The same thing happened when the next person, a woman, was called forward to be healed. I could see her complex and luminescent energy body, which looked like a glowing computer circuit board. I could discern a dark spot, a jagged interruption of the symmetry of the colors of her energy grid, and then *phssst!* I passed gas. Seconds later she vomited, and I heard the disembodied voice announce, *Illusion detached!* Even though I felt compassion for each person, as the pattern repeated itself, I could not help but laugh. Precognitive empathetic flatulent cleansing! I found the entire scenario hilarious.

I did not know it at the time, but John, my husband of twenty-five years, was having a hard time. In contrast to his first ayahuasca session, when he had experienced a beatific cosmic connection, this time he was undergoing a rough physical cleansing. While I was nearly swooning from heat, he was shivering with cold. He had one blanket over him and wanted more. It was only when don Luis motioned for him to come forward for the healing that I had any inkling, from my perch high in the jungle canopy with Mother Ayahuasca, that he was suffering. As he scooted forward, I could, with my physical eyes, just barely make out his silhouette in the darkness. With my spirit eyes, however, I could see streamers of energy coming from him, and I sensed they were historical currents, like ribbons of genetic memory flowing from him—or perhaps to him. I saw a group of his Mohawk ancestors paddling a canoe upriver, the longhouses that were their destination in the distance. I energetically saw memory plumes of his childhood, which had been physically and emotionally difficult. I sensed that he was shivering from the shedding he was doing, molting an exoskeleton of painful memories. Compassion rose within me, and I sent him waves of loving energy. Then my awareness seemed to black out, and I didn't come to until his healing was over. This pattern repeated itself several times during the night, especially when someone I knew and cared about was undergoing the healing. I would connect with his or her "story," understand it in a way I can't explain now, and then I would black out, not to regain awareness until almost the precise moment the healing ended.

That experience was especially strong with Karla, my sister-in-law. I knew Karla was suffering. Diane had helped her to the bathroom several times during the session, so I knew she was undergoing an intense purging. When don Luis called her name, she did not understand that he was asking her to come forward for a healing. Instead, she thought he was offering her more ayahuasca, which she refused. Since don Luis does not understand much English, confusion ensued. I understood what was happening but was not present enough to be of help. Others in the group quickly and quietly cleared up the confusion and Karla went forward to receive her healing. As she did, I felt overwhelmingly that she was getting more than she had bargained for. I sensed that at some deep psychic level she had agreed to clear some of the dysfunctional energy around her and John's family history. But now that she was about to do it, a part of her was balking at the enormity of the task Mother Ayahuasca was asking her to undertake. I energetically sent her love and support. I so sensed the tremendous difficulty of her undertaking that I vomited. (At least I think I did. I can't be sure now if it was psychic or physical.)

Then I blacked out again, not losing consciousness, only awareness. But something different happened this time. At some point, in my mind's eye, in a vision, I saw Karla having successfully cleansed what she has been asked to cleanse for her family. I saw her utterly spent, emotionally and energetically exhausted, pulling herself with her last vestiges of strength across the floor. She was dragging herself with her arms and elbows, too exhausted even to crawl. I saw her finally reach the edge of what seemed to be a low platform, but I couldn't see what this structure was. When I finally pulled my inner focus back, allowing the whole picture to come into view, I saw what I can only describe as her spirit guide looming over her. She was huge, twelve or fifteen feet tall, and angelic. Karla dragged herself to this guide's feet and collapsed on the edge of the platform, her face resting on her arms, one cheek turned so that I could see one side of her face. Her face was bathed in radiant light. Her dark hair glowed. I had never seen such beauty. The angel, or whoever she was, leaned down and stroked Karla's hair, then her cheek, silently acknowledging the incredible work she had just done. I could feel how proud she was of Karla. At that instant I also sensed that Karla had not only cleared some of her difficult family history but also two toxic relationships she has had with males in her life. I knew nothing about that, but I intuited the healing so clearly that I had no question it had taken place. (She later confirmed she had had two such relationships.)

Watching Karla at the feet of this angel was a kind of witnessing—of a miracle of love and compassion. I was enraptured. I thought of the Pietà, of the sorrowful beauty of ineffable humanity (the divinely human and the humanly divine). Again, I sent waves of love to Karla, and that is when I returned to some measure of normal awareness to see that Karla was actually stumbling back to her place, the healing over.

Others came forward, and I was witness to their healing. I don't remember when the session ended and the candle was lit because I was still floating somewhere up in the jungle canopy with Mother Ayahuasca. Slowly people began to gather up their belongings and stumble off to bed, but I did not want to move. I stayed sprawled in my chair, exhausted and soaked with perspiration. I felt the need to expose every square inch of skin possible to the air, to try to cool down. I had slid low in the chair, my legs splayed out in front of me. My arms were flung wide, flopping over the arms of the chair. I had the vague thought that I should be more modest, since I was wearing short shorts and a barely there tank top, and I felt very exposed. But I needed air, needed to cool down. I also felt intensely self-indulgent. Not sexual, but sensual. I was aware of my limbs, my legs tanned and muscled and stretched out in front of me. The bareness of my shoulders and arms. I became intensely aware of my body, not in the way of the temptress, but in the way of the worshiper. This surprised me, because I normally have a poor self-image and am working to be less critical of myself, but now I felt appreciative of my body, of its majesty. I wanted to stretch my limbs, arch my back, undulate my shoulders to feel my shoulder blades flex and back muscles stretch. But I didn't. I just lay there, limbs sprawled but still. I saw flashes of a black jaguar stretched out contentedly on a tree limb, his body muscled but provocatively sinuous. I identified with him, and I lay sprawled almost lasciviously in the chair, psychic counterpart to the black cat.

I couldn't seem to get straight, although I was no longer journeying either. I was caught in some state of mind and energy between the two. At one point Jack came over to ask how I was feeling. I remember answering, my eyes still closed, a hint of a smile on my face, "Jack, I'm floating in the river with no oars." I heard him chuckle, then translate my remark to don Luis, who was now himself stretched out on the couch across the nearly empty room. I heard don Luis's laughter. I heard myself laugh.

Some time soon after, John helped me up and we stumbled into the next room to our bed, where we slept fitfully. John was purging, so he was up and down to the bathroom throughout the night. I lay still, sprawled across the bed, my dreams little more than the slowly fading glow of the jungle electric.

The next day held a wonderful synchronicity, which I read as a sign that the jungle trip I would soon be taking was somehow going to be a deeply moving, if not life-changing, experience for me. We were gathered in a group on the veranda, relating our experiences from the session of the night before. Just as my husband finished talking and it became my turn, our hosts, Diane and Peter, rushed into the house and came back out with binoculars. They pointed with hushed excitement at the river, which was behind me. There along the far bank of the river was a great horned owl—my totem animal. I had never seen one so close. It was huge and was standing still in front of a log in the high green weeds on the riverbank. Our hosts exclaimed that they had never seen an owl that large so near the house and certainly not in broad daylight sitting out in the open next to the river. I silently welcomed my totem animal and made a mental and emotional note to really work to prepare myself for the jungle, for owl has never entered my life without my being put to some major, and usually difficult, personal test. So I considered myself put on notice, both by Mother Ayahuasca in the previous night's session and this day by great horned owl.

🌿 4 🌿

Other Voices,
Other Journeys

In this world that rushes and grows calm
I want more communications,
Other languages, others signs,
To be intimate with this world.

—PABLO NERUDA, "BESTIARY"

"What we need now are diaries of explorers. We need many diaries of many explorers so we can begin to get a feeling for the territory."[1] So wrote the intrepid psychonaut Terence McKenna about the need for reports from the field of psychedelia. In the journey I just related, I described what I saw, or intuited, while Karla and John were undergoing their healings. Now they, and others, will speak for themselves. Their stories and musings run the phenomenological gamut, from being pinned in the physical because of the discomfort of the experience to being freed through flights of mind and spirit. Their approaches to their personal experiences of ayahuasca range from the prosaic to the descriptive and from the philosophical to the transpersonal.

KARLA'S FIELD REPORT

I had very mixed emotions about having this experience. I was concerned about the physical effects—throwing up, diarrhea. I had experimented with acid in my younger years and really wasn't interested in doing that again. John told me that he did not get sick, ayahuasca was not like acid, and that he had sat in spiritual bliss the entire time of his first experience. Joan had told me that she did get sick, however.

I was interested in working with an Amazonian shaman and undergoing a profound spiritual experience. I was told it would be a different experience from what happens in meditation. So, with a mixture of excitement and trepidation, I decided to go for it.

Even after arriving at the destination, I was still thinking of backing out. I just knew I was going to get sick. But the environment in which this journey was going to take place was very beautiful and that relaxed me somewhat. I connected well with the others who were joining us and to our two guides for the journey. So I felt very safe.

We gathered in a circle and the shaman said prayers and smudged us. He then prepared the concoction that included ayahuasca but had other plants in it as well. I took my drink and sat back in my chair with my bucket (everyone is given a bucket in which to throw up). For a long time nothing happened. It reminded me of the old days when you were waiting to see if the substance you purchased was going to work or if you needed more. Most of the time you took more and the first hit kicked in and you were off on a mega-trip. I decided that I was not going to take more. I was getting a little rush from the "juice" and that was enough. In fact, I was hoping that what I was feeling was the extent of it. Other people in the group did take more. And as they got up to take more, the ayahuasca took effect within me.

I don't really remember many details. It felt like a freight train was running through my body. It was overwhelming, and I resisted it. However, I knew I didn't really have a choice, so I tried to stay with it. The colors were beautiful. I saw Ganesh, the elephant god of the Hindus. He is considered, among other things, to be the remover of obstacles. He told me to get on his back and he would help me. He was beautiful and had a very beautiful headdress in the blues and pinks and geometric designs that are seen in the artists' works of their ayahuasca journeys. Once, when I looked over at the shaman, I saw him as the plant growing in the corner and turning into a woman's face. She was very beautiful and powerful.

But I was very ill, and I had to keep going to the bathroom because I had diarrhea. It made it very difficult to relax. At that time I was having a problem with an ovary. I knew that ayahuasca is a purgative and used in healing. I was "told" (by an inner voice) that if I could keep the ayahuasca in my body for the whole time (not throw up), it would aid in my healing. The drumming and piping of the shaman were wonderful, and the music helped focus my attention on something other than how ill I was.

I know that purging is a very good way of clearing old emotional issues and that I was clearing family issues, but I don't remember specifics. I just wanted it to be over because I was so sick. The helpers were wonderful and guided me back and forth to the bathroom each time. They were very nurturing.

At one point I noticed others were getting another dose. Then the shaman began calling people up. I thought he was calling them to give them more ayahuasca, so when he called my name, I said, "No, thank you." Luckily, some of the people knew that I had misunderstood him, that he wanted to give me a healing, not more ayahuasca. So I crawled on my hands and knees over to him and he prayed and sang over me. I felt very grateful to him for his work.

Then I remember them closing the circle (the ceremony) and it was over, but I was still sick. So I went into the bathroom and was finally able to regurgitate, and I felt better immediately. I had a great night's sleep and felt great the next day.

I am grateful for the journey. There are no more problems with the ovary. I am sure there was a great deal of old emotional garbage that was released. It was a very intense spiritual and physical experience and a powerful healing. I believe ayahuasca is a quick way to remove many emotional layers. I felt very safe. Although I benefited from this ayahuasca experience, I would not work with it again. The physical response was too intense for me. I believe there are less drastic ways to achieve spiritual connection and healing.

JOHN'S FIELD REPORT

Ayahuasca is a great teacher. With every experience I've had with ayahuasca, I've gotten something out of it. There's no comparison between ayahuasca and other things I've done. Ayahuasca takes you "there" more quickly than any other modality—meditation, drumming and shamanic journeying, other psychedelics. You can get to places using those modalities, but ayahuasca takes you there and beyond. You can reach the doorway with other things, but ayahuasca takes you *through* the doorway. It takes you to your Higher Self, to the All That Is. You actually have that feeling of being one with the All, with the All-Knowing. Although sometimes that feeling is very fleeting, you're there. It gives you a sense of completeness; it's a very comfortable feeling, one where you can be in a place without judgment. Ayahuasca, most of the time, takes me out of myself, but at the same time it's both an inward and an outward journey. You can't separate it. It's all one. It's all inseparable.

For me, it's not like there are dark places with ayahuasca. It's just all good. That's not to say that there aren't dark things—they're there—but even the dark is good. The taste is not so great! The taste varies from session to session, but mainly I don't like the taste. I don't look forward to ingesting ayahuasca. The very first time I took it, it didn't seem that bad. It tasted rather like molasses. But the times after that, it wasn't pleasant. I just don't like the taste.

The physical experience itself is pretty much the same from session to session. At first, before the vine actually starts working and taking me to that place of enlightenment, before it really hits me, I always feel it in my body. It's very body centered. My stomach is always churning, and I feel like vomiting. It's not a nice feeling at all. But then, once I get to that first peak, that awful body feeling usually goes away. Not always, but usually it goes away. I have yet to vomit. Of the seven times I've worked with ayahuasca, there have been times I've felt like I needed to throw up or wanted to, but it just wouldn't happen. It didn't come. The only real purging I've ever experienced was with diarrhea during the second session. And that came after the ceremony, after the journey.

I was up all night in the bathroom. But by morning, when all the brew was out of my system, I felt fine.

Each session with ayahuasca is very different. There are similarities in content, but they're all unique. The first time I journeyed with ayahuasca, I was in ecstasy the whole time. When I felt ayahuasca flowing through my system that first time it was like going home. It seemed so familiar. I remember feeling, "Ah! I remember this." That whole journey was all about unconditional love and being in total bliss. It was about traveling and seeing people I know and conveying to them the message of unconditional love. It was about being connected through love. I felt I was communing with God. Well, actually, it was more than just feeling connected with the One; I was actually part of it all. There really was no separation. It was not like I was observing myself connecting with something; it was me being this. But when I was in that state, part of the One, then I would observe others from that perspective. Sending them the energy of unconditional love. Letting them know that they are always loved. But I was perceiving them from a state of *being* that energy grid. I wasn't journeying *with* the grid, I *was* the grid. The body, physical senses like vision— these were never a factor. The body had nothing to do with it. The eyes had nothing to do with it. It was just being.

The second time I journeyed with ayahuasca was the worst journey I've ever had. It was nasty. I was nauseated through the whole journey. But I couldn't throw up. It's not that I resisted vomiting, it just wouldn't come up. I was cold. I was shivering. I couldn't get warm, and I wanted it all to be over. It was just nasty from a physical perspective. But what I felt inside was that I was getting a cleansing, a healing. My intention for that session was for ayahuasca to cleanse me in whatever way I needed to be cleansed before I went to the jungle to work with ayahuasca. I felt that's what happened. During that journey, there were only a few glimpses of being in bliss. In the first session the energy grid was all around me, infused in everything, and the same happened in the second session—I was inside this energy grid, not just seeing it. It was like I was being cleansed from the inside out. When I felt that and could perceive that, I could feel bliss. But it was fleeting. The rest of the time, it was more a physical session, and not very pleasant. It was not a real spiritual session, but more a body experience. I was shivering, and not being able to sit comfortably, and so on. One person who journeyed with us that night, a physician, later described her experience as feeling like she had a high fever, and how when you have a high fever you can't ever seem to get comfortable. That's exactly what I felt, too. I couldn't get comfortable in my body. I felt fine the next day, but it wasn't pleasant during the session.

The sessions in the jungle varied; they were somewhere in between the feeling of the first and second sessions I just described. One time I would feel blissful and connected, and another time I would feel uncomfortable and like I was getting more of a physical cleansing.

Most of the visuals I have under ayahuasca are intensely colorful—pinks, reds, blues, greens—but they are abstract. I don't remember ever seeing any forms, like other people report. I haven't seen snakes, animals, plants, temples, and so on. What I see in my journeys are actual people from my life, actual things in my life. For me, the visuals are either very unformed or formed of very recognizable things and people. They're either just the colors and the energy grid, or they're people I know. Although I have sensed things like insects, I've never seen them. I could only sort of feel as if bugs were around. That happened in the jungle, but it wasn't about the actual bugs that were there. For example, one time it was more as if the butterflies woven into my poncho, which I had with me at the session, came alive and connected with me, making a bridge, being a catalyst, to my working with sound. It was rather a creepy feeling, an eerie feeling, that this poncho had tentacles, like bugs do, that were reaching out to me trying to get me to connect with it. I guess one time when I was having a hard time with my stomach, I felt as if there was a snake in there churning around. But I don't have visuals like most other people report or like are depicted in ayahuasca art. But I see the grid all the time. Eyes open or closed, I see the specks of light, the infinitely small specks of luminescence that form a grid, which is multidimensional. It's a geometric grid—one giant grid that connects and contains everything. You look around it and it is never-ending. It's uniform, and it appears to undulate only because it is beyond three-dimensional. It's multidimensional, so it appears to move only as you move through it, because you are moving through so many dimensions. The colors are brilliant, fluorescent.

Overall, ayahuasca has taught me quite a bit about myself, but it's hard to put it into words. I feel I've learned most about judgment, about *not* judging others, or myself. Not taking things personally, not taking others' judgments of me onto myself. I've gained a deeper knowledge that we all come from the same source, so I can now keep that type of thing in perspective more than I could before. It's given me more self-confidence. It's given me more trust. I've always tried to live from a place of trust, of knowing that everything is going to be fine no matter what the circumstances. Of not getting overly emotional or emotionally attached. Of not trying to force an outcome but just allowing things to be. Working toward a goal but not necessarily having to stay with a particular path. To bend like a willow as circumstances come up. Of not forcing myself in the direction I think I need to be going but just being clear about what I would like.

One of the most important things ayahuasca has shown me is the knowledge or the insight about how I work with sound. That this is what I am to be doing—working with sound in a combination of indigenous instruments and voice and intuition, using sound intuitively on individuals to help them repattern energy and align with their paths. Working with the vibrations of the body, mind, and spirit for healing at all levels. That all came together for me in the jungle working with ayahuasca. It all took form there. Primal Sound therapy, that's what I call my practice as a sound intuitive—it all took form in the jungle through the insights provided by ayahuasca.

Ayahuasca overall confirmed for me what I've always believed and trusted: I'm walking my path exactly as I need to be walking it. I may trip and stumble along the way, but I know I'm being guided, watched, assisted. I know that no matter what, everything will always be okay. Ayahuasca confirmed all that for me. When I talked about gaining confidence, for instance, one of the things I asked during my last session with ayahuasca was along the lines of "Who am I to be going out into the world, with no formal training, and working with sound to help people?" The answer I got was unmistakable and surprising. Ayahuasca made clear that I have been in training for years, since the time in 1994 when I walked the Inca Trail into Machu Picchu. Through all my work on the Andean path and in other spiritual pursuits. It gave me a different perspective on my spiritual path. It indicated that I've been diligent in my spiritual work and have earned the right to be of service to people in this way, with sound. Most people don't work with sound in the way I was shown to in the jungle. It's like my area to pioneer. It's my gift. Ayahuasca helped me see my interest in free-form sound as the gift that it is and to claim it with confidence.

In terms of feeling guided, I had one significant experience with ayahuasca in the jungle where I traveled in time. When I was younger, back in the 1970s, and I did LSD, I occasionally had what I call bummer trips. What these were, basically, were times when my consciousness, or subconscious, just wouldn't shut up. It would be telling me that I was wasting my time, I needed to leave my hometown, that if I stayed I would never amount to anything, that my path was elsewhere. It told me I needed to do something different with my life than what I was doing with it there. I finally listened to it and left. My whole life changed, which isn't so unusual, since most kids want to leave the place where they grew up. But I really started on my "path" only after I left. What I experienced during this one particular ayahuasca session was that this voice I had heard while under LSD back in the seventies was myself now under ayahuasca. That I had journeyed back to that time to counsel myself that I needed to move on. Back in the seventies, I was actually hearing my future self counseling me. It was an amazing insight, and an indescribable experience. I experienced that voice from the *other side*. Instead of being under LSD and listening to the voice, I *was* the voice coming through from ayahuasca in the future. It was a complete time shift. It's hard to explain the feeling of it, but that experience confirmed my feeling that I have always been watched over and guided—perhaps even by my self, or my Higher Self.

I am grateful for having the experiences of working with ayahuasca. But I'm not sure I will work with it again. I have journeyed under its guidance seven times, but I don't feel compelled to work with it again. I delayed working with it until the point when I felt I was really ready, and now I feel I have received what it has to offer me, to teach me. It's hard to explain. I can't say I'll never work with it again or that there isn't a lot left that it can teach me, but right now I feel complete with it.

ANDREW'S FIELD REPORT

My experience with more than twenty encounters with the Vine of the Soul has been nothing less than a progression of death and rebirth experiences. These have occurred through a series of reciprocating, oscillating if you will, karmic cleansings of the false self (Anatta), followed by deeper and deeper reidentifications with the True Self (the Christ, Atman, or Buddha consciousness). This processing generally occurs within a single session, but there have also been times while undergoing a double session (that is, back-to-back evening sessions) that the first session will concentrate on the necessarily prerequisite honest acceptance of my karmic frailties, faults, and transgressions toward life and consciousness. And the second session, often after a relatively rapid recapitulation of the previous session's "lesson," will then open with an invitation to the Higher Self.

From the very outset of my series of experiences with the vine, this process of penetration into the True Self through death of the false self has clearly been an act of remembrance, a kind of Platonic anamnesis, in which having been relatively cleared of the karmic dross of my inadequate and outright poor choices, I am allowed to remember (literally re-member) that totality, that unity, which has been dismembered or temporarily forgotten in the samsaric cycle of existence. The experience has time and again been truly a reidentification with the very essence of Being. But always the requisite has been the act of openly and honestly facing the trappings and illusion of my aggrandizement of the false self.

This oscillating, pulsating, reciprocating balance of a kind of systole and diastole of my vine experience has at times been most clearly represented by the image of the caduceus. In my search for the underlying unity of existence, it is as if one serpent of the caduceus has represented the destructive act of eliminating, Shiva-like, the false and illusory; whereas the other serpent of the caduceus signified the creative Brahma-like reestablishment of the real. And balanced in equanimity in the central rod of *sushumna** stands the Logos, the Vishnu-like eternal present, much like Isis thinly veiling the ultimate secret of Atman/Brahman. Again and again, ayahuasca, experience after experience, has engendered an initial out-breathing or elimination of the karmic dross of Anatta (the illusory self) followed by the in-breathing, leading to the re-memberment and reidentification with the Divine Source, the Christ/Atman.

Ayahuasca, the Vine of the Soul, the Vine of the Dead, has again and again led me through the Valley of the Shadow of Death into the presence of the Divine Light. Over and over it has taught me that to discover and truly remember the Divine Self, one must methodically and consistently purge and eliminate the ego trappings and karmic baggage of the false self. She is a divine omniscient teacher.

Yes, it is true that set and setting are of utmost importance. This is not a recreational venture but is for those who, Sufi-like, are in pursuit of the real. The experience needs to be entered into with a sense of reverence; thus the utter need for a spiritual setting. One's mental set or intention should be clear and focused. The power of focused, intense intention can carry one through the most difficult of experiences. But one must always remember, the vine in some very deep sense "knows" what one needs to see and understand. And as I have indicated, that often means what we need to face. The vine often will take us far beyond our seemingly exalted intentions. And it has been my experience that we often must first face the Dweller on the Threshold, our

---

* In the chakra system of energy, the *sushumna* is a major channel that rises along the spine from the root chakra to the base of the skull.

own self-imposed Gatekeeper, before the Silent Watcher (that is, the Angel of the Presence) will take action to reestablish itself at the very center of our psyche, in the very core of our Being. It is here that we rediscover the Pearl of Great Price, the Grail, the Lapis Exilis. It is here that we are reestablished in Truth, Beauty, and Goodness, which coalesce into a oneness revealing the divine sanctity of choice offered to each monad. It is at this point in the "Ceremony of the Vine" that categories, departments, concepts, and senses begin to cross over. One begins to experience synesthesia, as for example, one begins to literally see (as I did both with eyes open and eyes closed) the icaros (the songs of the plant) issuing forth from the mouth of the ayahuasquero. It is here that the *hieros gamos,* the sacred marriage, can take place. It is here that the shimmering, scintillating sheets of the most precious divine substance dance and undulate through one's consciousness in an exquisite display of colors, and one is catapulted into the presence of the Divine Mystery, set before the very throne of the Divine. For those who seek wisdom and union with the Divine, ayahuasca, the Vine of the Soul and the Vine of the Dead, is the great teacher. One enters the Path of Eternal Return by partaking of the Waters of Remembrance.

MICHELLE'S FIELD REPORT

My first opportunity to experience ayahuasca came when I knew almost nothing about it. It was 1995, and I was attending a conference in Brazil. I had no previous experience with psychoactives and was quite dubious about the prospect of entering a spiritual state of consciousness by ingesting such a substance. I had an opportunity to attend a service of the Santo Daime church, during which we would ingest ayahuasca. I couldn't imagine attending church for over four hours, and I certainly had no concept of how a psychoactive substance would play a part. It is only after several years of study with ayahuasca that I can look back on that first experience and understand how classic the effects were (that is, telepathic communication, visions of serpents, perceptions of energy and grids, voice in the ear, and so forth) that I experienced that night. I can certainly say it was the most profound, life-altering experience of my life.

It took roughly twenty minutes for the power to be felt. I heard a buzzing sound and began to feel light-headed. The energy was increasing by the moment as the pace of the ceremonial rattling, guitar playing, and hymn singing picked up. We were long past the point of return. I was suddenly terrified as I felt the intensity of the experience increasing. I was so overcome with nausea and fear that I had to walk outside the church. As I reached an area of plants right outside the door, I stopped and looked down. I realized I could see the energy of the plants. They were alive in a way that I never conceived of before. I saw the energy grids that I perceived as the life of the plants.

Suddenly the thought returned to me that I would surely die from this experience. I went through a motion as though vomiting, but instead of purging I experienced a vision of a large black snake with fluorescent colors on its back. As though I had been given a counteractive remedy, I suddenly had no nausea. As quickly as the terror had come over me, it disappeared. I felt arms around me from the back, although there was no human form behind me. I felt peace like I had never experienced before. I kept hearing my inner voice tell me, "Everything is fine, everything is fine." I returned to my chair in the church.

The experience of complete communication with what I perceived as the One or God began. It felt like a coming home and an experience of whole understanding—as it was before the forgetting of this life—and I felt a connection and completeness like never before. I had been granted the experience of returning to the One. I was trying to give words to the experience as it was happening. It was like seeing the one you love as most precious in life after hundreds of years, the intensity of feeling never fleeting. I kept saying, through my inner voice, "Thank you so much for letting me remember." I gave thanks like never before. I had tears streaming from my eyes. I was in ecstasy.

As I looked around the church, I suddenly had the perception of being all-knowing, as though I could perceive thoughts telepathically. I kept hearing my inner voice say, "You have a voice louder than you ever imagined without saying a word." I was aware of everything happening in minute detail. The message was that everything happens as it is supposed to happen. It is all perfect in that sense, and important. It definitely allowed me the opportunity to experience the world absolutely without judgment and with awe and wonder. I did not want the night to end. It was the most joyous experience of my life.

The wonderful blessing of this experience is that I can tap back into it at any time. It is not like a dream, where the intensity quickly dissipates. The experience was "real" in that sense. I was given a chance to experience what Buddhist practitioners and spiritual devotees of all varieties strive and work for in meditations, prayers, and study. Some may say that because it did not come through suffering and devotion it was not real but was only drug-induced wishful thinking. The only thing I can share in response to such suggestions is that I definitely saw and I definitely felt and I am forever changed as a result. I also believe that the experience involved a death of the ego. A complete loss of control, a getting out of your own way, is apparently required. I have since had a number of ayahuasca experiences where I did go down into the dark, the dreadful, and I did physically feel like death before I was granted the experience of visions. For this reason, one must be prepared for terror and have enough practice in maintaining one's center before embarking on such a journey. One thing is certain about the vine: there is no telling what you will get, but it will definitely be what you need. As one of the voices from a recent ayahuasca experience informed me, "There is no epidural for spiritual birth."

The progression of my experiences and the quality they now seem to consistently take on is quite something. The next experience I had after the Daime ritual took place in the United States under the care of an American shaman. The experience certainly took on a more raw, nature-spirit, if not Native American, tone. The serpent quality of the vine manifested in me, in my mouth, the pit of my stomach, in my ear, and in my visions. I felt as though I lost consciousness for a period of time, and when I came to, I was kneeling, moving my torso up and down like the head of a cobra. It was black, it was terrifying, and the sheer power that had me in its grasp was beyond my comprehension. I have returned as well to the state of ecstasy on a number of occasions and have had many experiences related to energy and the transmission of energy. I have, in fact, in the last few sessions, had the experience of volts of energy running through my body causing every muscle to contract. I would now, in hindsight, go so far as to say that the ayahuasca experience is in great part about energy and the tuning of the body vibrationally. I have experienced this so strongly that it is literally painful to come back from these experiences, and I cannot physically see or lift my head during the last thirty minutes or so of a session as my body tries to adjust.

I have had a total of ten experiences in a variety of settings. The experiences have been life altering in that I now know that we are capable of perceptions far beyond the day-to-day awareness most of us view as reality. Ayahuasca is a true teacher and is, to date, the finest teacher I have ever experienced.

One might ask, given the unpredictability of an ayahuasca experience and the harshness of its physical effects—not to mention the likelihood that sometime or another ayahuasca will take you places that are dark and frightening—why many people feel compelled to undertake the experience and then to repeat it. While the reports above provide some clues, they are too small a sample to answer this question properly. For a more definitive answer, we can turn to psychologist Benny Shanon and his book *The Antipodes of the Mind*. Shanon participated in more than one hundred ayahuasca sessions himself and interviewed dozens of people, both native and not native to ayahuasca-using cultures, who are experienced with ayahuasca. He found from his own and others' experiences that ayahuasca is seen almost universally as a teacher, and sitting in session is viewed as attending a school. One undertakes a "course of study" with ayahuasca during which one learns in ways not possible through other mechanisms or modalities. Shanon identifies the rewards of such study, and hence the reasons people continue to work with ayahuasca, as: (1) the pleasure of the experience and the joy gained through it, a joy that outweighs the often excruciating physical and psychical discomfort one also may experience; (2) the quest for knowledge and the revelation of truth that ayahuasca may impart; (3) the gift of deep personal insight and self-understanding; (4) the possibility of psychological insight and healing of the psyche; (5) the general sense of well-being and possibility for healing the body; (6) personal transformation; (7) the experience of transcendence and heightened spirituality.[2]

Although I have only "studied" with ayahuasca six times, I have experienced most of the effects listed above. While my motivation for trying ayahuasca a second time was mostly to see if my first experience was the norm for me (I was too naive then to know that there really is no such thing as a norm when dealing with ayahuasca), I continued to partake because I felt ayahuasca to be a teacher plant and a sentient being who could help raise my awareness on many different levels. I expect this is a motivating factor for most repeat experiencers. The most eloquent statement I have come across for explaining what one receives from ayahuasca and why one continues to study in the school of ayahuasca is in a hymn from an ayahuasca-using church: "I am drinking [ayahuasca] not out of curiosity / but in order to change / I am drinking not in order to aggrandize myself / but in order to find the light."[3]

The real conundrum concerning repeat experiences is, I believe, in trying to sort out how much of the visions one can trust. As one speaks with indigenous people about ayahuasca, one finds it described as a sort of trickster, both a truth teller and a liar. When I asked don Luis and Jack, they told me that I could trust 70 percent of the visions, should distrust 30 percent, and the other 10 percent one just couldn't make any determination about. When I pointed out the error of the math, Jack simply said, "That's part of the answer." Shanon, too, was perplexed about this same issue. When he asked an ayahuasquero how one can distinguish between what is real in the vision and what is personal projection and imagination, he was told bluntly, "In time, you will learn."[4]

This curiosity to know the real from the imagined is a compelling reason to continue one's tutelage with ayahuasca. Degree of experience does seem to be an important component not only of what one experiences with ayahuasca—the pleasure or the pain, so to speak—but also of how actively one can modify the visions and even participate in them. Shanon has gathered the phenomenological evidence that as one gains experience with the visions, one can more easily choose how intensely to immerse oneself in them and even to control them to some extent. I have surmised as much from my own discussions with people with long experience of ayahuasca. In fact, my own lack of experience caused me to think long and hard before writing this book. But I feel that even my own short experience with ayahuasca can demonstrate how one is in fact schooled by ayahuasca, and I believe that one does not have to be approaching mastery in order to offer an opinion about the course of study. Moreover, I believe that my experiences, and those of others reproduced in this book, can help solitary "homeschoolers" better respect the traditions of the lineage, including the dietary preparations and indigenous ritual and protocol that will soon be discussed.

❧ 5 ☙

Studying Through the Field of Love

So there's no turning back. One can't, one shouldn't remain in the attic of memory, precisely because of what that lost paradise means to us. Memory is an important piece of the luggage that helps us confront what awaits us when we wake from our dreams: the world of difficult light.

—ALFONSO DOMINGO, "THE MOTHER OF THE VOICE
IN THE EAR," IN *AYAHUASCA READER*

My second ayahuasca session had occurred in late July 2001. In October I would be leaving for the Amazon to do a full ayahuasca retreat, to partake of the Vine of the Soul in the old way, or as close to the old way as is possible for a modern Westerner. My two experiences of ayahuasca had upset the apple cart of my beliefs. I had thought I had a handle on what the "mystical" or "shamanic" world was, of what it was like to be immersed, for however short a period of time, in the otherworldly. Now I knew I had only a vague idea. The worlds I became immersed in while traveling with Mother Ayahuasca were more curious than any I could have imagined. Unlike my shamanic experiences, my ayahuasca journeys revealed glimpses of worlds or dimensions not even remotely human—in feel, sense, texture, or perspective. These glimpses were of "alien" realms, not in the sense of extraterrestrial, but of complete Otherness. In my shamanic experiences I had always looked through human eyes and through a human sensibility at dimensions that were, I see now, thoroughly anthropocentric, and I had never lost touch with the human perspective. Now I had caught glimpses of dimensions and modes of being from a perspective that felt as if I were nonhuman looking in on the human. It is impossible to describe this feeling because there is no language for it, and much of what I felt and saw was not just unfamiliar but absolutely unfathomable. For me this reversal of perspective was uncomfortable at best and terrifying at worst.

One thing was sure: I had come face-to-face with the issues of control and surrender. I learned that, so far, I was unable to give up the one in order to achieve the other. This is an ego issue common to many spiritual seekers, and I was turning out to be a stubborn student. Although I had worked for years on my fear issues, making what I thought was impressive progress, ayahuasca was showing me that I still had a way to go. So I was nervous about the upcoming jungle trip. We would be gone for sixteen days, ten of those in retreat deep in the Amazon jungle. We would stay pretty much in isolation in our individual huts, called *tambos,* and follow a strict diet. We would come together as a group every other night to share ayahuasca, for a total of five sessions. Every day we would drink a plant medicine "prescribed" to us by the ayahuasquero. This drink would not be potently hallucinogenic, only mildly and subtly stimulating.

I didn't know how I would acclimate to the foreign terrain and milieu of the Amazon. I am great in the mountains, which is where I had spent most of my time in Peru. I can endure cold well, but I am miserable in heat and humidity. I am not especially fond of insects. I tend to contract skin infections easily, especially in damp weather. Needless to say, my anxieties mounted as the date for our departure neared.

Then, in mid- and late September, all hell broke loose, within and without me.

I was working hard in my home office one day, trying to finish a frustrating editing project. I had a telephone interview scheduled for 9:30 that morning, and I was waiting for the man to call me. The appointed time came and went. At about a quarter to ten the phone rang. The man sounded awful. "Obviously we have to reschedule," he said, in a barely audible voice. "What?" I asked, confused. "Is something wrong?"

"Haven't you been watching TV?" he asked.

"No," I replied. "I rarely watch during the day."

"Go put it on," he said bluntly.

I hung up the phone and went to the den and turned on the television to see the World Trade Center towers in flames. No more need be said. Except that as I watched the horror, I recalled a strange feeling I had had that morning. About a quarter after eight I had gone out on the deck with a glass of juice and the morning newspaper. While reading, I suddenly felt a presence behind me. I felt that presence reach out and, from the left, decapitate me with a huge scythe or curved sword of some kind. I remember the thought popping into my head that Carlos Castaneda had said in one of his books that death comes from the left. I was creeped out, mystified as to why I had just experienced such a macabre image and feeling. I went indoors and for some reason looked at the clock: it was 8:40. I quickly showered and dressed and was soon in my office, as much in an effort to distract myself as to get ready to conduct the interview. Needless to say, once I turned on the television to the horrific images coming from New York City, Pennsylvania, and Washington, D.C., I understood the intuitive image and feeling, and I spent the rest of the day in front of the television alternately praying and crying.

A few days later, I was again in my home office working when the phone rang. I picked up the phone and the man on the other end of the line asked, "Is this Joan Wilcox? The Joan Wilcox who wrote the book *Keepers of the Ancient Knowledge*?" I replied in the affirmative, and the man went on to explain that he was looking for a copy of my book and could not find one (it was temporarily out of print). He was wondering if I had any copies, and if so, since he lived in the same town I did, if he could drive over to get one. As we talked, he expressed his interest in Peru, and I invited him to the house to talk further, look at some photos, and pick up the book. But since my husband's family was due to arrive on Saturday and I was frantically trying to meet an editorial deadline and prepare for their visit, I told him I would call him in a few days to schedule a meeting.

No sooner had I hung up the receiver than a strange feeling came over me, an insistent intuition that I should see him immediately. I am intuitive, even doing readings for people, and over the course of my life I have learned, the hard way, to listen to this inner voice, so I immediately called the man back (I'll call him Phil) and asked if he could come the next morning. He said he could.

Once we had discussed the tragic events of September 11, Phil and I had an interesting conversation about shamanism and healing and seeing energy. It turns out that Phil is a medical intuitive. We talked for nearly two hours, during which he "read" my energy field. He was fairly accurate in some things, and his comments about others were thought-provoking. During the course of our conversation, I mentioned that although I am trained in the Andean tradition to work with energy, I usually only intuit energy and rarely am able to actually see it. He asked if I would like to do an exercise; I agreed, and the result is that he reached the conclusion that my problem was not that I did not have the capacity to see energy but that I didn't want to. I was resisting seeing it. We talked about that for a while, and the subject soon strayed to my upcoming trip to the jungle. He asked if he could express an opinion—one that I might not like. I assured him he could say anything he wished, and he proceeded to tell me that in his intuitive opinion I was suppressing, or repressing, a memory and that if I did not find a way to face it, I might have a difficult time in the jungle. Up to that point, I had not expressed my apprehension about going on the trip, but now I wondered if the nagging feeling I had that I would get my energetic ass kicked in the jungle was what he was intuiting. He would not say what he thought the memory was about, and I did not get the feeling that he knew specifically, but he did make it clear that he felt it was something highly emotional and potentially frightening to me.

I was intrigued with his intuitive analysis, but not because I felt I had repressed a deep-seated trauma from my childhood. Although I am not denying that is possible, it just didn't feel intuitively right to me. Rather, I was intrigued because ayahuasca had shown me that despite all my work over the years, I still carry a lot of fear inside. Fear is a roadblock to self-expression and self-knowledge, and I knew that, for all the progress I had made in my life, I still had a long way to go in cleansing myself of it. Phil, curiously, had used words and phrases that I had "heard" during my ayahuasca journeys, and I could not shake the feeling that he was not here by accident. I felt that in some inexplicable way, he was part of how Mother Ayahuasca was preparing me for the jungle. I was growing steadily more sure that my next shamanic initiation was going to be about healing fear. I did not especially welcome the prospect of that test, but somehow it seemed appropriate. I had, as I have intimated earlier, gone through a three-year period in the mid-1990s that was a shamanic test, a period during which I had to risk everything that was important in my life and so had come face-to-face with many deep-seated fears. I had survived and even triumphed over them. Now it seemed that, on an intuitive level at least, I was about to reach even deeper, to be given the opportunity to clean up more hidden places within myself.

As Phil left, he made a prediction. "I sense that you are about to retrieve whatever this issue is," he said. "And soon. Like tomorrow!" This was Friday morning. On Saturday, five of my husband's family members were to arrive. "Oh, no! Don't tell me I am about to have a nervous breakdown in front of family!" I half joked. Phil laughed, and we left it at that.

Saturday came and went, and I had no recall of any kind. I was beginning to suspect that Phil was full of malarkey, although many of the things he had said during our conversation had hit the mark. In any case, my husband's family had arrived and we had stayed up late Saturday night visiting, and I was exhausted when I finally got to bed

Sunday evening. Just before dawn of Monday morning, it happened. I don't know that I would call what happened "memory retrieval." I hesitate to call it dreaming, although that is how most people might explain it. To this day, I do not know how to characterize the experience, although having had a few out-of-body experiences, many shamanic journeys, and by then two ayahuasca experiences, I can say unequivocally that it was none of the above, although part of one episode was out of body. All I can do is relate exactly what happened in the early morning hours of Monday, September 17, when I had a series of dream-visions that shook me to my core. I thought I had been frightened while journeying with Mother Ayahuasca, but these episodes gave me a real dose of terror, although I do not yet understand why they were so horrifying to me. To tell of them now induces no fear within me, and I cannot really see anything especially frightening in what happened. But to "live" these experiences was another story. I debated long and hard about whether I should even include these stories in this book. I value others' opinions of my credibility, and relating these experiences risks that. But I feel, deep down, that these dream-visions are related to ayahuasca, to what she was trying to show me about myself and the world, and about how I needed to approach the coming jungle trip.

FIRST DREAM/VISION/MEMORY

I am in the house I grew up in—we moved there when I was four or five years old. I am in the kitchen. I open the door to go down to the basement, which is finished and has four large rooms. I go over to an old typewriter. I haven't thought of that typewriter in forty years! I am surprised in my dream to find myself there with it now. It's old-fashioned, heavy, black metal, with round button-type keys. I used to always play writer on it. I am pounding away on it, and I can see the letters on the paper. They're just as they would be if a kid were typing: scrambled letters, random spaces, gobbledygook. I look at the black jumble of letters against the white paper, and it seems weird somehow. My sleeping self realizes that I am remembering something from long, long ago. At that realization, the scene suddenly shifts.

I am my current age (forty-five at that time) and on a bus, alone, the only passenger. I am sitting in the middle of the bus, on the left side, and I can see the bus driver's back but not his face. He's in a typical government blue bus driver's uniform. We are in a city, heading up a ramp into a tunnel. There are high concrete walls on either side of the ramp, which inclines rather steeply into the tunnel, although the tunnel itself is below ground level, as if there were another highway above us. Very odd. I notice a man walking in the otherwise deserted street: he has a slight build, and he wears a black suit, white shirt, and black tie. He has long silvery or gray hair, pulled back in a ponytail. He turns toward the bus and I catch a glimpse of his face. He looks familiar but not recognizable. He looks up at me through the bus window and seems surprised to see me, and mildly concerned. He half smiles and waves, as if he is tentative, unsure I belong here. Or more as if I am the last person he expects to see here.

The bus enters the tunnel, and as we come out the other side, we are still in the city, which is deserted around me, although I can see people across the next block, and they are going about their business, oblivious to me and the bus. I wonder if we are in Boston (I grew up in a suburb of Boston). What catches my attention is a bus-stop sign, white with blue, block-lettered words, BUS STOP, on it, that we are pulling up alongside. I feel anxious, thinking, "How will I know how to be back here at the right time? How will I ever get back here when I'm supposed to?"

The scene shifts again. Suddenly I am in my bedroom (of my current house), in bed, and it's night. I feel my husband begin to make love to me. It is very real, very visceral, and feels wonderful. I am responding as if this were real. It doesn't feel like a dream. I physically feel him, as he leans down on top of me, his chest meeting mine, his head moving down toward my right shoulder. He is about to whisper in my ear. I hear a voice (his? not his? not sure), and when I open my eyes I am shocked beyond measure to see not his face but the "face" of an insectoid "thing." The shape of its bald, bulbous head reminds me instantly of a praying mantis. The face is smooth, devoid of any characteristics. Elongated, tapering to a pointy chin. No real nose or mouth. But those eyes! Fathomless. Beyond deep. Not human but human. I am instantaneously terrified. Shocked to my core. Panicked even. I hear its voice, human, soft, but stern and somehow commanding, and it is saying something like either "We are / I am here to finally break the chain" or "It's time to break the chain, finally."

I try to scream for my husband, John, but my vocal chords won't work. I realize I am asleep (but am I really?) and that my vocal chords are paralyzed and that I have to wake myself up. I can feel air forming my husband's name straining against my vocal chords, but they are not working to produce any sound. I know my husband is in the bathroom getting ready for work and I am desperate to get his attention. The alien insect face is still close to my ear, and I finally wake myself up and call for John.

I am terrified. In total shock. Yet I am calm at the same time. This is a very weird feeling, because deep down I am completely terrified and shocked and confused, yet I feel centered and detached as well. I remember thinking that never in my wildest dreams could I have concocted such a scenario. It is simply shocking in its unexpectedness, its reality, its disturbing oddness.

I tell John what just happened and how real and unusual it is, and I feel like a fool. It is important to me that he believe me, and I'm embarrassed, even reluctant, to relate the dream-vision. He sees how upset I am, listens attentively, and is supportive, trying to calm me. I get out of bed and go outside onto the deck for a cigarette. I try to be quiet because my husband's family members are sleeping in various rooms of the house and I don't want to disturb them. Out on the deck, I am pacing, very nervous, shaken to the core. I look up at the dark sky and see the constellation Orion blazing, huge, above me. I am startled by this, for this is one of the few constellations I can recognize, and I know that the third star down in the belt is called Al Nitak and that I have always felt "attached" to that star. I learned a few years ago that this is one of the stars toward which the Giza pyramid is aligned. Anyway, this is the first time this season I have seen this constellation, and it is framed through an opening in the treetops of the woods behind the house, and it seems there just for me. In a way I cannot make logical connections to, it seems appropriate and meaningful that I am seeing it now.

I smoke and think about the possibility that I have just retrieved a repressed memory of some real event. Of course, I make the connection to alien abductions, although that possibility seems patently absurd to me at the moment. Philosophically I accept the possibility of human contact with extraterrestrials, but *my* having actual contact is another story altogether. I find it hard to accept that possibility, but I also cannot dismiss it, especially in light of my panic. I have to work to calm myself, and I do so by repeating to myself, "Okay, I am all grown up, so I survived whatever happened. I wasn't hurt. I am okay, and I am doing good work. So whatever this was, whatever may have happened to me, it hasn't affected me or harmed me. I am here, grown up, safe, and doing very spiritualized work with people."

I also start intellectualizing, rationalizing. I think that this is too, too weird. Maybe this is a screen memory for something deeper that I don't want to look at. I realize, now that the possibility is presenting itself in my own life, how skeptical I am of this whole supposed alien scenario, even though someone close to me has had such experiences and has worked to retrieve memories with Dr. John Mack, the Harvard psychiatrist who studies alleged alien abductions and uses hypnosis in his work. I keep thinking of her and knowing now what she must have been going through. No one can understand such terror until they experience the feeling themselves. I wish I could talk with her right now.

Then I try to dismiss the thoughts that this could be real. I think that perhaps this is a metaphor. I am struggling to find some explanation other than that I have just remembered something that actually might have happened. My terror also surprises me, because I have pushed the boundaries of my fears in so many areas of my life, have an extremely open mind, and practice shamanistic techniques and journeying that take me to otherworldly places. Why is this "dream" so terrifying? My ego is up in arms, already wondering what people would think of me if they knew this. It's my credibility on the line, so I try to rationalize possible psychological mechanisms for this. I think about Jungian archetypes, mythology, symbolic constructs that could explain away the dream's literalness. I think of ayahuasca's message to me during my first session, that "this is yours and not yours." But nothing feels right. It's all just an intellectual sham. This was real on some level and I think that I had better start dealing with it.

My husband is ready to leave for work and I talk to him about it some more. I am still shaking with fear. For some reason I find myself thumping my thymus area. John leaves. I am trying to be very quiet so as not to disturb my husband's family, so I decide to go back to bed, even though I am afraid to.

I lie in bed. Interestingly, I keep my robe on. Normally I don't wear anything to bed, but now I want the cover of clothing—it makes me feel better, safer, less exposed, as irrational as I know that is. I am thinking again of my friend who has had abduction experiences and how I saw something about her experience while under ayahuasca, and how when I related it to her, she confirmed that she had not told anyone about the event except her husband and Dr. Mack.* Coincidentally (or not, as the case may be), she was retrieving the memory during the same weekend I was journeying with Mother Ayahuasca and psychically visiting her. I am also aware that the praying mantislike face I saw is common to the UFO experience.

I am observing myself—my thought process and emotional state—as I lie there, the blankets pulled up nearly over my face. I marvel at the split self I seem to be: calm and centered and certain this is okay, and absolutely terrified and panicked at the same time. I think of my arro-

---

* There is one large portion of my first ayahuasca journey that I have not reproduced here for reasons of privacy. It involved telepathically contacting three of my friends. Two had no or little awareness of the contact. The other happened to be in Cambridge working with Dr. John Mack to retrieve memories of her abduction experience that weekend. While I was journeying with ayahuasca, I "saw" what she was remembering, although in a slightly symbolic and metaphoric way.

gance in the past when reading Castaneda or about alien encounters and how frightened people always seem to be when faced with the unexpected. I have been immersed in shamanism and I always thought that if I had Castaneda-like experiences (I have, but not anywhere near as strange as those he relates—that is, until I experienced ayahuasca), I would not quake in fear as he did but would try to embrace the wonder of it. I always thought that if I ever met an alien I would try to keep my wits about me and ask it about dimensional travel and God and so on. Now I know what an ass I was to think such things. Such arrogance!

SECOND DREAM/VISION/MEMORY

I must have started to drift off to sleep, because suddenly I am in a man's office. It seems to be the office of Dr. Mack (although I have never been there or had it described to me). I don't see him, just a female assistant. I hear myself say to her (not sure if they are my words or the "alien's" through me) "I am about to open a whole new window on your studies." I am lucid—I know I am "dreaming." Still, I think (in my "dream") that I am being egoistic again. I feel torn between thinking that something new is about to unfold about alien contact and that I am an egomaniac, feeling special or chosen. Then I think again about what a coward I am. I feel conflicted, but this passes. I don't know how much time passes, but I suddenly become even more conscious in my dream and I hear a voice, disembodied, in my right ear, say, "You are ready to remember the sounds now, aren't you?"

I actually hear those words, apropos of nothing I had just been thinking or dreaming. They are real, real, real. But the question, which feels more like a suggestion, *totally* and *instantly* terrifies me. I mean I am terrified to the core, more so than in the last dream with the green insectoid face at my ear. I instantly reject the idea of remembering "the sounds," and with my inner eyes, I looked downward and to my left inside myself. There, I see/feel a wall of liquid silver, undulating downward like water. It slams down on my consciousness at the very awareness of the question. Instantly, upon seeing that sheet of liquid silver closing down my mind/memory, I jump out of my body. Literally! I disassociate!

I have had some experience with out-of-body travel, but this is totally different. No smooth floating outward and upward. Not even a quick, effortless popping free. This time I slammed myself out! I find myself in my bathrobe (a different one than the one I had worn back to bed), hurrying down the hall, wanting to get as far away from my sleeping body as possible. It is dark and I am hurrying down the hallway—only I do not emerge into my den. I am in someone else's living room! I am startled. I recognize this bilocation right away, and I take a few steps forward into the room. I think (and this is a hazy, fleeting understanding or thought), "Shit! I'm out of my body and now I'm not even in my own house! I don't know *where* I am!" I am certain, however, that I am in this world, the "real" world I so know and love, actually having inadvertently astral traveled. I feel I am in New York City or some other cosmopolitan city, in a high-rise apartment building.

I can see the room clearly: It is a combination living room/dining room, and it is very tastefully, artistically, and expensively decorated. The walls of the dining area are a dark royal blue with white crown molding. There is a long, highly glossed, light wood dining table with six chairs. There are pieces of fine art, modern and abstract, on the walls. At the far end of the room, to the left of the dining table and at the edge of a wall that fronts an opening to another room, is a waist-high rectangular wrought-iron planter full of philodendrons and with a vanilla-colored metal barometer nestled in among the plants. I focus intently on the planter. The barometer, if that is what it is, is strange. It has a metal base and a single center post topped by a big circular metal face that has the barometer mechanism in it under glass. I look hard at it, but this all takes place in a fleeting second. Everything is *so real*. Somehow that planter and barometer cinch the deal that this is real—why would my imagination ever concoct such details?

I notice a man at the front right of the room. I think he is standing by sliding glass doors, but I am not sure. He is tall and stocky, very barrel-chested and big through the middle. He has brown hair combed straight back and cut very short and I think he has facial hair, a close-clipped beard and mustache. All of these impressions take place in an instant, and when I notice the man, I begin to plead with him, "Please, I need a cigarette. Just give me a cigarette!" He looks at me impassively and does not move. Yet I feel that he is compassionate, concerned for me. I am highly agitated, but I am not out of control or even raising my voice. I am more shaken than hysterical. There is a sense of my being desperate for a cigarette, as if tobacco is the only thing that will relieve my stress, will somehow ground me.

Suddenly I sense the presence of a girl, maybe eight years old, walking up from behind me, from my left. I sense her before I see her. I feel as if I know her, but she seems very odd, child and adult, human and machine, friendly and antagonistic. I am immediately wary of her. I do not want her here. I finally half turn to see her. She has a dark, very 1950s or early 1960s dress on, the kind with the puffed-out skirt; she has short brown hair and she is clutching a teddy bear in her left arm to her chest. (I recognize in some recess of my brain that from a psychological perspective she might be me when I was her age, although she looks nothing like me, nor does her personality feel at all familiar. I have no sense of identification with her at all, although somehow I am sure I know her.) She telepathically sends a message to the man about my wanting a cigarette, and I can hear it: "No," she says, "that's not a good idea."

I really dislike her. She is like an eighty-year-old in an eight-year-old body. A bossy little thing. She is coldly commanding, without the compassion the man has. I ignore her and plead once again with the man, "Please, I *really* need a cigarette!" I hear her again, in my thoughts, as she says to the man: "Remember the last time. . . ." I immediately visualize three or four chocolate-brown dogs, perhaps Labrador retrievers, jumping up, playfully, and knocking over an ashtray. There may have been a fire, but I don't see it in my mind's eye. I look toward the man again and plead rather quietly, almost under my breath, "Please, please just give me a cigarette!" He again looks at me

with compassion, and I know/sense that he does not have any cigarettes. But he looks to my right, his left, and I sense that my purse is
there with cigarettes in it and that I can probably have one. But then the
man looks back at me and says, with the utmost gentleness and compassion, trying to simultaneously quell my anxiety and explain what is
happening: "You do know that you are studying through the field of
love, don't you?"

His words stop me dead in my emotional tracks. They reach to my
innermost sense of self. The message is totally out of context and yet
seems so perfectly explanatory. I am stilled by those words, almost
immobilized by them, and it is as if my emotions (or at least my anxiety and fear) have been shut down. The clearest way to describe my
feelings at that moment is to say it is as if the world stopped. There was
nothing but those words reverberating through me: *You do know that
you are studying through the field of love, don't you?* I recognize the
profound truth of what he said, and I realize I have forgotten it.

Still, in that fleeting instant during which those words penetrate my
being, I also slam back into my body (which I catch a glimpse of on the
bed asleep as I reenter it) and wake up. Again, I am terribly upset. I
keep latching on to those words—I am studying through the field of
love—and I get the impression that whatever is happening, whatever
this means, it is huge, cosmic in scale, and it is in some sort of "divine"
order. That I agreed to study and this is the way it has to be done. That
maybe everything that has unfolded in my life since it took such an
unexpected turn onto the Peruvian path and into other shamanic areas
is no accident. Maybe I am indeed being taught through a field of love
that is ancient and penetrating and accessible in a way beyond our current understanding. But the memories of the "alien" are terrifying. Just
the thought of remembering sounds had slammed me out of my body.
What could be so terrifying about sounds? I am left thoroughly confused. I feel centered and calm and sure I can handle whatever is unfolding. I know that this is the time for me to remember, so that I can spiral
to the next phase of my work. It seems no coincidence that recently,
during the past year, my intuitive abilities had become heightened. But

at the same time, my terror is overwhelming. I cannot understand my reactions. Why am I responding with such heart-stopping panic?

Over the next few days, I could not get these two dreams-visions out of my mind. It was difficult to act the hostess for my husband's family, and I wanted nothing more than to retreat to my bedroom or office and read and write in my journal and meditate upon the emotions that had been stirred within me. I have to admit, however, that I was rather nervous about going to sleep, fearing more "dreams." I contacted a few friends and talked with them about possible meanings, and I was thankful for the much-needed perspective I gained from those conversations, but I was still left largely adrift in a sea of unknowing.

What I had experienced somehow seemed tied up with the coming jungle experience. Two ideas, especially, seemed important to me. First, that we each must remember that in this life we are all bound together and grow through the force called love, that even that which is frightening and threatening to us may be coming to us for our own good. Second, that somehow sound is important to opening consciousness. I ached to know more, to construct some context within which I could flesh out these tantalizing ideas. But, of course, the only way I could find answers, as I had been taught in my shamanic studies, was to live them. And so, in this uncertain yet committed frame of mind, a few weeks later I packed up and headed off to the Amazon.

PART TWO

The Mother of the Voice in the Ear

6

Off to the Amazon

This whole scene seemed scented by syrupy petal pies and bub-
bling ponds of decaying plant muck, a nose-puzzling mixture of
contradictory aromas (floral to fecal) perfectly befitting an
environment where cure-juices coursed alongside poisonous saps,
where the gorgeous and the marvelous repeatedly alternated with
the hideous and the dire, where brimming Life and pertinacious
Death held hands at the chlorophyll cinema; where Heaven and
Hell intermingled as they did at no other place on earth.

—TOM ROBBINS,
FIERCE INVALIDS HOME FROM HOT CLIMATES

We departed for the foreign world of the Amazon from a world that had itself become unfamiliar, and even to some degree unrecognizable. The airport terminal was palpably suffused with an eerie post–September 11 hush. It was nearly deserted except for those travelers who seemed falsely confident and deliberately cheery among the ubiquitous background of National Guard fatigue-green and the dark blue wave of airport security personnel and baggage screeners who hovered nervously in small, twittering groups around the screening belts like scurrying ants appearing purposeful but heading nowhere in particular.

From Greensboro to Miami to Lima we were screened, smiled at, and stared down. Common, everyday items—eyebrow tweezers, metal nail files, and pocket knives—were now banned items, and everyone was subject to search. Once, they actually performed a manual search of my carry-on backpack. The experience did not instill confidence in me that they could actually find concealed weapons or even recognize a potential one. During this search I had to step from behind the yellow line to help the security woman figure out how to open my compact (she was going through a small makeup kit). It still mystifies me that they confiscated metal nail files and tweezers but no one blinked an eye at a woman's compact, with its mirror that could so easily be popped out and broken and its jagged edge used as a deadly weapon. But preferring the option of powdering my nose under the brutal Amazon sun to making that point, I kept my opinion to myself. I did sheepishly point out, however, that the screener had entirely missed a zipped compartment in my pack and suggested that although there was nothing but mints and Kleenex in it, she might want to check it out. She did, especially carefully.

We did not mind the drill, and it is surprising how quickly we learned it. We had our belts unbuckled and hiking boots off before we even got to the second screening station. Soon, when standing spread-eagled as the screening wand passed over my body, I was able to predict almost to the second when it would screech, causing all eyes in the immediate vicinity to turn toward my back, where the screener would be manually feeling up the hooks and eyes of my bra closure through my shirt. As I said, we were supportive of the increased security and not the least put off by it. In fact, this was the best flying experience we ever had—empty seats on which to stretch out, no jostling for space for carry-ons in the overhead compartments, uncharacteristically attentive flight attendants, on-time departures and arrivals, and no lost luggage.

We met our friends Michelle and Andrew in Miami and flew together to Lima. The remainder of our group was to arrive on a later flight from Los Angeles, and we were to meet at breakfast at the hotel the next morning. Our group included two Californians, Henrietta, who prefers to be called Heni, and Patrick, neither of whom knew each other. (As I explained previously, most names are pseudonyms.) They are both in their midforties, and both have worked with ayahuasca many times before. In fact, Patrick had come with Jack and don Luis to this jungle retreat the previous year; and Heni revealed that she had been cured of late-stage cancer (uterine cancer, I think) during an ayahuasca session. Although I was not able to confirm that, I had no reason to distrust her claim.* Steven is a tall, quiet New Yorker who had also been in the jungle with don Luis and Jack the previous year. Also joining us was a young Midwesterner named Jeff. With Michelle and Andrew and me and John, our group totaled eight. Jack, who was to assist don Luis, was also with us; we would meet don Luis in Pucallpa.

After quick introductions and a buffet breakfast from which we chose foods compatible with the ayahuasca diet, we headed back to the airport. By eleven-thirty Saturday morning we were in Pucallpa, where we would spend the day and evening and repack for the jungle, leaving most of our bags behind. We could take only what we could carry in a backpack. At the Pucallpa airport—a single, small, but fairly new terminal—a battered red pickup truck pulling a long metal cart delivered the luggage to the carousel. I let John pick through the jumbled mass of bags to find ours, as I pressed my nose to the large plate glass window in wonder at what filled the bed of the pickup. It was piled staggeringly high with rough, slatted wooden crates filled with peeping and pecking chicks. Nine layers of crates tottered skyward and extended up and over the roof of the truck cab. I was mesmerized by their defiance of the laws of gravity.

---

* There are anecdotal reports of ayahuasca as a healing agent in cancer and other serious illnesses. Most well known is the personal account of the healing of cancer by Donald M. Topping, Ph.D., Professor Emeritus, University of Hawaii, as reported in two issues of *MAPS* (the *Bulletin of the Multidisciplinary Association for Psychedelic Studies*), vol. 8, no. 3 (1998) and vol. 9, no. 2 (1999); and in *Shaman's Drum*, 55 (2000). Serious research into ayahuasca as an aid to healing addictions, especially alcohol and crack addiction, is being undertaken by Dr. Jacques Mabit at his center, Takawasi, which is in Peru. See, for example, Jacques Mabit, Rosa Grove, and Joaquin Vega, "Takawasi: The Use of Amazonian Shamanism to Rehabilitate Drug Addicts," in *Yearbook of Cross-Cultural Medicine and Psychotherapy*, ed. Michael Winkleman and Walter Andritzky (1995).

Pucallpa itself is a ramshackle city teeming with people, stray dogs, aging cars spewing fumes, and three-wheeled "cabs" powered by loud, smelly engines or human pedal power. It is polluted in many ways, but worst of all by noise—car horns honking, vendors clogging the sidewalks (when there were sidewalks) and hawking their wares, dogs barking, radios blaring tinny, static-filled music. It retains vestiges of its reputation as a rough-and-tumble jungle frontier town, which writer Tom Robbins characterized as the "Vulture Capital of South America." It is, according to Robbins, "polluted, contaminated, decayed, rancid, rotten, sour, debauched, uncultured, and avaricious. It's also hot, humid, and disturbingly vivid."[1] Never having been to Pucallpa before, I have no basis for comparison and so cannot bear witness to any beneficial transformation over the years since Robbins wrote that description, but I can confirm that it remains "disturbingly vivid."

We arrived at our hotel at one-thirty that afternoon. It was a rather faded, antiquated building, but quite nice by what I took to be Pucallpa standards. The weather was decidedly muggy but not unbearable. I was happy to see that we had an air conditioner in our room, although I was dubious about its safety as I inspected the mass of thin, duct-taped wires that snaked from its innards and down the wall to an electrical socket. Our bathroom had hot and cold running water, for which I was thankful, for you learn never to take hot water for granted in Peru, even in Lima or Cuzco.

At four o'clock we headed to a restaurant, where we would be joined by don Luis—and what a feast we had! We had all been easing ourselves into the ayahuasca diet, which I will describe shortly, and so our meal was quite a surprise: two types of fish; a typical, and delicious, Peruvian *ensalada* of rice, red onions, sliced avocados and tomatoes, and fettuccine-like strips of hearts of palm, all drizzled with lime juice; and, finally, my mouthwatering favorite, green corn tamales with chopped red onion and hot mustard. Before we ate we looked to Jack for approval, and he smiled and told us to dig in "because everything goes downhill from here!" We laughed, but we knew he was serious—our jungle diet would be bland and sparse. Jack explained that although our meal contained spicy foods, our main dishes, the fish dishes, one of which was *paiche* and the other *doncella,* were in accordance with the ayahuasca diet. I liked the paiche in particular, and learned that it is a fish as large as sturgeon and is considered a delicacy. That dinner was also my introduction to *chicha,* a ubiquitous local drink made of corn that comes in fermented and unfermented varieties. We sampled unfermented chicha, since alcohol is prohibited for at least a week before partaking of ayahuasca. One sip was enough for me, for I found its sour taste disagreeable.

At the restaurant, don Luis had joined us with Fernando, his friend and a fellow ayahuasquero. Fernando is a mestizo of about thirty, handsome and articulate, although he speaks very little English. Although fully trained as an ayahuasquero, and a very good one according to Jack, he holds an everyday job as a professional in a field of mainstream medicine. We were also introduced to don Emilio, a *vegetalista* who, we learned to our delight, would be accompanying us to the jungle. Basically, a vegetalista is an herbalist, a healer who relies on his plant knowledge and may or may not also use ayahuasca. Don Emilio, Jack told us, is a skilled herbalist who is sought out by many people for his plant knowledge and healing skills. A short, thin, dark-skinned man of modest demeanor, he was also trained as an ayahuasquero, although he no longer frequently imbibes the Vine of the Soul. After dinner we retired to the courtyard of our hotel, where don Luis, Fernando, and Jack talked with us for more than an hour about ayahuasca. Fernando provided most of the information, with Jack translating.

Fernando began by citing ayahuasca's historical uses beyond healing: divining the weather, petitioning for successful harvests, finding animals for the hunt, locating enemies, counteracting sorcery, connecting to the spirits of the jungle for all kinds of information concerning both community life and one's individual life.

Then his remarks became more philosophical. "Everything changes for us once we define an objective for ourselves, which includes how to use this universe of plants and the body of knowledge that has been passed on from generation to generation. This is knowledge that can help us in our daily lives. Very often spirituality is considered abstract," he said. "But to eat is spiritual. Going to the bathroom can be spiritual. We must go beyond duality. My intention, and Luis's, is to see how we can use these plants for everyday life.

"You teach us," he said, gesturing toward us. "And we teach you. Many people come here to teach us—meditation, music as therapy, Reiki. We learn from you and you learn from us." He shifted gears then, talking specifically about ayahuasca. "Ayahuasca is only one plant. Its properties are better known by the public than are those of other plants, but it is only one plant. There is not a healer in Peru who uses only ayahuasca. They use many plants. The diet and using other plants are as important as using ayahuasca. I mention this to tell you how important it is to do the diet for the other plants, not just for ayahuasca."

He began to name other plants and their characteristics. "Bobinsana grows near the water. It has long and deeply penetrating roots. Its trunk opens into many branches. Many plants fall down, but bobinsana doesn't because its roots are so deep. I tell you this because many times the exterior of a plant tells you what happens when you explore it in your interior. Ingesting bobinsana makes a person more rooted in nature. And as the trunk of the plant opens up, so too does a person open up. That is why it is a teacher plant.

"*Chuchuhuasi* is tall, with a big trunk. It gives endurance to the body. Some plants give endurance and some are used exclusively for cleansing, to cleanse and purify the body. With *yahuarpanga* you must drink a lot of water. This plant induces vomiting. You keep on vomiting and vomiting. This cleanses your body. Vomit is a type of medicine. It purifies the body. Some plants heal emotions. For instance, *ushpahuasa*. Traditional shamans call it a rejuvenating plant, but it won't erase your wrinkles! It works to loosen the emotional parts and the memory. It opens the heart."

I listened carefully as Fernando and Jack described ushpahuasa. After my weird alien dream episodes, I had consulted two friends who, through various shamanic and intuitive tools, advised me that part of my trip to the jungle would be to learn to "feel more deeply" (although I was sure I had already felt terror about as deeply as I cared to) and to open my heart chakra. Both had also suggested that this trip would be about retrieving memory. Neither had known what the other's insights had been, so I had to respect the repeated message Spirit seemed to be sending me. Now almost the same words were being spoken by Fernando to describe this teacher plant, so I was especially attentive. I most assuredly wanted to work with ushpahuasa while in retreat in the jungle.

Fernando continued with his explanation. "These are a group of plants that are not given enough attention. Ayahuasca is best known, but all of these plants have their uses." He then veered off to discuss the ayahuasca diet. The diet, as was explained to the group by Jack weeks before our departure for Peru, is used to cleanse the system, and it should be started at least a week before the retreat. It includes abstaining from red meat and pork and cutting back on or also eliminating chicken and fish and eliminating salt, pepper, and most other spices, especially hot spices and chili-type peppers; sugar, including most desserts and pastries; and fats and oils. Also discouraged are yeast products; fermented foods such as soy and tofu, and pickled foods; acidic foods; citrus; and dairy products. In addition, alcohol is prohibited, as are coffee, tea, and other caffeine-containing drinks. Cold or iced drinks are also discouraged. One must also abstain from sex. No medicines are allowed, even prescription medicines, especially those that act as MAO-inhibitors or are tranquilizers or antidepressants. Most over-the-counter medications, such as antihistamines and cold remedies, are not allowed either.* So what is left to eat? Jack told us our meals during the retreat would be mostly plain rice, oatmeal or quinoa, and plantains. We would drink only water.

---

* The basics of the diet are age-old, having been followed by ayahuasqueros for centuries, and the diet has a complex biochemical effect on the body. Ayahuasca seems to increase serotonin levels, and the diet may work to decrease, and so regulate, the serotonin levels in the body. Vomiting and diarrhea can result from an overload of serotonin, which explains ayahuasca's reputation as *la purga*. This also explains the prohibition of the use of medications such as Prozac, which are selective serotonin reuptake inhibitors. Too much serotonin in the system can be dangerous, causing hypertensive incidents and other problems. A diet low in tryptophans, which are found primarily in carbohydrates, helps

Jack went on to explain that the term *the diet* does not refer to the food and medicine restrictions alone but also to the overall experience of going into the jungle to work with a single, or a few, plants. One undertakes a retreat to work with a particular plant, to get to know its effects and how to use it—to befriend its spirit and, if one is so honored, to accept its offer to become one's ally. Fernando picked up the thread of the conversation and explained, "The diet [retreat] is undertaken for a period of time. It may be eight days, fifteen days, one month, or three months. It depends on the effects on the individual body and is directed by the shaman. Every day the shaman comes to the student and gives him a plant. In general, you do one plant, and take that same plant every day for the duration of the diet. We will do this, but we will also add ayahuasca every other night, with one back-to-back session on two consecutive nights.

"These are the rules of the diet. Salt is the door to enter the diet and to leave it. You stop [eating] salt to enter the door. We'll be eating a bland diet of quinoa [a grain], oats, rice, and a specific type of fish, if they are in the river and we can catch them. We didn't make up this diet. It is old. It comes from many generations of use. It is empirical knowledge. Why this diet? I don't know. We believe it has to do with eating with no flavor. Your sense of smell gets very sensitive. Your body smell changes. Your sight becomes clearer. Your urine becomes very clear. It is similar to a fast. This diet plus the ingestion of the teacher plant empowers you. The diet creates the ideal context for the plants, [so they can] find a space prepared for them in our bodies. You are ingesting the water and active principle of the plant, but the plant is also a spirit. It has spirit, energy, soul. Ingesting plants is not

---

counter the increase in serotonin levels and is especially important when one is undertaking a retreat with its frequent, multiple ayahuasca sessions. J. C. Callaway writes that "brain serotonin levels do not approach toxic levels after ayahuasca alone." But he adds that people who are taking medications that act as specific serotonin reuptake inhibitors (SSRIs), such as Prozac, "would be wise to allow at least eight weeks to pass from the time of the last dose of an SSRI before ingesting ayahuasca or any other MAO inhibitor." See Callaway, "Phytochemistry and Neuropharmacology" in Metzner, *Ayahuasca*.

compatible with all things. It is compatible with isolation and the diet and the healer who will lead the ceremonies. To take the best from the diet, it is best to remain relatively isolated. This leads to introspection."

Here Jack weighed in, expanding on Fernando's advice and explanation. "You should put nothing artificial on your bodies," he advised us. "Use no toothpaste, body lotions, shampoo, soap—nothing that is not natural. They interfere with the sharpening of the senses." Michelle and I looked at each other. Our packs were about to get a lot lighter.

"The diet is not balanced," Jack admitted, "and it is not much [in portion size]. Your body may weaken some by the fourth, fifth, or sixth day. But you will feel much more perceptively and acutely. You will be more sensitive. When we finish the diet, we will have soup with salt, and our bodies will immediately recover their strength. But during the diet and the five ayahuasca sessions, your body may be very open. This is why we stay in the jungle one extra day. It would be too great a shock on your system to go directly back to Pucallpa. We will do ayahuasca every other day, except for the last two sessions, which will be on two consecutive days. Every day you will drink a plant teacher as well, which will be selected for you by don Luis and don Emilio, based on their reading of your energy. We will eat certain fish if they are available to be caught in the river. This is *boquichico,* which means "little mouth." We cannot eat most other types of fish while on the diet, especially those with large teeth or mouths, or those that are bottom feeders. They disrupt the diet. Normally, when we get to the jungle, you will receive your daily meal at about ten o'clock in the morning. You'll drink the plant teacher earlier, probably between eight-thirty and nine o'clock. Then you will eat. There is no other meal on the day of an ayahuasca session. On the off days, you will get a second, small meal in the afternoon, about three o'clock, probably of oatmeal or quinoa with no spices."

We asked a few questions and then the group broke up, some of us wandering to the far corner of the courtyard, where some Shipibo Indian women were waiting patiently in the lengthening shadows to sell their crafts, and some of us returning to our rooms to pack our backpacks. That's what John and I did. I removed all my toiletries, retaining only some Gold Bond medicated skin cream should I need it for insect bites or skin infections. At the last minute, in a surge of habit tinged with vanity, I tucked a small makeup case into my pack. As John eyed me tucking the makeup into a zippered pocket, he recalled the days when he worked for Deepak Chopra, a medical doctor turned teacher of Eastern spiritual arts, including Indian ayurvedic healing. He informed me of the ayurvedic belief that the skin "eats" whatever you put on it. So it makes sense, he said, that we would not want to use anything artificial during our retreat. I smiled and remained silent and did not remove the makeup from the pack. In an odd, inexplicable way, the makeup was a security blanket for me. Looking back, I suspect that in some unconscious way it propped up my illusion that if ayahuasca succeeded in stripping away all my inner masks, I could at least fall back on my familiar outer one.

At 7:30 the next morning, we assembled with our gear, ready to hit the road—and the river, since much of our trip would be by dugout canoe. The day was growing steamy, and perspiration quickly skimmed my skin. I wondered how I would hold up in the jungle.

As our drivers loaded the subcompact cars, cramming the small hatchback areas with our luggage and supplies like chefs stuffing turkeys with dressing, the Shipibo Indian women flocked around us, calling our names, which they had quickly learned, and tussling to get close to us to sell their wares. They are handsome women, their broad, flat faces haloed by the glow of their long blue-black hair, a fringe of bangs cut straight across their foreheads and just above the glinting olive black of their eyes. Their skirts, which tightly encircle their hips and fall to midcalf, are hand woven, beautifully stitched with the classic geometric Shipibo ayahuasca-vision patterns in their characteristic eye-shocking colors. Many of us had seen the same patterns in our own visions. In fact, I had seen such liquid-light geometry superimposed over people's bodies during my second session. Wherever the symmetry of the pattern was skewed or broken, I saw a density of dark, stagnant energy that, I was told and indeed intuited, indicates the presence of or potential for physical illness or emotional blocks.

Three of the Shipibo women called out my name in Spanish: "Juana! Juana!" The trio pushed their way toward me, the women quickly grabbing both my wrists and fastening bracelets made of jungle seeds around them. The bracelets were gorgeous, some elegant in their simplicity, others amazing in the complexity of their design. I thanked them, and mildly protested while trying not to hurt their feelings. I knew they expected money for these trinkets, but, not having been able to resist their entreaties and smiles whenever I left the hotel room, I had already purchased more jewelry than I wanted. They insisted now that these were *regalos,* gifts. I thanked them again as I crammed myself into one of the tiny cars along with John, Michelle, Andrew, and our driver.

It was a rough ride to our first destination, which I will not name in the interest of honoring don Luis's request that we keep directions to his jungle retreat private. Not far from Pucallpa, the badly pot-holed asphalt road gave way to red dirt tracks riddled with humps and ruts. The drivers, ours and those of the other two cars, were oblivious to road conditions, driving at reckless speeds and dodging the few oncoming trucks and cars that passed us in the opposite direction on the narrow road. I was in the middle of the backseat, with my legs up on the floor hump, and the ride was uncomfortable. Within an hour my backside was sore, but there was no room to shift my weight or stretch out. It took a few hours to reach the derelict, rough-and-tumble town that was our first stop. The dirt streets were studded with piles of rubble and broken-down cars. In the main square—a scrappy area of dirt pockmarked here and there with grass—clusters of townspeople were gathered, eating and talking. We were a curiosity to them, but little more. We ate lunch, which was quite enjoyable once you got past the unsanitary conditions of the decidedly run-down restaurant. As we devoured plates of plain rice and boiled chicken, children congregated at the entrance, peeking in at us and laughing. One adorable but brazen girl strode in and nearly climbed onto my lap. In Spanish she admired my earrings and asked why we were here and where we were headed. "*La selva?*" she asked without waiting for my answer. The jungle? She seemed to know don Luis. Soon she was joined by two friends, and

Heni and Patrick entertained them with songs. They reciprocated by singing to us in Quechua and Spanish. After lunch, Heni and Pat bought two oversized bags of hard candy and handed it out to all the children, who came running from every nook and cranny of the village as if there had been a sugar-radar alert.

We departed about noon—the river part of the trip was about to begin. We hauled our gear from the cars to the riverbank and waited while the canoe was loaded. We were on a tributary of the Amazon, and the river was wide, with brackish brown waters and a swift current. Our canoe was a long craft carved from a single mahogany log, with a blue tarp strung out to make a roof to protect us and our gear (and some of our food supplies) should it rain. Even though the boat was much larger than I expected, I could not imagine how it could accommodate us and all our gear and supplies. Surprisingly, we fit, along with Angelina, our cook, and two boatmen, for a total of fourteen people. There were wooden slat seats along each side of the dugout, with a narrow central aisle and a large open area between the front and rear sections of seats. The gear was piled in a haphazardly organized fashion in the open middle section, on a low wooden platform to keep it out of any water that might settle at the bottom of the boat. After some juggling of people and supplies to get the weight distributed evenly, the boatmen strung blue plastic tarp over the foodstuff and gear, and then we pushed off.

The weather was cool and overcast—a good day for traveling, and our hours-long journey was slow, lazy, and uneventful. The river grew relatively calm, and it curved in graceful arcs through the thickening vegetation. It was not long before we were surrounded on all sides by a profusion of green as far as you could see to the horizon. Occasionally we spied a small village, which usually was little more than a sparse grouping of thatch-roofed huts built up on stilts or platforms close to the river. Wooden signs sprouted from the thick bushes at the river edge of the villages, announcing their names, which almost invariably were Saint something-or-other. Now and then we passed another canoe; one was occupied by a couple of fishermen who cast handmade nets out into the water and another by a stone-faced man and woman, who appeared to be taking their produce to market. The only sounds were the distant squawking of birds and the annoying, sputtering whine of the outboard motor. Occasionally Jack and don Luis pointed out plants to us, especially bobinsana. Overall, the jungle was monotonously green—green upon green upon green. The panoply of statuesque and even gargantuan trees; the thick climbing or looping vines; the profusion of thorny or broad-leafed or fanlike bushes, especially along the river's edge—all combined to make the eye experience of the jungle one of differing textures rather than of colors. Occasionally we could see distant smoke, curling in gray columns into the sky, which was the only ground-level evidence of the blight of the jungle—slash-and-burn farming. Once we passed a huge pile of scrap mahogany clogging the riverbank and rising like a fortress wall—the detritus from illegal logging. The poaching of mahogany trees is widespread in the Amazon, and toward the end of our stay in the jungle, we would see evidence of it, as poachers floated huge logs down the river past our camp.

After a few hours, the canoe turned up a smaller tributary—the river along which don Luis's camp is located. It began to drizzle, but we were protected by the tarp. The bottom of the canoe, however, had slowly accumulated water, enough so that the hems of my pant legs were wet and muddy. I tried to keep my boots up on a wooden rib along the side of the canoe, but it was neither easy nor comfortable. Finally the boatmen steered us toward the bank and bailed out the canoe. I wondered if this meant we still had hours to go on the trip, but we were only under way again for about ten minutes when they pulled close to a sandy embankment. We had arrived, although I would have been hard-pressed to explain how anyone could know that *this* was the place, for every sandbar looked alike to me, and this one seemed no different from any other. We leaped off the boat one by one, trying not to rock it too much. There was about a two-foot gap with knee-deep water between the boat and the sandbar. A few young men had come out of the forest to help us. They had obviously been waiting for us, and they appeared to be nonplussed by fussy gringos who either did not want to get their hiking boots wet or were too lazy to go through the trouble of removing socks and shoes to wade ashore. So we leaped, one by one, onto shore. Lucky for us, the river was high enough for the boatmen to float our gear farther upriver to camp, so we were spared the need to hump our packs into camp.

The hike through the jungle to camp took only twenty minutes and was fascinating. This was it! I was finally *in* the Amazon. The canoe ride had been like coasting through a postcard. This was the real thing. The path through the jungle was narrow but well marked, and more hilly than I expected. The jungle up close is gorgeous, and viscerally provocative, for I could feel its fecund energy and almost smell its chlorophyllous juiciness. As I walked, the light kaleidoscoped from reflected brightness here to dank darkness there. I was astounded by the size of some of the leaves. Huge palms swayed over our heads, their fronds arching in immense awnings. There were elephant ear plants with leaves taller than I and truly elephantine in their broadness. Fat clusters of plantains hung from trees or made hulking mounds on the ground where they had fallen to rot. I had heard that this type of plantain is inedible unless cooked, and I can attest to the fact that even cooked they are disgusting.* The word is that even insects will not eat them. I would certainly come to believe that, although I never confirmed it as scientific fact.

At one point during the short hike, John called my attention to a bright red-and-yellow caterpillar that was twice the size of my thumb. I was disappointed that I did not see many flowers. It was the dry season, and so most of the flowering plants were not in bloom. We heard rather than saw birds. The jungle was a cacophony of bird calls: the irritating squabbling of groups of parrots, mynah birds that sounded like sailors whistling at pretty girls, *whoooowoo, whoooowoo*. At one point we had to ford a narrow but swift stream, with water about knee-high and a slick, rocky bottom. Most of us rolled up our pant legs and

---

* I do not know the scientific name for this type of plantain, but I can assure readers it is not the type commonly available in U.S. supermarkets.

removed our boots and socks to cross barefoot. Michelle crossed in her hiking boots, thinking that since the temperature was so warm and was almost guaranteed to stay that way, they would dry during our stay. But that was not to be the case. Even after ten days in camp, her boots were still sodden.

Before long we reached the edge of camp, where the cook's area was set up with wide, open-air wooden platforms about a foot or so off the ground and topped by thatched roofs. They served as supply depots, sleeping platforms, and kitchen. We took a water break, and that is when John noticed that my face was covered with a pink hivelike heat rash. I hoped this was not an omen of things to come for me. Don Luis and Jack beckoned us toward an ayahuasca plant, a thick, woody rope-like vine that twisted up a tree in a double helix. They showed us how the leaves grow in twos, one opposite the other. None of the vines was in flower. They also pointed out chacruna bushes nearby. Don Luis was growing both to make sure he always had a supply, even though his camp is carved out of virgin jungle and he has found wild ayahuasca nearby. It is becoming more and more difficult to find wild ayahuasca. There is such demand for it now that most of the ayahuasca used in ceremony is cultivated.

We followed Jack over a small, rickety bridge badly hammered together from logs, and then he led us up the trail toward the tambos—our shelters for the retreat. We were told that we would not be allowed to visit the kitchen area again unless we needed to for some health or emergency reason. Part of the retreat is to stay isolated from those who are not dieting, such as the cooks, although they too must be "clean" in order to be allowed to prepare food for those in retreat. Another taboo while doing an ayahuasca diet is fire, so the cook's area was off-limits for that reason as well.

Spread out along the trail were the tambos, small, rectangular huts built up off the jungle floor, with railings but no walls, and with thatched roofs that spanned out over the railings and sloped down close to the ground. Jack explained that the tambos were spaced out up the trail for about a half mile and that we should each choose one. Right about then I felt a sudden, painful stinging on my upper right arm. Then another! My upper arm felt on fire. I slapped in the general vicinity of the pain and pulled up my T-shirt sleeve to see three red welts. The pain was intense, as if someone had injected beads of molten lead under my skin. I moved away from the thatched roof of the tambo and discovered that I had just received my jungle baptism—by fire ants. The hellish stinging lasted about twenty minutes before it faded. Thankfully, while I saw plenty of fire ants during my stay, I was not bitten again.

Jack claimed the first tambo along the trail. It is where he always stays. Directly up the trail from him was the communal house, called a *maloca*. Basically it is a large tambo, but round instead of rectangular. This is where we would come together for the group ayahuasca sessions. Michelle laid claim to the next tambo up the trail, and I the one after that. We had agreed to be close to each other for moral support, and we both now decided that we wanted to be close to the maloca. We had quickly assessed the situation and decided that we did not want to be stumbling too far up the trail in darkness after an ayahuasca session. I actually wanted to stay in the fourth tambo, but it was infested with ants, and after having just been bitten by fire ants, I decided "no way." Don Luis moved into it the next day. John chose a tambo well up the trail, next to a small stream and almost directly over a waterfall. He ended up loving his site, although on one or two ayahuasca nights he stayed in the hammock at my tambo for hours or for the entire night because he was too disoriented or exhausted to hike up to his own.

As the others went farther up the trail to choose their tambos, Michelle and I retreated back to ours to begin unpacking. Among my first tasks was to hang out the "Amazon Hilton" sign I had made for my tambo and the "Miss Michelle's Salon" for Michelle's. It was our joke on Jack, since at one point he had, perhaps unconsciously, perhaps not, given us the impression that he wondered if we were too prissy for this trip.

My tambo was in a clearing just off the main path. It was about twelve feet deep by sixteen feet long, its wooden floor about a foot off the ground. All the tambos were handmade by don Luis's assistants and were open to the air. The framed doorway openings were inset among the rough wooden railings, and the peaked roofs "umbrellaed" down over the sides. When I stood in mine, the roof overhang obscured the view of the river in front of me and of the jungle on the other three sides. I had an unobstructed view, however, when lying in my hammock or on the wooden platform bed.

As I began to unpack, Chico and Mateo arrived—our camp aides. Chico, an apprentice ayahuasquero to don Luis, is about twenty-two years old and is a handsome, solidly built young man with a style all his own. He sported a hip pair of wraparound sunglasses, and his glossy black hair was cut in a bowl shape with a long top layer. He would fit in at any Lima discotheque. Mateo is a boyish twenty-year-old who looks more like sixteen. His is the spirit of a child. He would often break into a wide grin that hid nothing of his emotions or his curiosity. He loves to laugh, and as I would soon learn, he and Chico were inseparable. Even though they are adults, don Luis and Jack affectionately called Chico and Mateo "the boys," and we did too.

There was a thin mattress covering the wooden bed platform, and sitting atop it were a set of sheets, a pillow, a light blanket, and a mosquito net. I was delighted with the accommodations. What more can you ask for in the jungle but sheets? Chico helped me string up the mosquito netting and hammock, which we tied off so that it angled from the post behind the mosquito-netted bed at one end and swung toward the door-frame post at the other. The hammock was the color of orange sherbet and gaily bisected the tambo, although I had room directly in front of my bed and to the left side of the tambo to move around. There was a small, rough-hewn table and stool, and a tall, narrow bookcase-like unit with two shelves. All the furniture in camp had been crafted by Mateo or Chico from materials taken from the jungle around us. On top of the shelved unit was a plastic five-gallon container of water with a spout. So we wouldn't have to purify our water from the river after all. We had come prepared to do so, on Jack's advice, and I was relieved to know that safe water was not going to be a problem. My only concern with the water would be the huge, inches-long cockroach that took up residence on the jug. After a few days it didn't bother me, but it took some getting used to.

I spent the rest of the afternoon sorting through my backpack and the items in the many Ziploc bags it contained. Soon John came down the trail to visit. I was eager for him to help me find my "bathroom." I had not located it by looking around and I was not keen on wandering away from my tambo by myself. We each had found sturdy walking sticks for the precise purpose of striking the trail in front of us as we walked, which we were counseled would scare away any snakes. I had heard snakes hung in the trees in the jungle and could drop down on you, and so I felt I had only half my bases covered with the stick. With John for moral support, I tramped around my tambo and quickly found the faint signs of a path slightly behind and to the left of it. The short path led to a cleared area, where a wooden box with an opening cut in it was set over a three-foot hole in the ground. It was quite close to the trail, but the boys had staked huge palm fronds into the ground to screen it off. Again, I was content with the accommodations, although I made a mental note to remember to always go to the bathroom before I went to bed, as I did not want to wander here by myself in the middle of the night. I would soon learn that it is dark—pitch black—by about six o'clock, so all my best intentions in this regard were moot.

We met as a group that Sunday evening for our "last supper" together. The food was delicious and did not exactly conform to the dietary restrictions, but, once more, Jack told us not to worry and warned us that it truly was all downhill from here. This time he was telling the truth. The next day we would start our diet proper, which included staying to ourselves, in relative isolation. Jack gave us permission to visit each other, but he counseled that we should keep our visits and talk to an absolute minimum. So we took the opportunity this night to enjoy each other's company and marvel at the jungle. John noticed what looked like a huge lightning bug; it was odd, though, because it had two luminescent spots but they did not flash. When one landed on my walking stick, we noticed that it was a large, grayish brown mothlike insect whose two eyes were huge rings of luminescent yellow. While John marveled at it, I slapped at my legs, for something was—or many things were—crawling up one of my legs. Even though my pants had slide ties at the ankles, the bugs had found their way in. I felt sharp little bites but did not know what was causing them. The bites did not end up itching and they caused me no problems, which was good, since I would soon have many, many more, especially on my arms and legs.

It was dark as we headed back to our tambos, and before we left, we were each given two small packages, each containing a half dozen thick white candles—our night lights. Before we left, Jack also informed us that don Luis and don Emilio had chosen the plant teachers that each of us would drink every day, beginning Tuesday, two days from now. Those of us who had never before been in the jungle were assigned a tea made from the leaves of the bobinsana plant. Its effects are to ground you in nature yet also open your consciousness to new experience. Andrew had asked to diet with chuchuhuasi, the plant that teaches strength and endurance, and his request was granted. Steve, also, would diet with chuchuhuasi. I wanted to switch to ushpahuasa. It is a tea made from the plant's roots and its effect is to open your heart chakra to stimulate depth of feeling and to help you retrieve memories, especially of childhood. I was unsure if I should speak up now and ask for this plant teacher or wait and talk with Jack privately about it later. As we readied to leave, rather than actually making a decision, I let my chance to talk with Jack lapse as he headed out into the darkness toward his tambo.

John stopped at my tambo to help me settle in for the night. We had strung up a blue tarp at one corner of the tambo as a dressing and washing area for me. My tambo, and Michelle's, were right next to the trail, and so we had little privacy, much less than all the others had. John promised that the next day he would bring me some cord he had stashed in his pack to string up as a clothesline. We used two flat rocks as candleholders, melting some wax onto each and setting a candle upright into the hot wax. That worked quite well. Then John swung in the hammock and I sat on the little rough-hewn stool and we soaked up the atmosphere in silence. Occasionally we eyed each other, saying with our gaze, "Can you believe we are here?" While we remained silent, the jungle was alive with sound. It does not take long to realize that the experience of the jungle is not visual, for the vegetation is so thick you cannot see far in any direction and you have to search for an opening in the canopy to see the sky. It is, instead, an experience of sound, with hardly a quiet moment. Insects, frogs, birds, leaves falling—leaves *crashing,* I should say. Every once in a while a crashing sound startled John and me, bringing us to our feet in an adrenaline rush. We were certain a wild boar, anteater, or some other jungle creature was about to charge out of the darkness. It took us until the next day to finally figure out that the noises were leaves falling. The simple fact is that some of the leaves are so huge that they make a racket when they fall. Even after we knew what was causing these sudden explosions, it took us days to stop jumping every time it happened. I simply never got over marveling at it.

The insects soon made themselves a nuisance. It was not long after lighting the candles that huge moths and other flying creatures began their kamikaze raids. Tired of dodging giant droning winged things, we decided to turn in. I was hesitant at John's leaving, but I did not want to show it. He hung around while I changed into my nightclothes, a cotton tank-top T-shirt that reached almost to my knees. He kissed me before I hopped into bed beneath the mosquito netting, then passed my water bottle, flashlight, and handkerchief under the netting to me, and tucked the netting in tightly under the mattress. He blew out the candles, told me once again that he loved me, then headed into the dark.

I lay there immersed in the sounds. The sounds. The sounds. The jungle never sleeps. In fact, it is more alive during the cooler air of night than at any other time. There were the familiar sounds of cicadas and tree frogs. But there was also the choir of strange, rhythmic, and often haunting hoots, clicks, swishes, buzzes, twitters, swooshes, trills, whirs, and whistles. Still, I felt safe—there is no place that feels more secure than within the white cocoon of a mosquito net, even if it is hot—and I finally drifted off to sleep, feeling as if I were cradled within the arms of my Green Mother.

7

Growing Green

Spirits are an incontestable part of humankind's "experienced reality," and, regardless of what their "ultimate reality" is, cross-culturally they seem to represent the forces of transformation that can either enhance growth or inflict illness or even death. Therefore, they are by their very nature both good and evil, both guides and deceptors, both healers and destroyers, the creators of life and the servants of death. To seek out these transformative powers willingly, as the shaman does, brings one into intimate contact with the secrets of existence. To open oneself to these double-edge forces is thereby to transform oneself.

—RICHARD NOLL,
"SHAMANS, 'SPIRITS,' AND MENTAL IMAGERY,"
IN *SHAMANS THROUGH TIME*

I awoke early Monday morning, about five o'clock, the remnants of an anxiety-filled dream hovering at the periphery of memory. Try as I might to recall the entire dream, all I could remember was that I had been shopping, barefoot, and had not been able to buy anything, although I could not remember why. I left the store pushing an empty shopping cart and then feeling startled and confused as strangers came by, one by one, and dropped items into it. I ended up going home with all kinds of things that I did not buy and did not want. I played around with possible interpretations for the dream but none felt satisfactory. It wouldn't be until the next day, as I lay in my hammock thinking about my first ayahuasca ceremony in the jungle, that I understood the dream in a much deeper way. But that was tomorrow.

This morning, I quickly shrugged off the dream and puttered around my tambo. As I gathered up my clothes from where I had draped them over the hammock the night before, I realized my pants were too damp to wear and something had chewed a hole the size of a silver dollar through the left front of my T-shirt. I had planned to wear each set of clothes for several days, and now here was one set already unwearable, at least for today. The sun had not yet reached into my tambo area, but I hung the pants on the railing to dry and I gave up on the T-shirt, balling it up and tucking it into a corner of the shelf unit. I pulled a clean, dry tank top and sarong-type skirt out of my backpack. I decided to forego the river and bathe with premoistened towelettes, of which I had packages and packages. Then I dressed and selected one of my three paperback books, Karen Armstrong's *Buddha*. I swung in the hammock reading, with some difficulty, since my tambo was still in shadow, until about a quarter after seven, when Mateo came by balancing a large plastic sack on his shoulder. In Spanish, we greeted each other and exchanged pleasantries. His smile was amazing, lighting up the morning in its sincerity and sheepish humility. He slipped the sack off his shoulder and pulled a large, orange plastic bucket toward him (there was one in each tambo). I sat up and watched as he grabbed handfuls of small, dark, dull green leaves from the sack, half filling the bucket with them. He smiled again, an embarrassed sort of smile, and began describing a process while simultaneously acting it out (although knowing a little Spanish, I understood his instructions). He pretended to pour river water into the bucket, indicating that the water should reach just to the level of the leaves. Then he plunged both hands into the leaves, rubbed the leaves together, and proceeded to bathe himself. *"Guayusa,"* he said by way of explanation. I nodded my head, recognizing that he was naming a plant whose use Jack had described to us the day before.

Guayusa is an aromatic plant whose leaves are commonly used for medicinal baths. Ayahuasqueros frequently require that their patients bathe with guayusa before a healing session. Jack had described the aural and energetic cleansing effects of guayusa as like that of smudging with sage or sweetgrass in native North American healing traditions. He informed us that fresh guayusa leaves would be delivered to our tambos every morning, and we should half fill the bucket with river water, rub the leaves together to release their oils and aroma, and then rub the leaves over our bodies to bathe. At the very least, we should use the herb-infused water to refresh ourselves and cool off with throughout the day. At night or early in the morning, we should empty the bucket so it was ready for refilling. Although I had already washed and dressed, I took the bucket down to the river, dipped it in until it was half full of water, and then, once back at my tambo, did as I had been instructed. As I rubbed the leaves together, a subtly sweet smell arose. I scooped the water over my arms and face, then reclined once more in the hammock. When I next looked up, the bucket was crawling with ants. I wasn't sure what to do, so I grabbed one of my boat shoes—those cloth slipperlike shoes people wear at the beach—and brushed the ants away. I had brought some bug spray with me, but I was loathe to use it unless I was facing an infestation. (I have to admit that I did use it twice: once that day to spray around the entrance to my tambo, for the posts around the "doorway" were where the army of ants liked to crawl single file into my living area, and once a few days later to spray down into my latrine hole to keep the bugs at bay and to make doing my business bearable.)

I read for another hour but grew bored and "antsy." I wandered around outside my tambo for a while, but I was still not acclimated to the environment and did not feel comfortable wandering too far. Back at my tambo I became fixated on the huge, balloon-shaped mud nest on one of the tambo posts at about head height. I wondered if it was a nest of jungle bees. I had heard about them and did not want to be anywhere near them. But I did not see any insect movement at all in or around the nest and I was afraid to poke at it to see if it was occupied. I resolved to ask Jack to check it out later. I also noticed the mother of all cockroaches (at least it looked like a cockroach) that had taken up residence on the five-gallon water bottle. I shooed it away with my boat shoe, but it soon came back, and I decided that as long as it stayed put, I could live with it. It tended to scurry to the back of the bottle or the tambo railing whenever I opened the water spout, so I was never in danger of making contact with it when I needed water.

Soon these jungle novelties wore off and I wondered how I was going to deal with the inactivity of the retreat. I was used to being active, busy, occupied. I had once followed a daily meditation routine, and when my husband had worked for Deepak Chopra I had sat in meditation for up to six hours a day at one of his seminars. But I had long since abandoned any regular practice of sitting on the cushion. Before coming to the jungle, I had resolved that this trip, with its enforced isolation, would be a perfect opportunity to resume that practice, but now, only a few hours into my first full day in the jungle, I seemed incapable of quieting myself. It was not anxiety, although I am sure at some level it was, but more simply boredom. It was not yet even midmorning, and I had a long day ahead of me in which I knew I was going to do nothing. I went back to reading, and being a fast reader, got well into the Armstrong book, which seemed an answer for me.

The more I read, the more inspired I became and the more centered I felt. Indeed, its message of going inward, of observing the self and one's thought process, of being present in the moment, began to seem a perfect way to approach that night's ayahuasca session. I resolved that I would try to take just such a Buddhist stance while traveling with the Vine of the Soul: I would attempt not to get caught up in the geometry, colors, or emotions of the experience but would instead try to remain the observer of my own process. I practiced by staring at the river for a long time and simply observing the wandering of my mind, and, while I attempted to remain impartial and nonjudgmental of my own inner process, I was chagrined to see how self-involved and chaotic my thoughts were.

After a while I "observed" that I really, really needed to get up and do something, so I decided to check in with Michelle. I found her sitting on her mosquito-netted bed, reading. She had brought her net from the States, and it was much more transparent than mine, and so let in enough light to read by (although, Michelle reported, the tiniest bugs also found their way in; nothing ever made its way through my netting). We talked for a while and then I wandered over to use her bathroom. It was much more private than mine and had less vegetation encroaching on it. But, I noticed, my box seat was much finer than hers. I laughed to myself as I walked the short distance back to her tambo. "This is what I've come to after less than twenty-fours in the Amazon," I said to myself, "comparing the quality of latrine seats!" All in all, though, I liked the layout of her tambo area much better than mine, especially because there were fewer large trees immediately surrounding it and so the light was much better.

John soon arrived, and he and I set off to the kitchen camp, where we had been told we could each select a pair of rubber boots. The trail was always damp and muddy, and if it rained, rubber boots were a must. When we got there, however, I was badly disappointed. The two pairs of women's-sized boots were gone and the best I could do was a man's size 11. I took them, knowing I might need them and considering that if I wore the one pair of heavy hiking socks I had with me or even my boat shoes inside the rubber boots, I might be able to walk in them without tripping.

Since we were discouraged from socializing, we decided it was time to head back to our respective tambos. John walked with me to mine, and, remembering that he had brought the cord from his pack, we strung a clothesline across two posts on one side of my tambo. When I noted how dusty and dirty the floor was, John, ever the creative problem solver, rigged me a palm-frond whisk broom. It worked like a charm.

It was only ten o'clock—time seemed to have slowed to a crawl. Only minutes after John left, Chico and Mateo showed up with food. Since this was an ayahuasca day, this was the only food we were going to get. Mateo handed me a spoon and a small, reddish pottery crock. Chico reached into one of the two large white buckets he had and scooped out brown rice, filling the crock to the top. Then he reached into the other bucket and plopped a fish atop the rice. The fish was blackened from having been baked in hot coals, but it still had its head and its tail, although it was slit down the middle and cleaned of its insides. I stared at the fish's cloudy eye as Chico and Mateo headed off up the trail.

I had only the spoon with which to eat the fish, and since it was full of tiny bones, I soon discovered that fingers worked better. But it was messy, picking out those bones. I spread out a couple of the premoistened towelettes and used one to collect the bones and the other to continually clean my fingers. The fish was boquichico and was worth the effort—it was delicious. The brown rice was another story altogether. It was dry and devoid of any flavoring, even salt. I ate only a few spoonfuls, and I forced those down only because I knew there would be no more food until the next morning and I needed nourishment. I wondered what to do with the leftovers. Jack and don Luis had told us to dump any excess food down our latrine, but there was so much rice left that I feared it would attract a swarm of insects. I wanted to avoid doing anything that might attract insects, as I already had a huge red welt under my left buttock, compliments of some biting thing that was living at or visiting my latrine. They had also told us to cover any food we put down the latrine with earth, but my only digging utensil was my spoon.

I dumped the towelette on which I had collected the fish bones on top of the skeletal remains of the fish and the rice in my bowl, and headed to the latrine with my spoon. It took a half hour to cover the dumped food. My tablespoons of dirt had a long way to fall, and it was difficult to get the dirt to land where I wanted it. When the food was sufficiently covered, I cleaned the crock and spoon in the river. Dozens of tiny grayish-green fish swarmed, nipping at my toes and jostling each other for the bits of rice that littered the water. I made note of them, for I would soon have to take a bath in this river.

I returned to my tambo pleased that my chore was done, until I found out from Chico, as he headed back toward camp, that we would have to keep the crock and the spoon for our entire stay in the jungle. I worried momentarily about having used the spoon to scoop dirt and having only the river for washing. Then I got out the premoistened tow-elettes, one package of which was antibacterial, and thoroughly washed the bowl and spoon again. I rinsed them with water from the five-gallon jug, even though we had been urged to use that water only for drinking.

The rest of the day passed almost in a haze, as I alternately read or dozed or simply stared out at the unfamiliar world around me. Strangely, I still could not really see the jungle. It was a wall of texture but little more. I was as yet unable to clearly differentiate anything in the mass of greenery that surrounded me. It was as if I literally could not see the trees for the forest. Instead, the river attracted most of my attention. I delighted in the small swarms of vanilla-colored butterflies that skimmed the river's surface, moving in graceful synchrony; the slightly larger black ones with orange and yellow spots on their wings that lazily undulated by in groups of twos and threes; and the magnificent, solitary, and fast-flying morphos, with their stunningly blue wings. Within my own tambo, I was amused for a short time by two tiny grayish lizards—and, when they were not there, a black-and-yellow one—that sat unmoving on the basketball-sized nest I'd been looking at earlier, which I would soon learn was a termite nest. Occasionally their tongues would flick out, but I could never actually see what it was they were fishing for or eating. At one point I went over to get something from my backpack and scared a mammoth grasshopper-like insect off it. It half flew, half jumped to a railing, and it sat there for hours, completely unmoving. At some level I felt anxious about its sitting motionless for so long on the railing, facing my hammock as if it were observing me, for this weird praying mantis/grasshopper hybrid reminded me of the insectoid alien face I had seen in my dream-vision.

The memory of the alien dream-vision arose again later that afternoon. Although my eyes were not yet sensitized to the details of my environment, my ears were. So hyperalert was my sense of hearing that I thought once or twice of the alien's voice in my ear, asking me if I was ready to remember the sounds. I did not have to remember any sounds, for the sounds were everywhere, filling the air unceasingly. The jungle provides an almost constant background hum, with the insects and frogs providing the "white noise" of this world. Against the backdrop of that humming undercurrent, however, was a symphony of the strangest sounds I had ever heard. There was the bird whose call sounded like water slowly dripping from a faucet: *ka-boink, ka-boink, ka-boink*. Something—and I'm not sure if it was a bird, frog or toad, or insect—made an irritating grating sound, like a socket wrench ratcheting in a bolt. Another bird or insect made a call that varied in pitch and sounded like a radio whining as the signal was being tuned in: *weeeee eeeee ooooooo, weeeee eeeee ooooooo*.

Then I heard flute music. It was don Luis playing his Native American flute. He had moved into the next tambo up the trail, and the plaintive tune drifted through the trees toward me. His music reminded me of my husband, who also plays the Native American flute. A wave of sentiment washed through me, a soft but sweeping current of love, and I projected this feeling and energy up the trail toward John. In that most intimate of energetic moments, however, I was startled back to the material world by a sudden, tremendous crash. The adrenaline rush catapulted me out of the hammock, and I whirled in my tambo looking for the source of the sound. It took only seconds for me to realize that I had been spooked once again by nothing other than a huge leaf falling through the jungle canopy. At almost the same moment as my realization, Jack became visible on the trail. He was here for a visit, for his daily "check-in" round.

I offered him the hammock while I pulled the stool out from under the table. He swung in the hammock sideways so he could face me, his long legs dangling down and skimming the floor as he rocked. He handed me a flyer in which he had written about the jungle. Almost every day, during his rounds, Jack would leave us with a new flyer. They ran the gamut from prosaic, factual information about the diet to poetical musings about the nature of consciousness. I came to look forward to them and not only thoroughly enjoyed every one but always learned something new.

Jack stayed for only a few minutes, to see how I was and to inform me that we would gather as a group in the maloca at eight o'clock for the ayahuasca ceremony. I took this opportunity to ask him if I could switch my daily plant teacher, which we would start drinking the next morning, from bobinsana to ushpahuasa. He told me that he and one other person were dieting with ushpahuasa and he was not sure there would be enough. But he promised to check with don Emilio and don Luis, who were already in the process of making the teas. I asked him to tell me about ushpahuasa and he explained that it worked very subtly. It did not give visions but mostly stimulated dreams and gently stoked the fires of memory and feeling. Before he left, I also asked Jack if I could interview don Luis. Jack and don Luis are very wary of anyone writing about their work because they are serious psychonauts and healers and do not want to get caught up in the ayahuasca tourism hype or risk anyone encroaching on don Luis's camp. I explained that as a professional writer used to following the ethical guidelines of my profession and as a serious practitioner of the Andean spiritual arts used to respecting the wishes of the indigenous peoples with whom I work, I would have no qualms honoring any information restrictions they chose to place on me. Jack said he would talk with don Luis about it and get back to me.

It was nearly five o'clock when Jack left, and my tambo was already deep in shadow, so it was nearly impossible to read or take notes without the use of a flashlight. I decided to try to nap, since we would be up half the night in ceremony.

About six-thirty John came and woke me, and I readied myself to go to the maloca, gathering up my water bottle and flashlight, a handkerchief, and a long-sleeved shirt. I also took my notebook and tape recorder. We got to the maloca about a quarter after seven, and almost everyone from the group was already there. The maloca was arranged with wooden seats without legs—like wooden backjacks—topped with cushions. I chose a space close to the entrance, so I could get out quickly and with the least amount of effort if I needed to vomit. It turns out that most of us just poked our heads through the railings of the maloca when we needed to purge, but that first night I needed the security of knowing I could exit the maloca without having to stumble across it in the darkness. Jeff was sitting next to me, with Patrick and Heni also on our side of the maloca. Across the room, John, Michelle, Andrew, and Steve made themselves comfortable. Along the back of the maloca were seats for Jack, don Luis, and don Emilio.

By eight o'clock we were all in our places, and don Luis had set up his mesa with its variety of musical instruments and two plastic bottles of ayahuasca. He had already prepared the brew, so we were not going to have the opportunity to actually experience making the tea, which is a ceremony in itself. Most of us, I believe, immediately noted the differences in the color of the brews in the two bottles. The taller, larger bottle contained a blackish red liquid. The smaller bottle contained a very black brew. Jack began the evening with a laundry list of business and then, to our delight, announced that don Emilio and don Luis would take us on a nature walk Thursday afternoon, in three days, to point out various plants and their medicinal or healing uses. He then talked about the brews that don Luis had prepared, explaining that there were indeed two teas. The blacker tea in the small bottle was made from wild vine, as opposed to cultivated vine, and prepared with additional plant extracts and was, he said, quoting don Luis, the most potent brew don Luis had ever prepared. He called it *ayahuasca negra,* or "black ayahuasca," and quickly added, "You do not have to drink this particular tea at all. It is up to you. If you do, you cannot do so until the third or fourth session, and then you will only be allowed a very small dose at first—to see how it goes, to see how your bodies and spirits handle it. Tonight, we will drink the other brew, which itself is plenty strong." He also explained that don Emilio would be drinking the tea with us tonight, although he rarely uses ayahuasca these days, and it had been a long while since he had.

With that the ceremony began. The setting, of course, was perfect— a not-too-steamy night deep in the Amazon. My "set" was to stay in a place of impartial observing, not to get caught up in the captivating visuals but simply to stay present to and mindful of whatever arose in my mind, heart, and soul. The ceremony itself was normal in every way, with don Luis honoring the four directions, washing himself with a camphor-herb decoction, and passing the bottle for us to do the same. Then he began whistling an icaro into the uncapped bottle of ayahuasca. Soon he switched to a haunting melody that sent me to another place within myself. Don Luis offered the large bottle of brew to don Emilio, who sang into it. Then don Luis readied the small cup from which we would drink. As each person went up to drink, he or she consulted with Jack and don Luis about the dose. When it was my turn, I indicated I wanted a full dose. I had decided that I had come all this way to the jungle to be in Mother Ayahuasca's home and to meet her in whatever way she saw fit to approach me, so I was not going to hold back in any way. I raised the cup, blew my finest energies through it three times, and drank the foul-tasting tea. When I returned to my place, I sat with eyes closed and began to center myself, reminding myself that my set was to remain the detached observer. I also offered thanks to the spirits of the land and rivers for my, and the group's, safe arrival, and I offered a prayer to Mother Ayahuasca to receive me as her grateful guest and humble student.

The journey began much as the others had, with an eruption of color and pattern, although not in as staggering a way as it had during my first experience. I actually do not remember a great deal of detail about this journey, except that it was intense in a way different from all the others. It was more imagistic than visual, meaning that the patterns seemed connected to "understandings" rather than to identifiable images. The most important part of this session was that Grandmother Ayahuasca, whom I had seen as "White Ayahuasca" during my first experience, revealed herself to me again.

From the beginning of the journey, what I remember most is the sickening physicality of it. It was as if my body were vibrating at too high a rate, and I was overcome with this loathsome feeling of being on the edge of losing control. I am fully aware that control is my issue, and that the waves of fear I sometimes felt when I journeyed with ayahuasca resulted from my refusal or incapacity to surrender. Now it was as if ayahuasca were infiltrating every hidden crevice of my body-mind to see what was hidden there, to clean it out or, at least, to expose it to the light of my consciousness. If my consciousness would not acknowledge what ayahuasca was trying to show me, then my body had to register the knowledge for me. It was a visceral, on-the-verge-of-panic energy that made me feel as if my flesh and bones were in despair. Additionally, the more I allowed the visuals to carry me away, the more intense my "body-emotion" became. I absolutely dreaded the feeling.

At one point, apropos of nothing in my inner field of vision, which was swirling with shockingly bright colors and fantastically intricate patterns, the dark, reddish cockroaches appeared, scurrying across the kaleidoscopic page of my mind. As I have said, I know these critters. They are a decades-old dream symbol, representing my fears, doubts, and self-recriminations. But since I was determined to stay in the observer mode this night, I worked hard to pull my defenses back and just let my body feel whatever it was feeling and my inner eyes see whatever they were seeing. So, instead of becoming anxiety filled at the sight of the cockroaches, afraid of where in my emotional self they might take me, and banishing them, as I had when they had appeared in a previous journey, I pulled my emotional body back, with some struggle, and simply watched them. They skittered here and there, usually along the edge of my visual field. Some other separately observing part of me was amazed that I could actually remain detached and not get caught up in the anxiety these bugs usually provoked in me. I felt as if there were multiple me's, layer upon layer of observer selves. Soon the cockroaches scurried over an actual edge of my mind field and were gone. Then, abruptly, my entire field of vision coalesced into rows and rows of luminescent insects of gorgeously shimmering colors and phantasmagoric anatomy. These most beautiful of bugs were iridescent hot pink and silver, and they sported gossamer wings, curlicue feelers, feathery appendages, and a profusion of filaments that trembled in their delicacy. Like a scene from the Disney film *Fantasia,* the insects ordered themselves into an ethereal field of high-stepping dancers and performed for me. Their dance was breathtaking.

Sometime during the journey, and I have no memory of time or of order during this part of the journey, I became aware of Grandmother Ayahuasca again. She appeared to my mind's eye exactly as she had before—as an ancient, humpbacked indigenous woman. She was in a garden area, in a clearing in the jungle, and she invited me to come closer. She told me the journey with her this night was going to be a gentle one, and that she was giving me a gift that would help make it so. She did not actually hand me a gift or even tell me what it was, but I sensed that at some level it had already been given and accepted.

At about this time, I became aware of hearing an unfamiliar icaro. It was not one of don Luis's. I suddenly remembered that don Emilio was with us, and it was he who was singing, in Quechua. I also heard him mumbling and talking to himself, sounding as if he were drunk. He tended to slur his words anyway, and I could barely understand his Spanish because of this, but now he seemed to be in another world, talking to someone, carrying on a conversation beyond time and space.

The next thing I remember is urging myself to stay in the observer mode, to witness and not participate. At this point my inner ear seemed to be listening to a cosmic lecture, although it was not a lecture in words but in knowing. Some immense energy seemed to be hovering in the background of my awareness and its message was emphatic but impersonal. I understood, in a message that I had received before while "dreaming" with ayahuasca, that humans are the puniest of beings, profoundly inconsequential within the infinite scope of the universe. We consider our choices and decisions to be momentous, but in truth they are utterly meaningless within the grand cosmic scheme. We are less than dust motes in the vastness of some immense field, some force that is beyond our ability to truly comprehend it, but that connects us to everything. But we are also awesome in our beingness. Everything we think and do matters at the most integral level of the cosmos. At one level we matter; in fact, we are responsible for all that is. But there is also an All That Is that makes us and everything else, even itself, possible.

As before with ayahuasca, I was tumbling into paradox, and I understood at the core of my being that everything, *everything,* is an illusion. But that illusion is itself an illusion. It was as if I could grasp nested "mind boxes" of illusion within illusion within illusion, but the whole mind itself was one gargantuan illusion. I felt trapped in a fun house whose mirrors reflected "humanness" back a million times, a trillion times, one image repeating itself ad infinitum. I could not tell what was real and what was unreal, what was I and what was not-I. The feeling of being in some sort of free fall of beingness was overwhelming, and I struggled to pull myself back to a stance of observation.

As I groped my way out of the black hole of paradox, I once again heard don Emilio singing. He seemed very close to me, and I suddenly knew that he was the gift Grandmother Ayahuasca had given me. I realized that it must be hours into the journey and I had not purged, which was unusual for me. I sensed that don Emilio was working with the group energy, and with each of us individually. I sensed that he had been bargaining with the spirits in some way on our behalf, that he was taking on our heavy energy and processing it for us, making it less burdensome for us. I mentally thanked him, repeating *"Gracias, gracias"* and energetically sending him waves of appreciation and thanks. And then I heard his reply, with my physical ears, as he said, uncharacteristically distinctly, *"De nada, de nada."* It's nothing, it's nothing. He resumed alternately singing and talking, his voice rising and becoming sharp toned, as if he were arguing with someone.

Then all hell broke loose. Don Emilio seemed to lose his bearings completely. He began to holler, his words a mumbled jumble of shouts, exclamations, and exhortations. I saw Jack leave the maloca. He returned in a few minutes with Chico and Mateo, and the three of them half dragged, half carried don Emilio from the maloca.

After a few minutes, Jack returned and we all settled down and resumed our inward focus. But I felt the loss of don Emilio's energy, and within minutes I felt the bile rising. I twisted around and hung my head through the railing and vomited. In some ways the purge relieved the awful ayahuasca feeling in my body and I suddenly felt quite strong. But while my body felt revitalized, the purge seemed to unhinge my mind even further.

I took a sip of water, then sat upright in my space, holding my head in my hands and rubbing my face, as if I needed to make sure I was still there, in the body. The brilliant colors and fractal patterns, which had mostly settled down, erupted again. I tried to resume my observational stance, but the feeling that I was being sucked outward into another dimension was intensifying. There is so much about this journey that I cannot remember now, but I do recall the feeling of exhaustion and disorientation, of having gone deep and then of being rocketed outward to a different kind of depth. It was the difference between descending into a cavern in the earth and being propelled into the depths of outer space. I don't recall where I went, how long I stayed there, or what occurred while I was wherever I was.

Then suddenly another shift. These shifts came unexpectedly, and they tended to leave me even more disoriented. I was back at the garden clearing, but now I could see Grandmother Ayahuasca's house a short distance away. She was tending a fire in her home, a characteristic Andean hut with thatched roof. I could see her through the open door. I walked to the threshold but did not cross it. Grandmother Ayahuasca continued her task, as if I were not there. She was not ignoring me, for ignoring someone is an intentional act, and I somehow knew there was no such intentionality on her part. However, at the same time that I felt her indifference, I also sensed her attentiveness toward me. Paradox again. I heard her voice—not because she was talking with me, but more because she was projecting her thoughts into my mind. *I am through with you,* she said as she continued her sweeping. *You can be through with me, if you want. You do not have to drink again. It is of no matter. Everything is sacred. You can heal through meditation. You can heal through tai chi. You can heal through psychotherapy. You can heal through ayahuasca.* I got a real sense then of ayahuasca as her daughter. This was not the vine itself, not the Mother of the Voice in the Ear, but the mother of the vine, the Mother of the Mother of the Voice in the Ear. It was *Grandmother* Ayahuasca, and for some reason it was important I realize who was communicating with me.

She continued. *However you want to heal, you can heal. You simply need the intention to do so. So you do not need to go through this.*

I understood that "this" referred to my feeling sick and the indescribable ayahuasca body-feeling I so abhorred. *My second gift to you this night is the ushpahuasa, which you will begin drinking in the morning. It is what you really came here to experience. All you need to do is drink ushpahuasa. You do not have to drink ayahuasca.*

I was startled by this information. I did feel ushpahuasa was a plant teacher tailor-made for me, especially since the alien dream-visions. But I still did not know whether don Luis and don Emilio had agreed to let me switch from bobinsana to ushpahuasa or if they had prepared enough of the tea for me to do so.

In addition to being startled by Grandmother Ayahuasca's gift of ushpahuasa, I also felt relieved to think I might not have to drink ayahuasca again. But I wondered if this oh-so-convenient message was not just my fear duping me. My mental process began to dominate my head space. "Okay," I told myself, addressing myself in the second person, "this is not really Grandmother Ayahuasca talking—this is your fear. You just want an excuse not to drink the vine again. This is your unconscious's way of making it okay for your ego." I struggled for a few minutes trying to sort out whether the counsel I had received was a psychological trick on my part or was indeed a metaphysical message from a plant teacher. Then Grandmother Ayahuasca spoke again. She talked me through a multiple-choice test. A list with check boxes next to each of the choices appeared imagistically in my mind:

- ☐ Meditation
- ☐ Tai chi
- ☐ Psychotherapy
- ☐ Ayahuasca
    - ☐ A full dose
    - ☐ A half dose
    - ☐ A quarter dose
- ☐ None of the above
- ☐ All of the above
- ☐ Some of the above

It was a ludicrous test, and I knew the choices were each right and each wrong. I felt the energy of paradox flowing through me again and the insight that none of our choices matter and yet they all do. It simply did not matter if I drank ayahuasca again. I could go inward to gather my many selves together, to integrate, to heal, in any number of ways. The method made no difference. All that mattered was the impeccability with which I made a choice and lived its consequences. On a grand, cosmic scale along the continuum of eternity (or, in the eternal Now), my choices were meaningless. All that mattered was that in the face of meaninglessness I act with impeccability.

I was truly emotionally exhausted by now, and feeling extremely nauseated. At some point I finally laid back in my space and pulled my denim shirt over me as a blanket. I was through. The session was over for me even though I was still journeying, but not intensely at this point. I lay there for a long time, and finally someone lit the candle, signaling the formal end to the session. I checked my watch. It was only 11:45. Everyone was silent, and we stayed in our spaces for about a half hour before some people began to gather their belongings and leave. Jack came by to check on each of us, and John motioned to me that he needed help getting to the bathroom. He was still flying. He was very uncoordinated, and as I helped him up, I had to bear most of his weight and steady him on the short walk to the latrine. At one point a sliver of light came through the clouds and tree canopy and illuminated some leaves on the ground. John crouched down totally fixated on them, and it took me a while to get him back on track for the latrine.

John and I finally got back to my tambo about one in the morning. I was perfectly straight again, but John seemed to still be under the influence of the vine. I insisted he stay at my tambo, although he refused to take the bed. He crashed in the hammock and I changed into nightclothes and lay in bed under the mosquito netting. My stomach still felt squeamish and the dance of illusion and paradox still stirred my thoughts. But I fell asleep almost right away, and when I next awoke it was three o'clock in the morning and I was in the midst of a bizarre light show.

I was lying on my side facing the back of the tambo, and when I opened my eyes the mosquito netting was lit up as if someone had a floodlight pointed at it. I could see the dark shadows of leaves and vines and stems silhouetted against the white cloth. At first what I was seeing did not register, but when it did, I immediately turned over, toward the front of the tambo, where John was lying in the hammock. My entire bed was alight, and as I turned I saw not only the same shadows of dancing leaves and plants against the netting but also the silhouette of a tall, rather hulking man. He had on what appeared to be a skirt, for I could see the solid outline of a long sarong-type skirt. His upper body seemed bare, although I could not make out any features or details in the shadow. He was shaking a schacapa-leaf rattle about midway down the length of my body. I was totally disoriented but not frightened. In fact, I was miffed! I still felt sick to my stomach and completely wrung out, and I shielded my eyes with one arm and groaned inwardly. Whoever this was, I simply wanted him to get his damn flashlight out of my face. I thought it must be Jack, since he sometimes wore a nearly floor-length sarong to sessions, and I wondered if he had borrowed don Luis's schacapa-leaf rattle to come over and do a healing on me. But deep down I knew it was not Jack. And certainly it was not John. I did not care who it was, I simply wanted no part of it. I wanted the light out of my face and the sound of the leaf rattle out of my head, for its papery whispering was making me feel as if ayahuasca were rising in my body again, ready to take me on another flight.

The figure then moved slowly to my feet, still shaking the schacapa rattle. Now I was confused. I wondered how he could be at my feet, since the end of my bed platform abutted the railing at that side of the tambo and there was no room for anyone or anything between the bed and the railing. But I did not dwell on that thought. I closed my eyes and groaned again. Although I was perfectly rational and felt no residue of the ayahuasca experience within me, I felt the pull of the other-worldly. The dry rustling of the schacapa leaves was pulling me into an altered state, and journeying was the last thing I wanted to do at that moment. I thought about asking the person to leave, but I was too lethargic to make the effort. The figure, continuing to fan the leaf rattle along the length of my body, moved toward my head. I could no longer see him, but I could hear the rattle shaking on the other side of the mosquito netting at my head.

And then I went on high alert. I sensed or intuited that the man had turned toward John. Since the hammock was tied off at one end to the post directly behind my bed, he would have been at John's head as John lay in the hammock. I sensed that the man was massaging John's shoulders. Then things got even weirder, for I sensed that the man was getting into the hammock with John! "What the hell is going on?" I wondered. I should have gotten up at that point, but I didn't. I rolled over onto my back and strained my ears to hear anything that might be happening, and that's when the song began—the most beautiful icaro I have ever heard, unlike anything don Luis or don Emilio had ever sung. It was otherworldly in its beauty. I was even more confused now, for I was sure this was John's voice singing, and John normally cannot carry a tune. I tried to see through the mosquito netting, and that is when I realized it was no longer illuminated. The shadows of the plants were gone, and I saw a large blob of light sort of sailing along what I knew to be the trail. Whoever had been here was leaving.

The icaro continued for about ten minutes more, and I had to fight hard to stay present, for every haunting note seemed to want to lift me away to other states of being. I simply did not want to go. I had had enough. But I restrained my impulse to ask John to stop singing. "This song is a gift," I counseled myself inwardly. "No matter how deeply it is stirring me up, I have no right to interrupt him. If he needs to sing, he needs to sing." So I endured the icaro, appreciating its mellifluous beauty but refusing to allow it to coax me into its mystery.

8

The Jungle—Inner
and Outer

*The forest is not only the immense regulator of the world's climate,
a fantastical natural zoo, a rich repository of important woods
and remarkable vegetal species; more than that, it is an area of
intimacy with the Divine. The natural world is the habitat of an
enormous spiritual energy that remains untouched to this day.
Each living pulsation of the forest produces a profound therapeutic
effect on the people connected with it. This living connection
anticipates the felicity that will be encountered living in the new
era, as human consciousness surpasses human destructiveness.*
—ALEX POLARI DE ALVERGA, FOREST OF VISIONS

Tuesday I awoke early, at about five o'clock, as would become my pattern while in the jungle. John was asleep in the hammock but woke as I emerged from the mosquito-netted bed. He looked more than strung out and did not really feel like talking, but I was eager to ask him about the early-morning light show and visit I had witnessed.

"Who was here last night?" I asked, not wanting to lead him in any way.

"What?" He seemed confused. "When?"

"About three this morning."

"No one. Why?"

I told him about the lights, the shadows of leaves and vines, the man wearing the skirt and shaking the schacapa-leaf rattle, and the icaro.

"There was no one here. But I did sing for you," he said. "I was lying here half asleep and half awake, and I felt that you needed a healing, and I felt this song coming through me, so I sang. Did you like it?"

"It was gorgeous," I said. "But I resisted it, because it was pulling me back out into a journey and I was too exhausted to go. But it was more beautiful than any icaro I've heard from Luis or Emilio. Do you remember it?"

John thought for a moment before replying. "It's sort of like it's right at the edge of my memory, but I can't sing it now. Did it help you? You seemed sick last night. And by the way, thanks for helping me. I was out of it, almost all night!"

We joked about how "inebriated" John had been from the brew and about his fixation with the leaves as we had made our way to the latrine. He seemed to remember the entire night, even though he had been very high. How could he have failed to see the lights or the man in my tambo or hear the leaf rattle?

"I thought the man was right at your head, and that he massaged your shoulders. I thought he got into the hammock with you! You don't remember any of that?"

"No," John said, obviously struggling to recall anything from the early morning hours. "I just got a strong sense that you needed healing and I felt I could heal you through sound. And then the song came."

John then went on to tell me of his own profound journey during the ayahuasca session. He, too, had felt intimately connected with don Emilio. He explained that in particular he felt he was being taught how to heal with sound, and it was partly don Emilio's energy that was forging the connection between sound and healing for him. He described to me how his alpaca poncho, which he had taken with him to the session, seemed to come alive, reaching out to him, the border of woven cerulean blue butterflies undulating with life. John talked enthusiastically, fired up not only by his passion for how sound can be used in healing but also by the insight that he was being called to work in this way.*

That made a lot of sense, for John had long been drawn to indigenous instruments and had quite a collection. Plus, he had two sets of Peruvian whistling vessels, which are replicas of ancient Chimu vessels and have odd vibrational characteristics when someone blows into their double-chambered bodies through their narrow spouts. The whistling induces meditation-like brain wave patterns and complex vibrations inside one's ears and head, and John had given numerous workshops with the vessels.†

John was ready to head back to his tambo. He was wiped out and wanted to clean up and then sleep. So he gathered his things and left. I swung in the hammock, contemplating the strange events. I scrutinized the tambo and surrounding area with a skeptic's eye, trying to figure out the physics of the light show. I had thought someone had been shining a flashlight in my face, but now I realized that to have cast shadows, the light would had to have been *behind* the man and the vegetation. That in itself seemed unlikely. But I surveyed the area as if it could have been a possibility and I noted that except for several very tall trees in the immediate vicinity of my tambo, all the bushy vegetation was cleared to about ten feet on three sides of the tambo. The trail ran directly in front of it. On the other side of the trail, the land sloped down to the river, although it was fairly heavily vegetated. It seemed impossible that a light could have shone at bed level and cast shadows of plants on my mosquito netting. And even if somehow it had, why had there been no shadows of the railings, table, shelf, and water dispenser?

Next I considered the source of the light. If it was not a flashlight,

---

* Partially as a result of his jungle experiences with ayahuasca, John has created a form of sound healing he calls Primal Sound therapy. See his field report in chapter 4.

† To learn more about the vibrational characteristics of the whistling vessels, see Daniel Statnekov, *Animated Earth* (Berkeley: North Atlantic Books, 1987), and his research, much of which is available on the Internet. Also see Don Wright's Web site: www.entheosound.com.

it must have been a natural source. But surely it had not been the moon. The sun faded early, so that I could hardly read in my tambo by about four in the afternoon. There was no way I could believe that moonlight could have streamed down through the jungle canopy with such luminosity, notwithstanding the fact that the tambo's thatched roof sloped steeply and was fairly close to the ground at the back of the tambo. Plus, the bed had been illuminated on *all* sides, and I had no way to explain that.

And how was I to explain the man with his skirt and leaf rattle? I kept thinking it had to have been Jack, with don Luis's schacapa-leaf rattle. But I could not imagine Jack coming to my tambo so many hours after the session to heal me. It made no sense, and I had never had any indication that Jack did more than assist don Luis, never mind did healings himself. So, physically, the entire scenario made no sense and seemed to have no even quasi-rational explanation.

I was left to consider that the entire episode had been an ayahuasca-induced vision. After all, if it had been physical in any way, John would have experienced it as well. Yet he had not. But I was not willing to claim it as a vision. I am familiar with many types of altered states of consciousness, and this experience was not one that had been induced by a psychoactive plant.*

---

* I want to stress that I was definitely not having an ayahuasca-induced vision. Most of the people to whom I have related this experience respond with, "Oh, so this was a vision." It wasn't. I was completely straight, although still sick to my stomach from the ayahuasca session and feeling tired and physically weak. I have experienced many types of altered states, some on a regular basis. I have practiced shamanic journeying for many years, practiced meditation, and experimented with out-of-body (OBE) techniques and lucid dreaming. As anyone familiar with various types of altered states can attest, each has its own unique quality of "mind," and it is unlikely one would confuse the state of mind during a dream, for example, with that of meditation or a shamanic journey. This same point will be crucial to understanding an experience I relate later in this book about my final ayahuasca journey, for the second part of that experience also did not result from my ingestion of ayahuasca. During it, too, I was in a qualitatively different kind of altered state, much more akin to that experienced during a shamanic journey—a quality of consciousness anthropologist and shamanic teacher Michael Harner has coined the "shamanic state of consciousness."

To deem it so would have been a cop-out. I had been nearly back to normal consciousness when I had left the maloca. In fact, except for the exhaustion and the lingering nausea, I was completely coherent and grounded, able to help John and take care of his needs. I had felt "straight" by the time I went to bed. There was simply nothing about this experience that had any of the qualities of an ayahuasca vision. Still, I was not quite ready to accept it as real either.

Frustrated by my inability to make sense of the light show and night visitor, my mind wandered back to the shopping dream, in which I had been left to return home with items foisted on me by others. The dream made sense in relation to what I remembered of the previous night's ayahuasca journey. I felt it was symbolic of how we all enter this life barefoot and with empty carts—walking in clean and unfettered by illusions, beliefs, opinions, judgments, and prejudices. But we accept ways of knowing and being from other people, especially those close to us, such as our family, friends, teachers, and religious authorities. We end up living our lives carting around all this stuff (behaviors and beliefs) we really do not want and did not choose for ourselves.

My analysis was interrupted by Chico and don Emilio, who arrived carrying various large pitchers and containers filled with dark liquids— the other plant teachers. We each had a plastic water pitcher and plastic glass in our tambo, and I fetched mine, thinking that don Emilio was going to fill the pitcher with bobinsana, since those taking it could drink as much as they wanted and whenever they felt like it throughout the day. But he motioned away the pitcher and pointed at the glass. As I held it out and he filled it three-quarters full, he said, smiling, "Ushpahuasa." So Jack had relayed my request and it had been granted. I thought back to the session, when Grandmother Ayahuasca had said she was granting me a second gift, ushpahuasa, which I would begin drinking in the morning. Her prediction was being fulfilled.

The tea was blackish green, and bits of plant matter floated in it. It did not have much of a smell. Don Emilio must have been impatient for me to drink, for he pantomimed throwing his head back and swigging from a glass. I quickly blew my energy through the plastic glass three times and then swallowed. The room-temperature tea did not taste bad going down—it certainly was not as repulsive as ayahuasca—but as soon as I swallowed, a rank, vegetal taste roared up my throat from my stomach and I felt like vomiting. All I could think of at that moment was, "I *asked* for this? And I have to drink it *every day?*"

Don Emilio began to talk in his hurried, slurred Spanish and I could barely understand a word. Chico remained silent. With some effort, I finally understood that don Emilio wanted to refill the glass, so I would have some ushpahuasa to drink later that afternoon, but I graciously declined. I told him in Spanish that tomorrow I would drink more, but for today, one glass was enough. He nodded okay, and he and Chico moved on to the next tambo.

I brushed my teeth, hoping to erase the taste of the ushpahuasa, but since I had no toothpaste but only water to brush with, I did not succeed. My stomach felt mildly upset, and I decided I needed to distract myself with a bath. I put on my bathing suit and headed to the river. I ignored the tiny fish nipping at my toes, knees, and elbows, and managed to wash myself and my hair in the river. Of course, I had no soap or shampoo, so it was more a rinse than a bath. After I dried off and dressed, I lay in the hammock, again contemplating the previous night's events. But I came to no conclusions, except to ask Jack about it later in the day. The only person who in any way came close to matching the shadowed silhouette was Jack.

The day was cool (as jungle temperatures go), with low humidity, so after a couple of hours, my hair was actually dry, something I had worried about because my hair is long, thick, and curly. I decided to take a walk over to visit Michelle, who, it turned out, was having a hard time of it. She did not feel at all connected to the jungle, felt that Jack and don Luis were more distant than normal, and felt completely out of sorts. The food repulsed her, and she was not eating at all. Andrew, her husband, was there and we changed the subject to the previous night's session. They related their experiences and I shared mine, including the early-morning light show and healing visit. Both thought it must have been a spirit energy that had shown itself. Michelle and I

BEAR CUB BOOKS

INNER
TRADITIONS

BEAR & CO.

Inner Traditions • Bear & Company

P.O. Box 388
Rochester, VT 05767-0388
U.S.A.

Please send us this card to receive our latest catalog.

☐ Check here if you would like to receive our catalog via e-mail.

E-mail address _____

Name _____ Company _____

Address _____ Phone _____

City _____ State _____ Zip _____ Country _____

Please check the following area(s) of interest to you:
☐ Health   ☐ Self-help   ☐ Science/Nature   ☐ Shamanism
☐ Ancient Mysteries ☐ New Age/Spirituality ☐ Ethnobotany   ☐ Martial Arts
☐ Spanish Language ☐ Sexuality/Tantra   ☐ Children   ☐ Teen

Order at 1-800-246-8648 • Fax (802) 767-3726
E-mail: orders@InnerTraditions.com • Web site: www.InnerTraditions.com

talked about ayahuasca, and how awful it made us feel. I told her about Grandmother Ayahuasca's message that it did not matter how we healed as long as we did and that I did not have to work with ayahuasca again unless I wanted to. I explained how attractive that option was to me, even though I could not imagine coming all the way to the Amazon and not participating in the sessions. Michelle thought the message a reasonable one. She had "dreamed" with ayahuasca many more times than I had, and she thought now that she, too, was through with it. In fact, she said, she just wanted to go home. I did not know what to say in response, except to offer support and to urge her to hang in there. This was only our second full day in the jungle, and we had to expect that it would take some time to adapt and acclimate.

Andrew and I ended up taking a walk over to Jack's tambo, to express our concern that Michelle was not eating and to seek his advice. Michelle is thin and small boned, and her refusal to eat concerned us both. True, the food was not very tasty, but it was edible if one had the willpower to just force it down. Some even liked it. For instance, incredible as it was to me, John and Andrew actually liked and indeed looked forward to the oatmeal.

Jack, naturally, urged us to make a special effort to get Michelle to eat. He did not seem too concerned otherwise, telling us that each person acclimates emotionally to the jungle at his or her own pace. But he did want to be kept informed if she continued not eating. He then changed the subject, apologizing for don Emilio's disruption of the session, expressing his—and don Luis's—opinion that don Emilio had gotten out of control and had not been able to handle the ayahuasca at all. "He's getting old and a little frail," Jack explained, "and he doesn't drink the vine very often anymore."

I was mystified. I had felt completely connected to don Emilio, and I explained to Jack how I felt don Emilio had helped me, cleansing my heavy energy. I explained how I had not vomited as long as don Emilio was in the maloca, but shortly after he had left, I had purged. I also told him how emotionally and energetically attached John had felt to don Emilio as well. Andrew expressed many of the same feelings. Jack was kind in his words and his tone, not condescending at all, when he said that perhaps that was our own individual perceptions. As for him and don Luis, they considered don Emilio as having totally lost control. "He was wailing about being attacked and about the police chasing him. He was shouting that a woman was coming to rescue him," he recounted. "That's when I went and got the boys, to help me remove him from the session and to take care of him. He won't be drinking ayahuasca with us again, although he will be joining us for the sessions."

Jack then changed the subject, beckoning us to come outside so he could show us an unusual tree. We walked behind his tambo to a particular tree, which I would now be unable to identify. "This is *sangre de grado*," he explained. "That means 'blood of the grade.' But *grado* is a degradation of the Spanish word *drago,* which means 'dragon.' It is really 'blood of the dragon.'" He pulled out a pocketknife and made a small cut in the bark. A dark red sap oozed out. "See," he said, wiping some of the sap from the bark, smearing it on his palm, and mixing it around with a fingertip until it began to froth slightly. "When you cut into the bark, it bleeds a red sap that doesn't harden. You soap it up in your palm, then apply it to a cut, where it forms a second skin, which is antiseptic. It's like nature's Band-Aid!"

After the demonstration, Andrew and I left, he returning to Michelle's tambo and I to mine. Chico and Mateo delivered the morning meal about ten, just as John was coming for a visit. He had come to take me to the waterfall, which was a wonderful place to bathe, but since I had already bathed, he went off by himself. I laid out my table to eat. The boys had delivered two baked plantains and a fish. I laid out the two towelettes and began the delicate work of picking the dozens of tiny bones out of the fish. It was slow work. It could take minutes to clean a piece of fish the size of a thumbnail. But it was worth the effort, as the white meat was delicious. I bit into a plantain thinking it would taste rather like a banana. I had had a plantain once in Florida, and it was good, not as sweet as a banana but tasting quite similar. So I bit into the plantain with relish, and was instantly disappointed. This type of plantain is nothing like the kind you can get in the States. It was dry and bland. The only way I can describe its taste is by asking you to imagine what it must taste like to bite off a piece of cardboard and chew. I placed both plantains aside and finished the fish, knowing that since this was not an ayahuasca day, we would be served additional food in the afternoon. (We were: quinoa with a scattering of bite-sized carrots and plantains, and another fish—a virtual feast.)

Strangely, although I had been eating next to nothing, I was not very hungry and ended up discarding most of the food. I was hesitant to keep throwing food down my latrine, so I tossed these morning left-overs into the jungle, knowing that the insects and small jungle creatures would have a feast. But I did not do that often, as don Luis and don Emilio preferred that leftover food be dumped down the latrine and not thrown into the jungle.

For the rest of the day, I lay in my hammock reading, dozing, or staring out at the river, where throughout the day a large bluish gray bird dive-bombed from a branch to the river to catch fish. It kept me amused for a while. Mostly, however, I read or slept, or mused about the strange events that had taken place in my tambo. About four o'clock Jack came by on his rounds. Here was my chance, so as soon as he was settled I asked him if he had visited my tambo in the early-morning hours. He had not. I described my experience to him. He listened without interrupting me and then asked, "Are you an especially intuitive person?"

I replied that I am. His reply was emphatic: "You were visited by a jungle spirit. He came to heal you."

I was left to ponder his pronouncement for the rest of the evening, for since it was not an ayahuasca night, we remained alone in our tambos. I was not sure how I felt about being visited by a spirit, especially such a large, humanlike one in the middle of the night. I felt both spooked and honored. I wondered, "Why me?" What in me needed such healing that a spirit had arrived to undertake the task? Had it worked? Or was the visit more a preparation for something, a cleansing because I had some important or difficult personal work to do?

Steve and Jeff wandered by at different times, and we exchanged a few words, but I spent most of the evening alone, swinging in my hammock, thinking of the otherness of the worlds that ayahuasca and the jungle itself were showing me and wondering what in the world would happen next.

Wednesday was more of the same, mostly swinging quietly in the hammock, letting my thoughts drift, sleeping, reading. The days seemed to meld one into the other. It was more humid on Wednesday, with a few brief thundershowers. Everyone but me was wishing for a classic jungle monsoon storm, especially Steve and Patrick, who had experienced several such storms last year when they were here. They had described the spectacular downpour and dazzling lightning. But I loved the dry and relatively cool weather. I joked with them that I was the weather shaman, and maybe, if they were lucky, I would order a great thunderstorm for Saturday, which was not an ayahuasca day, so I wouldn't have to leave my tambo and deal with jungle mud.

Wednesday was the first time I had food cravings, although I did not feel especially hungry. As I lay in my hammock, I would find my mind drifting to green corn tamales, pancakes with syrup, and fried cheese. Fried cheese! I never eat fried cheese, so I don't know why I suddenly craved it. When the day's meal arrived, I felt especially disappointed, for it was oatmeal, Amazon style. If I disliked most of the food we were being fed, I especially disliked the oatmeal, even more than the plantains. As with all our other food, it was not salted or spiced, and it tasted disgusting. Perhaps it was the texture that so grossed me out, for it looked like wallpaper paste and tasted like I imagined wallpaper paste would taste. After a few tablespoons I could eat no more. That left me with plantains. Only today they were boiled—what a difference that made. They had some semblance of moisture to them, and so I could split them down the middle and scoop out the center meat and actually eat half of one. Other than that, my entire meal went down the latrine—with great regret on my part, since, being an ayahuasca day, this was the only meal we would get. I have to admit, in the interest of being faithful to the truth, that later that day I found a low-fat, wheat-free apple spice breakfast bar in the bottom of my backpack. I ate it, but it was not the delicacy it appeared to be. It was sickeningly sweet. I had not had sugar in more than two weeks, and I felt sick to my stomach after eating it. I also felt a small measure of guilt.

I spent some time down at the river, since I was craving sunshine. But Jack came by and told me that it is forbidden while on the ayahuasca retreat to do much work or to be exposed to the sun for more than a few moments at a time. So, back to my tambo I went. I sat on the floor, leaned against the railing, and marveled at the jungle. I had grown quite comfortable with it in some ways. An emotional tie was forming. Neither horsefly bites nor fire ants nor bugs too strange looking to describe bothered me much anymore. I had ceased to worry about snakes dropping from the trees, and I could not have cared less that the termites were working the wooden post above one corner of my bed and the mosquito netting there was covered with black wood dust. The ushpahuasa seemed to be doing its subtle work. I drank two glassfuls Wednesday and was in an almost continually dreamy state of mind, feeling centered and quiet inside. My rational mind seemed to have begun settling down. As I sat there, I talked into my tape recorder: "I'm sitting in a backjack on the floor of my tambo, and the river is flowing lazily by. It's the color of coffee with milk. I can hear the rush of the waterfall, and the birds and insects singing. So many oddly beautiful sounds. Sunlight is filtering down through the trees. There's barely a breeze, and there are very few bugs right now. Why would I want to be anywhere else in the world?"

At six o'clock Wednesday evening, we met in the maloca for the second ayahuasca session. Don Emilio agreed to tell us about his life and training, but first Jack and don Luis spoke. They told us that in a traditional plant diet, one is supposed to follow the restrictions for as many days *after* the retreat as one did the sacred plants. Since we would be in retreat for ten days, ideally we should continue the diet for ten days after we left the jungle. I knew that was going to be a challenge. During my morning food fantasies I had been almost able to taste the glass of ice-cold chardonnay I was going to order as soon as we got back to Pucallpa.

A few of us asked questions, and Jack asked me to relate my experience of the "jungle spirit" visit. Everyone listened intently, but the only comment was a joke that I lived in the "haunted tambo." I had to agree, in some respects. Besides the eerie and sometimes smelly termite nest that festooned the post of my tambo, I had been forced running, but not screaming, from my tambo one night when a large bird flew in. Because of the steep pitch of the thatched roof, it could not find its way out and was trapped up in the rafters. But I had not known at the time that it was a bird. All I knew was that *something* was trapped and making a racket near the roof of my tambo. I had not waited around to find out what and had dashed out into the darkness with no flashlight. I had called down to Michelle, and Andrew, who was visiting there, had called back, "Come on down, Joan. We're here." I called back into the darkness, "Andrew, come quick—and bring your flashlight and a big stick!" Andrew came to my rescue, but in the end, the bird flew out on its own.

What's more, there was a red *lupuna* tree right outside my tambo. Ever since we arrived don Emilio had been trying to tell me something about the tree, but I had been unable to fully understand him. All I could make out was something about a short, red man. I finally asked Jack about it, and he told me there are two kinds of lupuna trees, white and red. Each variety has a spirit attached to it: the white lupuna spirit is an elderly man who is kind and helpful; the spirit of the red lupuna is a nasty dwarf with a red beard who, if disturbed, chases you and tears out your stomach or intestines if he catches you. So my tambo had the reputation of being the center of weirdness, and the jungle spirit visitor simply cinched the deal.

Don Emilio talked for nearly an hour and a half, with Jack translating. He told us how his grandfather and father had trained as vegetalistas and had in turn trained him. How his wife assists him, and how one daughter and one grandson in particular are also learning to heal with plants, even with ayahuasca. He described how specific plants are used to treat particular conditions and illnesses. For instance, he uses *sanango* to help physically disabled people recover their mobility. "Even people who have been unable to walk for five years or more can be cured with sanango," he claimed. "We treat them with these teas of plants and also make baths for them. Then after two or three or four months, they can get up and walk again." He described the use of yahuarpanga to treat addiction, especially crack and cocaine addiction. "We give them yahuarpanga, which forces them to vomit, and it is very effective in healing addictions. After we give them yahuarpanga, then I invite them to eight sessions of ayahuasca, and each night they take ayahuasca. Then finally I give them eight days of ushpahuasa. That usually takes care of the addiction."

Don Emilio focused on ushpahuasa for part of his talk. When he undertook his first retreat with this plant teacher, he said, he dieted for one month and refrained from eating salt for two more months. "The plants give you their songs," he explained, and then began to sing an icaro. It was a haunting melody, low of tone and slow of cadence. "The song I just recited for you was the song ushpahuasa taught me. Ushpahuasa has very big, black spirits. As you take ushpahuasa and lie down, you see these big spirits surrounding you and they are the doctors, the doctors of this medicine. They use the schacapa rattle and like to heal at your feet." I sat there dumbfounded. What he had just described sounded very much like my spirit-visitor experience.

When it came time for questions, Andrew asked about ushpahuasa's reputation as a rejuvenating plant. Don Emilio said, "Yes, ushpahuasa clears and cleans you. It clears your eyesight, makes you see clearer. I am sixty-five years old, don't wear glasses, and I recognize everybody I see! A lot of people in their fifties lose their eyesight. They can't understand or recognize what they see. It's also good for hearing. It prolongs your hearing as well. It removes any pains you have in your joints and legs. There is a man in [names a village] who was in bed for five years. He could not get up. But he wanted to marry this widow. And he could not because he was bedridden. So I gave him ushpahuasa; he drank ushpahuasa and soon he was no longer bedridden. I asked him later if he married the widow. He said no! He did not!"

Since don Emilio was on the subject of ushpahuasa, I jumped at my chance to ask him about my experience. I was fairly convinced now that an ushpahuasa "doctor" had come to perform a preparation ceremony for me. I told him, with Jack translating, what I had seen and that the spirit visit had occurred only hours before I had first started drinking ushpahuasa. "Do the spirits of a plant come unbidden like that?" I asked. "Can they come to prepare you to *receive* the plant?"

"The spirit of the plant is called the 'Mother' of the plant," he explained. "It appears to you like a spirit, with shape and form. It may come and blow over you, touch your feet, heal you. Then when you start taking the plant, you diet and follow the routine, and you sometimes will begin to hear the song of the spirit. Then you continue to follow the diet, and you go to the latrine and put all your excess food in there and you follow the diet. Then the spirit will come back, as you keep on taking the plant. If you diet well and you follow the correct procedures, you should begin to remember things. You gradually begin to see the spirit of the plant, and you remember it."

So, Grandmother Ayahuasca's promise of a second gift had been fulfilled more fully than I had anticipated—not only by my being able to switch from bobinsana to ushpahuasa, but also through the ushpahuasa spirit who had visited my tambo. I thought of John's singing the gorgeous icaro, and I realized we had shared this experience in some deep and profound way, even though John had not seen the spirit as I had. In our shamanic work of the Andean mountain tradition, John and I function as a *yanantin,* the complement of two different energies; in this case, the male and female. During the spirit visit we had achieved *japu,* the perfect fusion of yanantin energies, each playing our role: me intuitively receiving the spirit of ushpahuasa and John intuiting the icaro of this sacred plant teacher.

I did not have much time to contemplate don Emilio's explanation,

for the ayahuasca session was about to begin. We drank at about
seven-thirty, and feeling a little overwhelmed by all my experiences, I
decided to take only a half dose. But as with the last session, I resolved
to stay in my observational self. Although I have read and heard the
advice of many psychonauts that it is a good idea not to get sucked into
the visions—that you can learn more about yourself by remaining
detached and observant of your own inner processes—I was beginning
to wonder if doing so was not keeping me from going deep enough
within myself to heal whatever in me needed healing or revealing.
Maybe I had to follow the green magic wherever it took me, fully
immersing myself in the experience in order to get the most from it? I
did not know, for I was too new to the use of entheogens.

All I know now, as I write this account, is that despite my resolve
to remain observant, I have very little memory of this particular session.
I remember the jaw-unhinging yawns that can be characteristic of
ayahuasca use; visions of ancient temples, mostly Aztec or Mayan,
some of which had elaborate figural inscriptions over doorways leading
to labyrinthine passageways; the vibrating energy grid that seems to be
at the heart of all matter; and the power of the icaros to modulate my
visions and emotions. In fact, my experience of the icaros was sublime
during that session. I was acutely aware of how the colors and patterns
responded instantaneously to a shift in the undulating melodies, the
haunting whistling, and the whispery vocables. I understood what I had
read in one of Terence McKenna's books about how language (sound)
becoming visual and figural may be a function of evolution. I was visually gliding and sliding through the music and it through me. I felt as if
I were being psychically operated upon by a surgeon whose scalpel was
sound.

At one point the musical surgery became almost physically real, as
don Emilio came over to Steve, who was sitting at my left, only eight to
ten inches from me. Although it was dark and I could hardly see their
forms, when don Emilio began singing, I knew it was into the crown of
Steve's head. Don Emilio sings almost exclusively in Quechua, and his
icaros are long and repetitive, with a more somber quality than most of

don Luis's. I began to feel the spillover of energy from the healing. A heat began to rise to my left and drift into my field, like a fog encompassing me. I began to sweat profusely. As don Emilio's songs became more forceful, strident even, I felt waves of energy swirling around me. The nausea was rising in me, as was the physical and psychical discomfort. I literally felt a heaviness being lifted from Steve, hissing off him like steam and drifting toward me. I felt a fever rising in me, and a humming sound within my head began to drift ever higher in pitch and intensity. I remembered Jack telling us that we often pick up the energy or the "dream" of the persons sitting next to us or directly across from us, and I was aware now that I was fully in the spillover of Steve's healing. John was to my right, and there was no energetic contact at all from his direction. But I was beginning to feel overwhelmed by the heat and energy coming from Steve and don Emilio. I had to move, to put some distance between us, but there was nowhere to move without being disruptive. John was immediately to my right, so there was no real room for me to shift over. The wooden backjacks the boys had constructed as seating in the maloca were permanently attached in groups of three, so our seating was fixed. It was so dark I could not see in front of me, but I knew don Luis's mesa was not too far from my feet. Worst of all, I had very little control over my body and did not feel well enough or coordinated enough to stand and walk without causing a ruckus.

I thought for a moment of my Andean training in *hucha mikhuy,* a technique of "digesting," or cleansing, heavy energy through the navel chakra and then feeding it to Pachamama, Mother Earth, but I was incapable of centering myself enough to perform this energy digestion. As my discomfort intensified, I thought about calling out for John or Jack to come assist me, but, again, I did not want to cause a commotion. So I endured. I was no longer capable of detached observation. I was at the mercy of the energy now blasting me from my left, and I simply had to endure it as part of my experience. After what seemed like forever, don Emilio's songs ended and he returned to his place. It was with much relief that I heard Jack rise to light the candle, signaling the end to the session.

I did not hang around long. I almost immediately returned to my tambo. The steamy night air was a relief from the suffocating heat of the healing energy. I washed with the guayusa-infused water, then sat in my hammock and centered myself, and by about midnight I felt returned to normal. John came by, kissed me goodnight, and headed back to his tambo. I felt better by now and was not tired, but the kamikaze insects were zeroing in on my candles and immolating themselves, so I decided to go to bed. I tried reading by flashlight but was uncomfortable, so I clicked it off and just laid there, in the somewhat stuffy womb of the mosquito netting, listening to the night sounds.

For some reason, and I don't know why, I suddenly felt that I should call in the jungle spirits. All week my closeness with the energy of the jungle had been growing, until now I felt fully identified with it. In fact, I felt part of the jungle, especially at night, when I would lie awake and allow myself to be enveloped in its night talk. So I silently projected my thoughts out into the night, saying, "If you are there, spirits of the jungle, and you will come with my highest good and well-being as your intent, I welcome you now." Almost immediately I sensed a woman step out of the jungle toward the foot of my bed. I saw her in my mind's eye, and as I looked into her eyes, her face—that of a young, healthy woman—changed in rapid succession from one face to another, in a myriad of countenances, male and female, old and young, until the woman's face formed once again. I could no longer clearly see her features, and I stared with my mind's eye, trying to bring them into focus. When that did not work, I softened my inner vision, hoping that would help. It did not.

Then I realized the face was a distraction—I was not supposed to see it clearly. While I had been so focused on the faces, my hands had begun to move, as if they had minds of their own. My hands were splayed out, palms flat and a few inches over my body. They were moving from chakra to chakra over my lower three energy centers. They felt disembodied, moving of no volition of mine, and I thought of Castaneda and the hand gestures, the magical passes, of the Yaqui way of knowledge. My right hand hovered, quivering over my womb, then slowly moved up to my navel, then up to just below my breastbone, then up and over my left breast, and finally down to just below my rib cage. Up and down and over they moved. I understood that by occupying my mind with trying to see the faces, I had been freed to allow my body to work on itself intuitively, in some kind of chakra cleansing. With this realization, my mind and emotions were flooded by an archetypal energy, the energy of the Divine Feminine. I sensed that I was clearing energy not just for myself but for "womanhood." As my hand moved over the womb area and solar plexus, I was clearing issues of will and power. I was clearing marriage wounds. I felt a surge of understanding about how women can be damaged and wounded and left feeling disempowered through their ties to unhappy marriages and domineering spouses and stultifying cultural expectations. Although I did not feel that these were characterizations of my own experience with men and with marriage, the observation felt personal and archetypal simultaneously. I remembered the voice from my first ayahuasca session: *This is yours and not yours.*

I must have dozed off, for I awoke around two o'clock and could not get back to sleep. I got up and went to the latrine, then cooled off by rinsing myself with guayusa water. I decided to stay outside in the hammock. After I got comfortable, I turned off my flashlight and once again gave myself over to the night. The rush of the waterfall seemed more subdued than it did during the day. A breeze rustled the leaves and palm fronds. The world hummed with insects and frogs. On an emotional level, the ushpahuasa seemed to be opening me to the nuances of the jungle, for I was feeling, at last, that I was not an intruder or even a visitor, but was instead a supplicant praying in a green cathedral. Still, I also knew that the jungle was full of ambiguity.

During the day the jungle can be pure magic, always ready to spring a surprise, either breathtaking or death making: a gorgeous butterfly or a deadly snake, a rare orchid or a poisonous plant. But in the daylight you can deal with it, even attempt to master its magnificence. In the light of day, you can hoodwink yourself into thinking that you might, with the proper fortitude and adequate patience, achieve dominion over the tangled profusion of life here. But at night, such hubris seems . . . seems . . . what's the right word? Vulgar? Hackneyed? Pretentious? Offensive? At night the jungle is alchemical, transforming itself from a landscape into what poet Gerard Manley Hopkins would call an inscape, ushering one from the exteriors of life to its interior spaces. It is at once threatening and evocative, for one cannot help but be impressed with the grandiosity of its night life and yet also made small by one's own vulnerability. The jungle at night is tantalizing in its secretiveness and flagrant in its imperviousness.

As I lay there, something beyond my sentimentality seemed to be softening me toward the jungle. It was as if at night the jungle became something darkly anthropomorphic, a creature that could stalk me but chose instead to gently rub itself against the hard edges of my being, marking me with its scent and drawing me toward its hidden den. As I listened to its aliveness, I thought of a provocative passage from César Calvo's book about ayahuasca. Although I did not remember the words verbatim, their meaning drifted through my mind as I lay there wondering what I was really doing here alone, in the dark, in the jungle. Calvo had written about how it is impossible to listen to everything in the jungle, for what one hears is not only the cacophony of living things of the jungle but also the echo of all that humans have been and all that we will be. The jungle at night is the sound of memory, he wrote. "Memory is much, much more—don't you know? True memory also holds what is yet to come. And what will never come; it also holds that. Imagine. Just imagine. Who on earth could hear all of it—tell me? Who could listen to it all at once and believe it?"[1]

With these thoughts drifting through my awareness, I finally crawled under the mosquito netting about three o'clock and settled down to sleep.

When I next awoke, the netting was ablaze with light. The shadows of leaves and vines and branches quivered against the white cloth. I flashed back to Monday night's experience and became frightened. The spirit doctor was back, and just the thought of him scared me. While a few hours ago I had sent out an energetic invitation to the jungle spirits, now I wanted nothing to do with them. Pressing the fright back, I mentally thanked him but asked him to leave. "I'm sorry that I am so afraid," I apologized, "but I am, so you need to leave." Almost immediately the lights went out, as if someone had flipped a switch, and I was back in the dark. As I rolled over and tucked myself into the fetal position, I chastised myself. I was disappointed with myself and the fear that seemed to control me. As I have said before, I had always inwardly scoffed at spiritual adventurers like Castaneda, who had been so frightened, even after years and years of work with his Yaqui master, of experiencing anything the least out of the ordinary. Now here I was, acting like a child afraid of the bogeyman in the closet.

"What," I asked myself, "is so frightening? An hour ago you were swooning in the sweet embrace of the jungle and now you are afraid again. It's not like you haven't seen spirit lights before." But there was a difference. The spirits I had felt over the years during ceremonies or initiations were just that—feelings, intuitive contacts with presences and inward communications with them. And when I had experienced actual physical manifestations of energies, they had rarely been personal. The amorphous bluish spirit lights I had seen at Machu Picchu had been at a distance of several feet. They had only vague form and they were not interested in me. Another time a similar amorphous blue energy had coursed through me, like a giant blue condor, but that experience, while physical, had been momentary and emotionally impersonal.

That the spirit had come unbidden also bothered me. During shamanic journeying or while doing ceremony in Peru, I had always been the one to initiate the journey or seek out contact, and even if I had been surprised by a specter, as I had while walking the Inca Trail, I had rarely met any even mildly threatening presences. This experience was different—not only was the spirit here and in a very physical form but he was here expressly for *me*. I could not face the intimacy of the situation. What is more, most spirit contact I had experienced had always involved some form of communication. The spirit had always indicated outright or intimated more subtly why it was showing itself. This dark, hulking presence was mute. For all these reasons, I simply could not allow myself to relax into a posture of receiving, despite the fact that this spirit did not feel threatening.

As I lay there, I realized that I had to do something about my anxiety, about my fear, and that there was no better place than here, in the jungle, and now, with the opportunity to allow the green magic to heal me. So I resolved that at the next ayahuasca session, which would be Friday evening, I would go for it. No more detachment: I would take a full dose and aim for full immersion. No holds barred.

❧ 9 ❧

Finding the Light in My Heart of Darkness

Go to your bosom; knock there, and ask your heart what it doth know.

—WILLIAM SHAKESPEARE, *MEASURE FOR MEASURE*

Thursday dawned cool—by jungle standards—and breezy, and despite having been awake most of the night I felt rested and refreshed. I remembered a dream I had had, of a bakery in my hometown where as a child I always used to go with my mother to buy Italian bread and pastries. I hadn't thought of that bakery in decades, but in my dream I was there, waiting to be served. The cases were filled with mouth-watering confections and crusty loaves of bread hot from the oven. But no one would serve me. The train—there was a station a block down the street—arrived and the store became filled with commuters. I was pushed aside. I awoke feeling ushpahuasa had taken me back to my childhood, and I marveled that even in my dream I had been forced to keep to the ayahuasca diet! It was only much later that I saw the dream in another, more serious light—that I had been too timid to ask that I be served. I saw parallels between that passivity and the anxiety that had pushed the spirit doctor away from ministering to me. What sweetness had I denied myself?

Don Emilio and Chico came by my tambo about eight-thirty with the ushpahuasa. I drank a full glass, and Chico poured another that I would drink in the afternoon. About nine-thirty the food arrived, a bowl of brown rice and a plantain. I could have as many plantains as I wanted, but I took only one and could manage to force only half of it down. These days a quarter of a bowl of rice and half a plantain felt like a lot of food. Although just the morning before I had had green-corn-tamale daydreams and last night I had been drooling over Italian pastry in my dream, today I felt no hunger. But neither was I feeling weak. John and some of the other men were losing weight and feeling weakened, and so Jack had agreed to serve food twice a day even on ayahuasca days. But I felt fine. In fact, I felt stronger than when I had arrived.

Today we would meet at one o'clock at the maloca for the nature hike. I lounged in the hammock in my usual position, facing the river and staring into nothingness, until a black buzzing thing caught my attention. A hummingbird? I had not seen many, and most of those I did see were during visits to John's tambo. The dark whirring thing circled the trunk of a young palmlike tree directly in front of my tambo. When it alighted on a branch, I could see it was not a hummingbird at all but an odd, oversized beetlelike insect. It was only slightly smaller than a hummingbird and its exoskeleton was glossy black. Its longish "beak" reminded me of a hummingbird's, as did the whir of its wings when it flew. But it was definitely a beetle of some kind—definitely the weirdest bug I saw in the jungle, except for the "fairy bug," a miniscule feathery insect that I would not get a close look at until the next day.

Later in the morning I heard a startling sound—disorienting but vaguely familiar. It took seconds for me to recognize it as an airplane—the first "civilized" sound I had heard in nearly a week. The rest of the morning passed quietly, with a short visit from Andrew and another from Heni.

At 1:00 we all met at the maloca and headed off up the trail, with Jack, don Luis, don Emilio, Chico, and Mateo as our tour guides. Most of them carried machetes. John photographed the trees, vines, and bushes while I took notes as don Luis or don Emilio explained their medicinal uses, but it turned out to be nearly impossible to match up photographs and description later, so I am at a loss now to adequately describe each plant. The jungle truly is a pharmacy, and I was impressed with the wide range of medicines that were available in the short half-mile or so hike we took around our tambos. There was o*chahuaha,* whose bark is mixed with ushpahuasa to make an ointment to treat snakebite. The oddly curving and ground-hugging *uña de gato,* or cat's claw, has antitumor and anti-inflammation properties. The rubber tree, called *renaco,* oozes a white sap that is mixed with alcohol and drunk in order to cure rheumatism. Healers also apply the sap directly to joints to ease swelling and pain. Don Emilio pointed out a leafy vine that seemed decoupaged to a tree trunk. It was *trumpetero sacha,* or trumpet wood. Vegetalistas boil the leaves and stems and then bathe babies who are on the verge of walking in the cooled waters. The bath imparts strength to the babies' legs. I was particularly touched by this plant and its use, not only because the vine appeared so completely fused to the tree around which it wrapped, but also because it had never dawned on me that medicine could be used in such a tender and supportive way. To make babies' legs strong! To help them prepare to walk! I was overcome not only that the jungle offered such a gift to parents but that vegetalistas had discovered this gift at all.

As we continued up the trail, don Luis showed us *aguaje,* a palm tree with edible fruit but whose trunk sports sharp spines from which, he declared, sorcerers make a tea that gives them the ability to see devils. *Estoraque* leaves are also used to make a tea, but this tonic is made to impart sexual potency to the men who imbibe it. *Chamburo* attracts luscious, fat worms that the locals fry and eat. The worms supposedly are delicious and provide protein and rich oils to the inhabitants' diets. The name of the yahuarpanga plant, which we had already heard so much about as an inducer of vomiting, literally means "leaf of blood," because it oozes a red sap. To prepare the medicine to treat addiction, the healer grinds the leaves in a food mill and then steeps a tea. Usually only a quarter cup is enough to begin a prolonged purging, and the purge is continued by ingesting water. Don Emilio also explained that if someone is blocked emotionally, he or she would be given yahuarpanga followed later by ayahuasca.

They also showed us *juster sacha,* a relatively rare creeper vine with distinctive heart-shaped leaves that are boiled to make a tea, which then must be left out overnight to be exposed to the dew. Only then is it ready to be used to treat kidney problems. *Vacu pisceni,* an elephant ear plant, is actually irritating to the skin, but if you "half cook it and then wrap it around a body part," don Emilio explained, "it protects you from sorcery" or cures an illness caused by sorcery. By wrapping the stricken part of the body, Jack elaborated, you draw out the sorcery-induced evil that is causing pain or problems. We were shown many more plants and trees, but everyone seemed to be losing strength, so we returned to our individual tambos about two-thirty.

Not long after our return, the afternoon meal arrived: quinoa and plantains. I took very little and ate even less. After dumping the leftovers down my latrine and washing the crock and spoon, I dozed in the hammock. By four-thirty my tambo was in shadow, and by six o'clock it was dark. I went to bed at seven-thirty, not wanting to be bothered by the swarms of insects that the candlelight attracted.

I awoke, as was now my jungle routine, about two-thirty in the morning, feeling sad. All of the plants I had seen and learned about that afternoon seemed to march to the forefront of memory, one by one displaying their magnificence. While I still felt intimately and emotionally connected with the jungle, I was sorrowful at my lack of knowledge, my intellectual disconnection from this world. I was indeed a stranger in a strange land, and to think anything else would be to dupe myself. I had gotten to know some of the plants that afternoon, but I realized now that I would never know much. "I'm here but not really part of what's here," I bemoaned. "I know little more than someone walking the streets of New York City." I wanted to know more. I wanted not only to be identified with the jungle, which I was emotionally and energetically, but also to be able to identify that which it comprised. I knew it only as a profusion of green, not as individual plant medicines with their own unique healing spirits. I thought of the vine whose leaves are made into baths for babies about to walk. I was filled with gratitude to Mother Earth, who had thought to provide such an amazingly tender helping medicine for her children. That gift was beautiful to the point of sadness to me. I contrasted cultures, marveling at the poignancy of a culture that could discover and treasure such a medicine and disgusted with my own culture, which was profoundly disconnected from and even contemptuous of the natural world. We had no recognition of this kind of gift from nature to our children. We had no real clue about the immensity of the healing capacity of the plants around us, and we did not seem to care enough to find out. And even if we did, we did not honor these gifts; we only exploited them. I was overcome with emotion and lay in the dark weeping for our blindness, our stupidity, our loss.

I felt melancholic and rather teary eyed all day Friday. I tried to rouse myself from feelings of pity for myself and for humanity in general by staying busy, but there was not much to do. I visited John, and we marveled at the blue morpho butterflies that flew so solitarily around his tambo. But it was difficult to visit. We truly were into the spirit of the retreat, and we felt the need to be solitary, so I returned to my tambo after only ten minutes. The short hike left me feeling weak, the first time I had felt any ebbing of my strength. Around a quarter to ten the boys delivered our morning ration, and what a surprise it was—rice with a boiled plantain, a slice of avocado, and a chicken thigh! Just the sight of protein lifted my spirits, and although the chicken thigh was mostly bone with only a little stringy meat attached, I savored every morsel. The avocado was luscious. The plantain and most of the rice went down the latrine.

I drank my second glass of ushpahuasa in midafternoon and spent the rest of the day lazing in the hammock. That's when I finally got a good look at the insect I had come to call the "fairy bug." It was tiny, hardly larger than a gnat, but somehow still discernibly fluffy. As I lay there one hovered close to my bare forearm, and inexplicably, I had microscopic vision—I could make out the finest details of this bug, even though I am farsighted and have to wear glasses to read. It was like a tiny black puffball, and skittish, for if I moved my arm in the least, the bug floated back, keeping its distance. After a while it would come close again, hovering, as if it were checking me out. This game of back and forth went on for almost half an hour, and during that time I was able to study this curious creature. It truly was a fairy bug. It had a black body with a slightly neon bluish tint to it. Its miniscule feet were actually shaped like pontoons, which seemed so riotously oversized for its diminutive body that I marveled that the creature could fly at all. Its body was adorned with curlicue feelers and long, curving, silken filaments. For all its delicacy, this was the most complex-looking bug I had yet seen. I sketched it in my notebook but could not achieve a semblance of its etherealness. It was the highlight of my afternoon.

We gathered for the evening ayahuasca session about seven. We talked for a while, with Jack checking in with each of us. I learned the reason that don Luis asks us to sit relatively upright during the sessions, with straight spines: to lie down tends to more easily invite dark visions. Plus, you can drop off to sleep while journeying with ayahuasca and get lost. The shaman might have to come rescue you as your body sleeps but your spirit wanders off. Don Emilio announced, through Jack, that he would conduct healings during the session, so we should be prepared for him to approach us in the dark. Jack also made a last-minute announcement. Tonight, if we wanted to, we could drink the ayahuasca negra, the black brew, but we would be given only a small dose.

Don Luis blessed both bottles of brew and whistled his benediction to ayahuasca, and don Emilio blew the smoke from jungle tobacco through them. They each sang icaros into the bottles. Then don Luis and Jack dispensed the doses. I was prepared to go for it this night, but the dose of the black brew seemed very small. Jack said I could take more later if I needed to. But I didn't, for I was the second person to be healed by don Emilio, and that healing was more transporting than any larger dose of ayahuasca could have been. It was an energetically wondrous experience.

Don Emilio sang most of the icaros, and his songs propelled me into the fun house of fractal forms and scintillating colors. The circuit boardlike grid pattern that overlaid everything was especially intense and intricate and was vibrating at a tremendous rate. The ancient temples appeared, as did the rows of splendorous silver and hot pink insects, dancing their ethereal dance. But this time I did not get sucked into any of the visuals. It was not that I was making a special effort to remain detached; I just was.

When don Emilio approached me in the dark to begin the healing, I was deep into ayahuasca dreaming but yet not lost in those dreams. He knelt in front of me, but it was so dark I could only just make out his shape. He leaned over me and began stoking my hair and head. Some type of aromatic granular crumbs fell as he did so, and I later learned that during his healings he rubs ground cinnamon bark on his hands and on the people he heals to cleanse them. He began singing an icaro into the top of my head, and I was mesmerized by the song. It was in Quechua, and I did not recognize many of the words, but its slow, repetitive tune was hypnotic. I can only reproduce it phonetically, but it sounded something like: *zuma, zu-ma, tut-ta-ma-ra, koi, ma-ri, koi, ma-dra-me-ra, kori-sa-ma, depa, depa, sapa ma-ri, kori ma-ma-man-ah-ah.* Don Emilio's voice was deep and a bit gravelly, but the song's unfamiliar syllables were sinuous, encircling me like a snake, slowly coiling their liquid light around and through my energy body.

When he finished singing the icaro into my crown chakra, don Emilio moved to my hands. At first I did not know what he wanted with my hands as he fumbled with them, trying to get me to assume a certain posture. Soon I was sitting more or less upright with my hands together but open, as if I were cupping water. He gently rubbed my palms with cinnamon bark and then leaned his face into my hands and began to whistle in a hauntingly slow and almost somber manner. Then, as he began to sing an icaro into my palms, the most amazing scenario unfolded, and to this day this healing remains one of the most memorable and deeply affecting shamanic experiences I have ever had.

As don Emilio sang into my hands, I almost immediately felt

energy collecting around my heart chakra, drawing all my attention there. In my mind's eye I could see into my chest, which was a deep void, an empty and ancient cavern encircled by ribs. It was dark, with a faint red glow at its bottom, which seemed far, far away. Slowly, as don Emilio sang, the glow intensified and became whitish gold. It gathered strength and mushroomed upward, filling my heart chakra with a soft but still powerful luminescence. Soon my entire chest cavity was aglow. When this light reached a peak of intensity, nearly blinding my inner vision, I suddenly felt as if my chest were a barrel wrapped with metal bands, and physically I felt the bands snap one by one. *Pop! Pop! Pop!* As each steel band broke loose, I felt lighter, freer, liberated! When the last one snapped, I took a deep breath. It was an automatic gesture, spontaneous, with no intentionality on my part. I simply *breathed,* the most wondrously full and expansive breath I have ever taken. I was incredulous. The feeling was too wondrous to translate into language, although in every way it was a revelation. "*This* is what it's like to breathe!" I marveled. I realized that I had never taken a true breath in my life. "*This* is how the universe breathes. *This* is what is meant by the breath of life." I never wanted the feeling of expansiveness, peace, well-being, and at-one-ment to end. I felt immeasurably expansive and exquisitely alive. I felt drunk with happiness for having taken this one, true breath. I was utterly free at every level of my being. Joy filled me, and I felt fresh, clean, whole—lost to my ego self and at one with the All That Is.

I never wanted to lose that feeling. But don Emilio was moving to my belly. He lifted my shirt to expose my skin and began singing into my stomach, just above my navel. The glow at my heart chakra began to fade, and with it the feeling of unbounded freedom, although that sensation, which was both emotional and physical, remained as an afterglow, and does to this day. I sat in awe in its aura as don Emilio finished singing into my belly, bared my feet, and began singing into the tops of my feet.

He carried out the same process of healing on each of us, and it took what seemed like hours for him to move around the circle. By the time he got only halfway around, I was fighting to stay awake. While in the glow of that breath, the breath of the heart, I had been awakened to life and to being. Now I felt as if I were fighting to remain conscious. I do not remember many visuals at this point, but I do remember the voices. I seemed to be floating in a bright blackness, fighting off a profound need for sleep, when out of nowhere and apropos of nothing, a voice began to offer comments about who I am, what I believe, how I act. The voice was disembodied and unidentifiable, and it spoke without a trace of judgment, neither condemning nor congratulatory. *You're such a flirt.* A single comment and then nothing. Moments later, another comment. *You're way too hard on yourself.* Silence, then another observation. *You don't laugh enough.* The impartial assessments continued intermittently. *You're kind and supportive of others. . . . Why do you think you are unattractive? . . . You are blessed in your friendships, and others are blessed by your friendship. . . . You have the capacity to be a powerful teacher. . . . Why don't you believe in yourself?*

After a while the voice stopped, and I sat in the darkness feeling as if I were floating in a black void—until don Emilio got to Jeff, who was sitting in the circle directly opposite me. I had heard Jack talk about the intricate energy configurations that can take place in a circle of ayahuasca dreamers, and I had experienced such a spillover of energy when don Emilio had healed Steve in Wednesday night's session. Now I was to experience Jeff's energy from across the room. As don Emilio began the healing, singing the by now familiar crown chakra icaro, the Vine of the Soul seem reactivated within me and the visuals arose like an iridescent wind sweeping across the barrenness of my mind.

As don Emilio sang into Jeff's head, Jeff began to moan and then talk in gibberish—or perhaps in tongues. His words were unintelligible yet seemed to have an odd kind of sense to them. I felt a stream of energy connecting him to me, and the heat began to rise. Within moments I was loosening the slide ties at my pant hems and pushing the pant legs up to my knees. I took off my long-sleeved shirt and bloused the neckline of my tank top in an effort to cool myself. I reached for my handkerchief and mopped my brow. I was boiling! But the energy stream from Jeff to me only intensified.

I felt myself sitting up straighter. Whereas moments earlier I had been slouched over, struggling to stay awake or conscious, now I was hyperaware and fully alert. I planted my feet on the floor with certainty and extended my arms out so my forearms were resting on my knees. That is when the metamorphosis began. With a creeping slowness, I felt my back harden, as if it were morphing into a carapace. Soon I had the reddish black exoskeleton of a beetle, with wings that felt delicate but not gossamer. The feeling of transformation was alarming, but there was nothing I could do to stop it. My arms and legs were no longer mine but were jointed bug's legs, with rows of tiny hairlike barbs along them. My eyes grew enormous, and I could see don Emilio across the room singing into Jeff's head as if both were illuminated by a black light. Stubby antennae sprouted from my head. I did not *feel* like a giant beetle, I *was* one—and I remained one for Jeff's entire healing. I do not remember thinking or feeling anything—not heat, not energy—during the remainder of his healing. I have no memory of morphing back into Joan. In fact, the rest of the session is a blur, and I was nearly asleep when Jack finally lit the candle at about one o'clock. I stumbled back to my tambo and slept deeply—the first night since my arrival in the jungle that I slept through the entire night.

🌿 10 🌿

Intellectual Interlude

Anthropologists are fond of reminding their students that
shamanism, not prostitution, is the world's oldest profession.
—MICHAEL BROWN, "DARK SIDE OF THE SHAMAN,"
IN *SHAMANS THROUGH TIME*

Saturday I was fairly zoned out, not wanting to do much but stay solitary and quiet. My first-day worries that I would grow bored had long since vanished. I was in the rhythm of the jungle now, fully into the retreat and loving it. This day went much like all the others: I drank ushpahuasa in the morning and afternoon, forced down a few mouthfuls of disagreeably bland food, and visited with John, Michelle, Andrew, and whoever else came along the trail. Jack had told me a few days before that don Luis had agreed to my request for an interview, so I spent some time preparing a list of questions and readying my tapes and recorder. Jack and don Luis arrived for the interview in late afternoon. As usual, Jack translated for don Luis, who was characteristically quiet. In the interest of retaining the flavor of the interview, I reproduce it here almost verbatim. I had interviewed six Q'ero *paqos,* or practitioners of the spiritual path, for my book *Keepers of the Ancient Knowledge,* and it had been extraordinarily time-consuming to coax them to talk in more than bare-bones sentences. Don Luis was equally succinct.

Joan: Don Luis, would you tell me about your decision to train as an ayahuasquero? It takes an extraordinary level of commitment, doesn't it?

Luis: I've been doing this for twenty years. It is a very dedicated discipline.

Joan (to Jack): Would you ask him to elaborate? Whom was he trained by? He does not have to reveal anything he does not want to, of course, but I would like him to share more about his training if he will.

Luis: The first four years I was trained by my *maestro,* don Tomás [pseudonym]. And then he introduced me to several other maestros, and the second one taught me about—not so much about ayahuasca, but about the diets and plants, how to use plants in diets. Then I also dieted many times with don Emilio, whom you know. With him I did the longest diet that I've ever done, which involved fourteen plants.

Joan: I'm wondering why ayahuasca is above all the other plants. We were talking the other day about how ayahuasca is the power and chacruna is the light, and how one can't access the light without the power.

Luis: Ayahuasca remains the most important plant, and, as many healers call it, it is the Mother of All Plants.

Joan: Most sacred things, whether a plant or something else, usually have a myth, a creation myth, attached to them, about how they were given to humans. Is there such as legend about the first contact between humans and ayahuasca?

Luis: The Shipibo-Conibo tribes, with whom I have trained, have a myth that ayahuasca comes from an albino snake. It was the gift of an albino snake. They manifest that idea in some of the designs that you see in their ceramics and cloth. Other cultures and tribes have different stories, but I don't know them.

Jack: Let me elaborate a little for you. One story I heard, which is also a Shipibo story—and these are all legends, myths—is that a woman once, in legendary times, took a liking to going to the river to bathe with chacruna leaves. She loved it and bathed with it many, many times, until one day the spirit of the chacruna bush appeared to her and asked, "Why are you using me all the time?" The woman said, "Because I enjoy you so much. You make me feel better. You cleanse my body and make me feel very good." So the spirit of chacruna said, "Well, since you are being so faithful, I am going to give you a gift. Go back to your people and tell them that if you blend me with ayahuasca and boil us and drink us, you shall be able to see the spirits." The woman went back to her village and told the story, the elders cooked up a batch of chacruna and ayahuasca, and that's how they began to see the spirits.

Joan (laughs): Which leaves me wondering once again why ayahuasca is so valorized over chacruna!

Jack: Well, many of them tell you, as I said before, that ayahuasca has the power, the energy, while chacruna gives you the light to see. You can't access the light without the power. So ayahuasca is seen as the Mother of the plants.

Joan: Please ask don Luis if he would speak about what he actually sees and feels during a session. Is he sensing group energy or individual energy, or both? Is he directing people's journeys? Would he describe what goes on for him physically as he leads an ayahuasca session?

Luis: More than seeing for me, it is feeling. I can feel the energy. Sometimes it is high, sometimes it is low.

Joan: Is that the group energy, or an individual's energy?

Luis: Both. Sometimes the group, and sometimes for individuals. It's always a collective and an individual experience.

Joan: Would you share some more of your feelings about that?

Jack: Let me interrupt for a moment. There's a number of issues—sometimes you see the individual as a bundle of energy and sometimes you see the individual with an overlay that makes that person appear to be someone else or something else. You could see a person, for instance a woman, as a man, with the overlay of her dressed as a man, who is dressed in a robe. Or you could see a woman as a woman, but not as the woman who is sitting there. She's some other person. Sometimes you see an energy pattern, like a printed circuit board, overlying the person, which, incidentally, is the pattern you see in the Shipibo pottery and textiles. The idea is that the lines that form the so-called circuit board need to be even and balanced, need to have order. Where you see the lines twisted or curved or distorted, that's a signal that there is something wrong in that part of the person's body.

Joan: You said the first time we were in session together that ayahuasca finds out where we are crooked and makes us straight. I love that metaphor! Although now that I've seen this energy grid for myself, I know you meant that literally.

Jack: Yes. Well, in general, there's often the idea of ayahuasca "straightening" you out. It doesn't mean morally straightening you out; it means straightening out the energy lines that have become distorted or displaced by disease or affliction or sadness or whatever. The disease or problem makes you crooked, and you need to be straightened.

The other thing they say is that you often don't see anything, you feel it. You would connect to an individual and feel the energy. If it's a woman, say, and there is something wrong in her left breast, you may not see it but simply sense it at an energetic level. It comes in different ways for different people. But all of these are ways of working with ayahuasca.

Joan: I'm curious about how the tradition has changed over time. Luis is training others now. The practices, the techniques, what people expect—how are these changing? Is there a modernization taking place in the training and practice?

Luis: Everything changes! But one thing that I have noticed is that more people in the cities are interested now and take ayahuasca. Whereas some decades ago ayahuasca was not a thing of the city and was actually looked down upon as something primitive or savage or not for "nice" people.

Joan: When I was interviewing the Q'ero, for example, I found that many of their ancient traditions are dying out, because so many of the young people either don't have the discipline to stick with the training or they simply are not interested. They want to head down from the mountains to the cities to live the good life. Do you find this to be true in your tradition as well?

Luis: Yes, I see it happening constantly. It is not only the loss of the ayahuasca tradition, but it is the loss of the knowledge of plants, of all the healing plants. For example, I see it among the Shipibo. If their children have a fever or an infection or some kind of disease or trouble, they don't have any fancy medical facilities or clinics to go to. But they don't know what to do themselves anymore either. Meanwhile, there are all the plants surrounding them that could heal some of these afflictions, but they no longer know about them. Sometimes I find myself in the situation of seeing these things and telling them about some of the plants—me, an outsider, coming to the village to tell them about the plants they originally knew about!

Joan: Well, Westerners seem to be flocking to ayahuasca territory. There's a lot of information being published. It's in danger of becoming a recreational pursuit. What do you think of this, of foreigners looking for ayahuasca? What are the benefits of this and what are the dangers?

Luis: There are all kinds of people drawn to come here. Of course, there is the quota of crazies who want to come here and become instant shamans. Become medicine men overnight! But that is only part of it. In general, I feel that it is not a bad thing, because what happens is that most Peruvians themselves are really not interested or they don't even know about ayahuasca. Or they consider it superstition. So some of the foreigners, some of the interested and serious foreigners, are helping to keep this tradition alive by coming here and learning about it. So, for the most part, I think it is a good thing.

Joan: Have you reflected upon the different motivations for ayahuasca's use? It seems that native people come to you for healing, for the healing properties of ayahuasca and other plants, whereas many foreigners seem to be on some kind of vision quest.

Jack: Let me correct your observation before I translate for Luis. Let me modify your question, for many people here also go to ayahuasca for insight, visions, and so on. Not only for healing.

Joan: I guess I want to revise this to an open-ended question. It's hard for me to formulate some of these questions because of my own ignorance. I was wondering what don Luis thinks it is most important for foreigners to know about ayahuasca, about using it.

Jack: Like warnings or precautions?

Joan: Not really, although those, too. Mostly just important aspects for approaching journeying with ayahuasca. We're relatively ignorant of its use. For instance, I could not have learned so much about the diet and how it affects the ayahuasca experience unless I had come here to the jungle and done it. Same with the icaros. I cannot now imagine journeying with ayahuasca without icaros as part of the journey. But most of us will not get this chance. Young psychonauts in the States are dreaming with ayahuasca in cramped apartment living rooms, by themselves, with the stereo on. There are so many aspects of "proper" use and of the ceremonial set and setting that we don't know about. I can't really formulate a perceptive question about this, but I think it is important for us to know what you or don Luis think about all this.

Jack: In my opinion, no one should use ayahuasca without having someone there with him or her who knows the tradition and is able to manage the session.* You must be careful of people who are distributing ayahuasca as a drug. It is not!

Joan: Okay, let me narrow this discussion down a bit. When we were talking the other day about how we should approach what we see during a journey, you told me, Jack, that we can trust some of what we see and feel. Other parts, however, we should just observe and not judge. Just accept them without need for analysis. Does don Luis have anything to say about how people should process—I guess that's the word—an ayahuasca journey?

Luis (laughs): That is a difficult question! You must take it part seriously and part not too seriously!

Jack: My feeling is that people should never do ayahuasca by themselves. Ayahuasca is a group activity. It should not be led by anyone who has not had adequate training. I feel it is dangerous to do otherwise. People may be overdosed. Nervous breakdowns and spiritual

---

* In her essay "Relative Truth" in the collection *Zig Zag Zen: Buddhism and Psychedelics*, edited by Allan Hunt Badiner (San Francisco: Chronicle Books, 2002), Brigid Meier writes of the importance of having a trustworthy guide during the use of psychedelics. On page 130 she counsels, "It is crucial to have a qualified guide, one who is experienced and who is also impeccable. The best guides admit that they know nothing themselves and have no desire to lay a trip on you; they simply create a safe, mindful set and setting conducive to further awakening. They are almost like midwives gently encouraging you to explore and/or release while possessing the knowledge of how to perform psychic triage should the need arise."

breakdowns can happen. The person who is leading the session has to know how to deal with these possibilities. If they don't, they could damage the participant.*

Now, in terms of the diet. If you are going to do an ayahuasca session, you don't go through the diet we are going through here. Doing a session in the States or elsewhere, a single session, is like ayahuasca 101. In the ordinary session, you fast for the day or most of the day, abstaining from excessive fats, salt, sugar, meat, and so forth. You go do the session and that's it. You might not do another session for six months or a year. What you are going through here, in contrast, is ayahuasca 201! Now you are getting into the background and the rigors of it. Like, if you go to church, you can go to one Mass. But if you want to become a member of the church associations, become one of the parishioners, you have to go to a different level of commitment. Normally you wouldn't do the diet like we're doing it if you are going to do one ayahuasca session. Now, even with one ayahuasca session, it

---

* Research into the benefits and detriments of ayahuasca use continues. Some studies have produced new warnings and revealed long-term benefits. For example, in "Herbal Drugs of Abuse" (online: www.stuaff.niu.edu/csdc/herbaldrugs.htm), under the heading "Ayahuasca Vine (or 'Yage')," the following warning is given: "The biggest physical danger of ingesting Ayahuasca is a hypertensive crisis caused by elevated levels of tyramine in the blood if an MAO inhibitor is taken in conjunction with dietary tyramine. A hypertensive crisis can lead to headache, hemorrhagic stroke, myocardial infarction, rupture of a preexisting aneurysm, and to death. Other drugs (such as MDMA, amphetamines, migraine medicines, and over the counter cold medications like ephedrine, dextromethorphan, etc.) can lead to a hypertensive crisis as they will not be metabolized while taking Ayahuasca. Lastly, certain natural herbs such as Yohimbe, Ephedra, and possibly St. John's wort can have similar negative interactions when used with Ayahuasca."

On the beneficial side, in *Psychiatric News* (online: www.psych.org/pnews/98-08-21/two.html), researchers claim, "Ayahuasca was found to be relatively safe because of its minimal impact on cardiovascular function and other physiological processes. Receptor binding studies found an increased density of serotonin receptors in platelets of long-term ayahuasca users versus controls. Neuro-psychological testing of memory and concentration found 'no evidence of deterioration compared with normal controls' and 'some indication of better function among the ayahuasca-using subjects,' according to [Charles] Grob."

helps if you do the diet. Of course! Your body will be well prepared. It's cleaner and clearer. So you can get more out of the session and have less hassle with your stomach.

As for the other, the suggestion that this should never be done as a recreational experience. To say that it's Friday night, so let's get together and do ayahuasca—that's a misuse of this sacred plant.

Finally, as to the other part of your question. There really is no answer as to what it is you are seeing. You ask twenty people and they are going to give you twenty different answers: from it's the spirits of the dead, to it's the spirit of the plant, to it's your own imagination, to it's the gods of the future. There is no answer to that.

Joan: Well, one aspect of my question was about the "process of processing," if you know what I mean. À la the therapeutic model. You and don Luis do not do much processing with people. Other ayahuasqueros, from what I have heard, do. But what I am getting at is that if a person sees a psychotherapist, it could take years to become aware of a deep-seated problem and work it through to some kind of integration or resolution. Ayahuasca seems to show you your stuff very quickly. Some people kid that ayahuasca is like thirty years of psychotherapy in three hours!

Jack: Yes, I think that is true. I've seen it, and in my own experience I know it's true. But I think what happens is that it brings up all the layers of one's personality, one's psyche. It's formulated and brought up so that you can access it, feel it, and perhaps deal with it. It can be, and it very often is, very effective in dealing with psychological problems that would take much longer to get into in standard talk therapy, if they ever surfaced at all. As you can already attest!

Joan: I've never been in therapy, but I can certainly affirm that ayahuasca is a lightning rod for the psyche! Now, let me ask another general question. The plants all have spirits. And ayahuasca's spirit is at the top of the hierarchy, the Mother of All Plants. Can you or don Luis talk generally about jungle spirits, perhaps from the Shipibo tradition? And do ayahuasqueros have totem animals, like allies, particular spirits that assist and protect them?

Luis: Yes. The idea is that all things in the jungle have spirits—animals, snakes, plants. The snake mythology is very important, and in the case of the Shipibo, the most important and powerful creator spirit is the water snake, which gave birth to all things. But in general all animals have spirits. All living things in the jungle have spirit.

Jack: Let me add something. The snake is very important, and there are two types of snakes. One is the Yacumama. *Yacu* means "water," so it's the Mother of the Water. Classically it's the anaconda, a huge, non-poisonous snake, which kills by strangulation. It can get quite large. . . . Then there's the Sachamama. *Sacha* means "wood" or "forest," so that's the Mother of the Forest. The Sachamama is visualized as being a huge snake that lives in the woods, under the earth. When it comes, you feel the earth trembling, and all of the sudden this huge snake comes and it's magnetic. It has radiation coming out of its mouth and can swallow you up. Sometimes, also, when you are in the forest and Sachamama comes, you find yourself suddenly on top of her, on her back as she rises from the earth, and you ride her back.

So, there are these two snake spirits. And, of course, all the animals have spirits. Here, the jaguar is at the top of the food chain. It's the most powerful animal. Nothing preys on it; it preys on others. It is, therefore, seen as the most powerful spirit. From there on down the food chain, each spirit has its place and function. The general idea is that the powerful entities, the spirits of the forest, manage the forest. The jungle or forest is managed by the spirits of the place, who are the teachers.

Joan: Does don Luis have a particular spirit ally, as native North American medicine men and women often do?

Luis: Yes, it works the same way here. We invoke and use the animal and plant allies. I do not have any special one. I feel that I have many, and I use many. I do not work with just one particular ally.

Joan: In the Andean tradition, there is the concept of the three worlds, the *ukhu pacha,* or lower world; the *kay pacha,* which is this world; and the *hanaq pacha,* which is the upper world. Are these levels found in the Amazonian tradition? If they are, what do they associate these three levels with?

Jack: I'll ask him that, but I can tell you, no. It's more like the forest . . . well, let me put it this way: the vision in the Amazon is horizontal rather than vertical, in a spiritual sense.

Joan: Well, the reason I ask this is because in some of the ayahuasca visions I have had there seems to be an upper world of some kind, with spirits who are very ethereal. And then there seems to be a lower world of some kind, with spirits who are more chthonic. I was associating this with the three worlds of the Andean tradition.

Jack: Well, in that sense, yes. In a sense there are the air spirits, water spirits, and underground spirits. Like there are bird spirits, and water and lake and river spirits, and forest spirits both above and below ground. But this doesn't necessarily imply the three worlds. The visual world is horizontal here, I think. This is my own speculation. This is because here you don't have a clear horizon. In the mountains you do. Here the horizon is fifty yards, so you don't see beyond, and you're concerned essentially with what surrounds you rather than having a concept of up and down. There are among the tribes some vague notions about a creator god, whatever that might be, in some cases a jaguar and in others a snake, who gave rise to mankind and so on. But not in the sense of the three worlds. At least, not that I know about, and I'm sure Luis doesn't know either.

We had been talking for a long time, and don Luis seemed bored. So I ended the interview with him and he left for his tambo. I continued talking with Jack for some time. One of the topics of our conversation was icaros.

Joan: So, when you were first given an icaro, was it a momentous occasion?

Jack: Well, no, actually. It doesn't happen in the beginning. The tradition is that if you work with ayahuasca, or another plant teacher, long enough, especially if you are doing the diet, then eventually the plant will give you a song. And it's really nothing very special. All of a sudden, when you are in a session, in the middle of a vision and all that . . . you sort of . . . a little melody comes into your head.

Joan: So it's not a revelatory thing, an intense identification with the plant?

Jack: No, no. At least not in my case. You just suddenly hear a song, a melody, and you say, "Oh, I don't know where this is coming from!" And you try to remember it. It's as simple as that.

Joan: Ayahuasqueros' icaros are powerful for me. They really influence, even control, what I feel or see at certain points in my experience. They use the icaro to invoke the plant spirits, right? Or to change the energy? The power of the plant is carried in that melody?

Jack: Yes. The tradition says that you use the icaros to heal, and it's basically about healing. And many of the icaros are connected to specific plants, and you use a specific icaro to heal a specific illness or problem. You can also use icaros to purify and cleanse, as don Emilio was doing last night. To bless a person even. As don Emilio did with you. With you, he wasn't clearing any illness, he was charging or empowering you. You can also use icaros to charge objects, like a vase or a scarf or something . . . to give that object powers and energies and vibrations the object would not normally have. So the object is charged by the icaro.

The boys arrived with the afternoon meal of brown rice and boiled plantains, so Jack headed back to his own tambo to eat. About five-thirty, in the growing darkness, I was hot and sweaty from the humidity, so I went down to the river and bathed. By six-thirty I was under the mosquito netting, reading by flashlight. I fell asleep early, and again slept deeply, not waking until early morning.

🍃 11 🍃

The I That Sees

In psychology one possesses nothing unless one has experienced it in reality. Hence a purely intellectual insight is not enough, because one knows only the words and not the substance of the thing from inside.

—C. G. JUNG, *AION*

Sunday night was to be the first of two consecutive sessions of ayahuasca. Before we began that evening, Jack, don Luis, and don Emilio held an impromptu question-and-answer session with us in the maloca. We were to take the ayahuasca negra brew again this night, so someone asked about the potency of brews made from wild versus cultivated ayahuasca. Jack consulted with don Luis for several minutes, then explained the gist of their conversation. There are many kinds—or "colors"—of brews, he said, and then listed several: "There's white. There's yellow. Then there is the dark ayahuasca and the jaguar ayahuasca. . . . Ayahuasqueros say there is a difference. One is denser. I really can't explain it clearly. But when you ask them if all the mixtures are the same [because all ayahuasca is chemically alike], they say, 'No, no, no, no! This one is different from that one. The vine weighed more. It's thicker. This one is very light, that one is very strong, or that one will overwhelm you!'"

Jack smiled, shrugging his shoulders, and then spoke for himself.

"Well, chemically there is no difference. Whether there is a difference for other reasons, it may well be. But you can't chemically tell one from the other. Of course, ayahuasqueros speculate. When you ask why is this tea stronger than that one, they say maybe it is because it was made with wild vine while that one was made with cultivated vine. Well, maybe. But there's no evidence of that. There's no factual evidence of that. A botanist would tell you that that's not true. But you know, if you go by the plant flowering or the conditions of the leaves, they [the ayahuasqueros] will tell you they are different. For all I know, maybe it is and maybe it isn't."

Of course, I wanted to know if I had misheard don Luis the other night, when he had said that the black brew was the strongest he has ever made in his twenty-year career as an ayahuasquero. Jack confirmed that don Luis had made that statement. I then steered the conversation in a different direction. "Luis told me in the interview we did that he dieted for fourteen plants. What span of time did that diet encompass?" Jack translated for don Luis. "He says that he did the diet for fifteen days. Of course, he did other diets for other plants, one plant at a time, but that time he did the diet for fourteen plants all at once! He did that with don Emilio, who prepared the plants."

Andrew and some of the others then asked don Luis about his background and training, questions I had asked during our private interview. He did not provide much information that was new, but he did reveal that he was "led to this life by fate." He explained, "I had no prior inkling. I did not know that this was what I would do. Fate led me to it. My family history is that my grandfather was a healer, using plants. My father was a healer. So it is in my blood, but I did not think that I too would be a healer. The first plant I started with was San Pedro, the cactus. Then I started taking and studying with others, and here I am!" He also mentioned, in response to a question about his personal relationships, that although he had once had a serious relationship with a woman, he is now resigned to being alone, declaring, "I am married to this life as an ayahuasquero."

Andrew then asked about don Luis's reaction to the terrorist attacks on the United States, since don Luis had been visiting New York City and had been only blocks away when the two hijacked airplanes slammed into the World Trade Center Twin Towers. "I was very close to it," he said. "I saw it firsthand. It was an enormous tragedy. I felt the full impact of that event. But it was an experience that none of us can conceive of how to handle. What is important for me is to be here in my world, in my universe, doing what I do. Really, I can't handle a question like this."

Heni changed the subject by asking don Luis to elaborate on what he experiences during a session and how he prepares for one. "The plant itself is very motherly," don Luis replied. "But sometimes it is also fatherly, because it can also kick you!" His statement made me think of the harshness of my experiences with Red Ayahuasca, which felt like the male manifestation of the plant, and the more nurturing connection with White Ayahuasca, which I perceived as Grandmother Ayahuasca. Luis then switched tacks to explain how he prepares the tea, with Jack interspersing a few of his own comments during the translation.

"The old way of preparing the brew was to make it in an earthen jar or cup. They are still being used, but they are very unreliable because they are locally made and they crack very easily. They can develop leaks and all of these types of things. That's the old way of doing it. But now we prepare the ayahuasca in metal pots. Ideally, it should be a steel pot. Usually, I begin with a big pot, like thirty liters or so. I put in both plants, the ayahuasca and the chacruna. With ayahuasca, you need to cut the vine, and you need a vine that is at least two or three inches thick. You cut it into foot-long pieces. You hammer them and squash them, until it's like rope, like a sisal rope, very stringy and with strands. You dump all of that into a pot and then add the chacruna leaves."

Jack jumped in, saying, "There are all kinds of formulas, but the usual one runs between fifteen percent [by weight] of chacruna to eighty-five percent of ayahuasca. That can be adjusted up to fifty percent chacruna and fifty percent ayahuasca. A very light brew would be the fifteen to eighty-five ratio. A strong brew would be fifty-fifty. Now, the fifteen to eighty-five ratio is low in visionary quality and high in vomit power! The fifty-fifty brew is typically high in visionary power and lower in vomit power. So, that's the range, and each *curandero* [healer] chooses the proportion. There are other plants that are also added sometimes. There is bobinsana, chuchuhuasi, and other additives, other power plants that are not necessarily involved in the process of MAO inhibition but make special recipes for specific purposes.

"Now, you dump all this into the big pot," Jack continued, "and boil it for twelve hours. The best brews are done with very little heat. You don't want a huge fire. You just heat it and let it cook. Some people boil it for five hours, some for eight. There are variations. I like twelve hours.

"Then, during those twelve hours, you at some point take out all the solid material. You put it in another pot, with fresh water, and boil it again until the water evaporates. So, now you have two boils. Then you mix the two boils, and eventually boil it all again—boil it down to these large bottles of medicine. You can filter it through a cheesecloth or a T-shirt or whatever. That removes all the solid matter. And you end up with the medicine."

Heni wanted to know about the ceremony for cooking the brew. Were there songs and prayers offered? "Yes," Jack responded. "They pray and sing over it. It's not a specific prayer or song. They each have their own. And of course, like everything else, there are variables. First is the proportion of the plants [chacruna and ayahuasca]. Then there is how long you boil them. And at what temperature. There are choices about what other additive plants to include. So, there are all these variables, and no two brews are the same. Myself, I prefer something close to a fifty-fifty ratio [of chacruna and ayahuasca]. Some people say that is too tough, in terms of the visionary properties. It's horrible, they say. They'd never do that! Some other people might say fifty-fifty is not enough. So, it's not codified. There is no formulary really. It's an oral tradition, but mostly it's personal procedure.

"For example," he continued, "some ayahuasqueros will separate men from women during a session, with men on one side of the group and women on the other. Some pray, with a lot of Roman Catholic prayers. Some see that as a corruption of the experience, as making a church out of it, as bringing in a foreign influence." He paused, reflecting for a moment, then resumed his explanation. "You can take ayahuasca in full fluorescent light sitting in a hard-backed chair and you can sit all night and pray. For some this is a crazy way of doing ayahuasca, a corruption. But for others, all that matters is the result. So, you get all these variations. Here, in the Peruvian and Colombian Amazon, and even in Ecuador, the way you do ayahuasca is the way we are doing it."

I was curious about Jack's comment about the separation of men and women. In most Native American ceremonies in which I have participated, for example, a Stone People's lodge on the Diné reservation in Arizona, the sexes are separated, one on each side of the sweat lodge. And menstruating women are forbidden to participate in ceremony because they are considered to be at the height of their power and so could overwhelm the people or sacred objects around them. I asked Jack about this in terms of ayahuasca ceremony. He talked with don Luis for a moment and replied, "Yes, here generally they do not want menstruating women to come to ceremony. The idea is that the woman during the time of her period is in a very, very high state of energy, of powerful energy. Two or three things can happen because of this. And I can sort of testify to this because it happened to me," Jack said in an aside. "A woman came to a session and didn't tell us ahead of time that she was having her period. One of the things that can happen is that she'll feel no effect whatsoever, even if she takes several doses. The other thing that can happen is the opposite. She gets unbelievably blasted and overwhelmed. It can be disturbing for everybody else. Another thing that can happen is that she feels nothing and the people on either side of her also feel nothing.

"Luis also confirms this. He says that for a woman in that condition, in the natural process of eliminating her menstrual fluid, the ayahuasca can have a strong impact, and it can affect her menstruation, in some cases causing excessive bleeding."

Andrew took us back to the proportions of the brew, asking what don Luis's preferred measure is. Our brew, Jack responded, is "getting close to the fifty-fifty proportion." Then he went on to explain about dosages. "At that percentage, you take a lot less," he said. "If you were using a forty-sixty or thirty-seventy mix [chacruna leaves to ayahuasca vine], you would have to take more. With the classic of fifteen to eighty-five ratio, you take about a third or half of a cup, with a cup meaning a cooking cup. Not like this cup we are using, which is much smaller. In my view, that proportion is not preferred, for me anyway, because it increases the chance you will vomit."

The conversation was veering from one direction to another, but I found it fascinating. Heni came back to a question that I had asked during my interview with don Luis: What does he see during a session? His reply was slightly more informative now. "He says," Jack translated, "that he sometimes see shadows and things. But in his particular case, he mostly senses things. This varies. In some cases he sees, but at most times he senses energies. He feels what is there." Jack again offered his own insight, saying "You are going a little bit into an area most ayahuasqueros are hesitant to discuss. If they see something you need to be aware of, they usually will tell you. If you need to take care of it or something, they will bring it to your attention. But it's not the kind of experience like you would have with a Western doctor, where the doctor will show you an X ray and say, 'Well, you have a black spot on your lung. Here it is.' It's not equivalent to that. It's energetic."

Michelle then spoke up, explaining that her experience of ayahuasca is both vibrational and energetic to the point that she feels as if electrical currents are running through her limbs. She asked don Luis to speak to the vibrational aspects of ayahuasca. His response was enthusiastic, if not very enlightening. "Yes! Absolutely! I absolutely feel the same things, the energy, the vibrations." Jack then offered his own opinion. "The most important aspect of a session is the behavior of the ayahuasquero: how he prepares for the session, if he believes in the work of the session, if he sees spaces, follows the journey, sees or feels the spirits coming through the spaces, and then controls what is happening."

Heni wondered aloud if don Luis ever loses control of a session.

Jack translated the questions and don Luis admitted, "Yes and no. But I *have* to stay in control. I am given the key to what a person is experiencing, and I can *choose* whether to use that key to open that door. I can get caught in it or not. In some sessions, with some ayahuasqueros, I wouldn't recommend you participate for this reason. Some people who do it in their backyards—you can hear all the noises of the city, the neighbor with the television on or the radio blasting, and so on. We have to do many sessions like that because we heal people who live there. But I don't like doing it like that. This is the way I like to do it— here in the jungle. This is the pleasant way of doing it!"

Jeff then asked another question that I had asked earlier in the private interview, if don Luis senses a difference when leading a session with Peruvians or with foreigners. "Human behavior is human behavior!" he exclaimed. "It is universal." He nearly doubled over laughing. "The question is not understandable to me," he exclaimed as he regained his composure. "There is no difference!" He broke up laughing again, then, still chuckling, he began to prepare for the ceremony, bringing the discussion to an end. After the blessings and the sacramental preparations over the brew, he and Jack administered small doses of the black brew, and in the darkness we each took flight.

I took a larger dose of the black brew than I had the previous session, and as I sat quietly, eyes closed, and felt the vine seep through my system, I reemphasized my resolve to go into the session full tilt, asking Mother Ayahuasca to help me heal my fear. My set was also to experience ayahuasca not only as an aid to my own healing but also as the sacrament that it is. Although I approach every ayahuasca session with reverence, I had never set a specific intention to experience the vine as a natural sacrament. Tonight I did, speaking this intention silently to Mother Ayahuasca. The setting tonight was different, too, for the jungle storm I had laughingly told Jeff, Patrick, and Steve I would order up had arrived, a day late. It was spectacular, with a steady but not torrential rain, rumbling thunder, and brilliant flashes of lightning.

Unfortunately, nearly a year later as I write this book, I cannot reproduce this session, although this night was to be my breakthrough, one of the most intense nights of my life. I remember everything that happened after the session when I returned to my tambo, almost as clearly as if it were yesterday, but I have little memory of the session itself, except for the chorus of frogs that after the rain sounded like a thousand tiny glass bells tinkling. Usually on the day after a session, I would take notes or speak into my tape recorder. But Monday, the morning after this session, I was so wiped out that I did nothing but doze in my hammock and relive the events of the night before—but not the actual session, so it is lost to my consciousness. But the rest of the night is not. My experience that night was to last nine hours: first with the ayahuasca journey that exhausted me but about which I have little memory, and then with an altered state of consciousness that was precipitated by an ego surrender and lasted until the first light of dawn on Monday.

The ayahuasca session must have been a wild ride, for I was emotionally and energetically exhausted by midnight, when it ended. Just as John had relied upon me after the first jungle session, when he had journeyed deeply, this night I relied totally upon him. I could hardly walk. I lay in my place in the maloca at the end of the session, unwilling to move and feeling more nauseated than ever before, although I had not vomited during the session. I remember at one point during the session getting up and standing over the railing of the maloca, leaning on it really, with my head hanging over it, waiting for the purge to begin, but it had not come. Instead, I had latched on to an icaro, which felt as if it were being sung just for me, and note by note it seemed to pull me back from the need to vomit. The song kept me on my feet, hanging on to the railing for support, and it cleansed me, so I did not have to purge. By the end of session, however, I was feeling a different kind of sickness. It was not only physical but also energetic, as if I had waged a battle that had sapped me of everything except the last vestiges of consciousness. I was literally sick at heart at some deep level. But I did not really know why then, and I do not now remember much of the session.

Somehow, by about a quarter to one, John had managed to get me back to my tambo.

There was no way I could sleep. Although I was physically sapped of strength and feeling a deep emotional anxiety and foreboding, consciously I was fully alert, back to normal awareness. In one sense I was rational and "straight," for I was aware of my surroundings. I was not seeing colors or visions, and my visual reality was not distorted in any way.* But at another level of awareness I was in a fight for my life. I felt sick to the depths of my being. I couldn't fathom from where within me these waves of despair were arising, and I became alarmed as the feeling intensified.

John tried to get me to go to bed, but I wouldn't go. I sat on the stoop of my tambo, my elbows on my knees and my head in my hands and I moaned. I just moaned. I felt as if I were being sucked into the dark, into death, into some beyond from which I might never return. I struggled against this dark beckoning energy, afraid of what might happen if I succumbed to it. I sat there for a long, long time, with John just standing helplessly behind me, not knowing what to do. Don Luis came by, on the way to his tambo, and he asked if I was all right. I smiled and said yes. He said something humorous about the red lupuna tree that bordered the trail in front of my tambo, and I laughed weakly, more from social obligation than from understanding his joke. Then I went back to moaning. Using my voice seemed my only defense against the waves of darkness that swept over me. There was nothing I could do for myself, except fight to stay alert to whatever was trying to draw me away. Moaning, even at the level of whisper as I was doing, seemed to reassure me that I was there, planted on the stoop of my tambo, in the physical, and able to maintain an edge of sanity. I knew I was in a

---

* I believe the part of my experience chronicled here—the entire intuitive flight I was about to take—was not an ayahuasca-induced vision but was a different type of altered state of consciousness precipitated by whatever ayahuasca had opened within me during the session. This experience had more of the qualities of a shamanic journey than it did an ayahuasca journey. See the footnote in chapter 8, page 142, for a fuller explanation.

spiritual and energetic crisis, but I had no idea what it was all about and so I did not know how to help myself.

Suddenly one of my husband's family members appeared to my inner eyes. She appeared as a young girl, and energetically she was writhing in anger at her father's death, which had occurred when she was about thirteen. Her entire life has been colored emotionally by that loss. I could also see her as she is today, in her midseventies. I saw her sitting with her older sister, talking and laughing. But I knew that beneath that gay exterior and deep within her was a wounded child who was furious at the universe for having taken her father from her. Then one of my close relatives appeared energetically. She had suffered an abusive childhood, and I was smothered by the combined weight of the despair, anger, and resentment pent up within these two relatives. I remember shaking my head in defiance of the energetic cleansing I felt I was being asked to undertake on their behalf. "Noooo!" I remember hearing myself moan. Then I remember declaring to ayahuasca, perhaps to the universe, "No, I won't do this. I won't clear family stuff right now. This is my boundary and I won't cross it. I'm willing to clear my own stuff, but not theirs."

Some part of me knew that this inner vision was not a psychological screen. I was certain that my seeing my relatives was not a way for my ego to transfer my own inner anguish onto others in an attempt to make that pain conscious to me. No, this was definitely some sort of psychic connection to two people close to me, and I knew that as much as I would have liked to help them on an energetic level, I did not have the strength to do so. As I defiantly stated my intention not to process family history, I felt the nausea rise physically and I retched, but there was nothing to come up. Still, the very act of trying to purge seemed to lift the oppressive darkness from me, and a whole new kind of darkness descended, what I can only describe as a visible darkness. This glowing darkness was alive and vibrant and mysterious, slightly forbidding, even threatening, yet also beckoning to me from its depths in a motherly way, infused with a sense of caring and nurturing.

I was split between two dimensions. In one reality I was totally straight although physically sick and weak, sitting on the stoop of my tambo in the dark with the barely visible jungle surrounding me and John hovering over me. In the other reality, I was alone on the stoop of my tambo teetering on the verge of emotional oblivion, struggling to stay in contact with the self I took for granted as "myself." The jungle was a glowing darkness, alive and visible and present in minute detail. Then, from the darkly shimmering vegetation, fairies emerged, dozens of colorful and ethereal fairies.* I don't believe in fairies, so I balked. I tried to deny their presence, but they would not leave. They continued to emerge from the jungle from everywhere, filling my inner and outer vision. I cannot really waffle about this—calling it a vision—for it was real at some level, even though I did not believe in the "little people" then, and I am still not sure that I do now. But they were there, emerging as sprites of light, beckoning to me, urging me to release myself into their care.

I was alarmed. I could not understand how I could be straight—turning to see John standing behind me; noting the mundane details of the tambo, which was illuminated by a single candle; observing and monitoring my psychological and physical condition—and yet all around me the jungle spirits were emerging as tiny fairies, who were beckoning me as if they had come specifically to show me something or to take me somewhere. The split reality—although superimposed reality might be a more accurate way to describe it—had a physicality to it unlike anything I had experienced while under the influence of

---

* Although my immediate understanding of these tiny beings of light was that they were fairies, they were not like any of the "little people" of Celtic lore that I am familiar with. They were of varying sizes, but all were miniscule, indeed insect-sized in most cases, and they had both humanlike and insectlike qualities about them. They seemed to flit in the air, from heights that just skimmed the earth to several feet above it. They emitted light, or were cloaked in light, so I could not make out any real details of their appearance. Each had its own color: some blue, others pink, green, yellow, silver. I was certain they were individuals, but they also exhibited hivelike qualities or some other kind of group consciousness. My emotional state at the time was such that I was not interested in examining them. I was certain they were "fairies" and since I didn't believe in fairies, I was in a crisis of belief.

ayahuasca, and it was unlike any other state of consciousness I had so far experienced in my life. I felt enthralled and threatened simultaneously.

But the weirdness was only just beginning. Shock of all shocks, a woman friend from North Carolina appeared in my mind's eye—as the Queen of the Fairies. It was as if I were scrying, seeing her in a crystal ball. She was not physically here with me, as the fairies were, but was instead reaching out to me through the energetic veils to make this most important contact. I was quite literally shocked. She was the last person I would have imagined in this role. What's more, at the time, I did not even know her very well. We were more social acquaintances than close friends. But there she was, reclining on her living room couch in the glow of a candle, her legs tucked under her, her physical countenance soft and tender, but her emotional presence strong and commanding. She, too, seemed split. It was as if she herself did not know what she was—this was some hidden personality that had emerged from deep cover within her to make contact with me. She seemed amused both at my reaction to seeing this aspect of her revealed and at her other self, which seemed asleep to this part of her, with no idea that she really was this other person, this Fairy Queen.

"Joan," she coaxed in a silken voice, "Come! Come with us. Relax. Relax. I'm here to take care of you. You can trust me. I'll help keep you strong." She beckoned me with outstretched arms, her fingers long and agile, coaxing me toward her. "Come be with us. You are ready. We have something to show you. It is time for you to see."

I laughed to myself. This was ridiculous! "She is the Queen of the Fairies," I was exclaiming to myself in disbelief. "The Queen of the Fairies!" But my laughter suddenly did not seem appropriate. In a flash, I understood that this was a woman who has immense power. In everyday life she may not know it, but in the dreamtime she is a power to behold. The fairies, in a multitude of tiny shapes and luminescent colors, flitted around me. They had substance, they had flesh, they had personality. Although my friend, the Queen of the Fairies, seemed distant, the jungle fairies were alive and real, and all around me. They, too, were coaxing me. I could hear them, although I am at a complete loss as to how to describe the sound—and the emotions it evoked. There was a backdrop sound that was a high, electric-like hum that also somehow had color to it. At some level the fairies functioned only as a group, with a hivelike existence. I took this electric hum to be their collective voice. But they also had individual personality and voices. It is difficult to describe the nuances of the synthesis between their sound and the feeling it evoked within me. It was not laughter as much as it was gaiety, not the call of a challenge as much as the pull of opportunity, not a suffusion of love but rather a flow of compassion. They had made a bed of leaves for me. They urged me playfully and gently to surrender to them. "Come with us. Come with us, Joan," they coaxed in whispers, their voices and demeanors caring and reassuring. "Let go! Let go! Lie down in the bed we have prepared for you. We will take you where you need to go. There is nothing to fear. Let go!"

I fought with every ounce of energy I possessed not to be seduced by them. My rational mind, will, and ego were up in arms. I knew I had to go, but I would not release control. How could I, when I did not even believe in fairies and when, as far as I was concerned, I was no longer ayahuasca dreaming? I felt normal in every way, except for this other dimension that seemed to intersect my normal space-time and was so ardently and darkly, and yet so lovingly, competing for my participation in it. A battle began, between my waking, conscious, disbelieving self and the part of me that knew I had better not miss another opportunity to transcend something within me that was holding me back. It was a metaphysical confrontation, and yet my body was physically sapped from waging it. I was exhausted and near despair from a sinking feeling that I was about to lose control. And yet I wanted to give in. I wanted to just breathe into a surrender. I was in spiritual battle deep within myself, and the fairies were my only witnesses.

My eventual release took every ounce of willpower I could muster. It sounds paradoxical to say that, but that's how it was for me. It took an enormous expenditure of my energy to override my need for self-control. The struggle was intense, almost cataclysmic in my interior spaces. It felt like a battle to the death. But finally, with a deep breath—almost, but not quite, like the expansive breath I had taken while don Emilio had empowered me with his healing—I allowed my defenses to fall, willed my ego to release its grip on me, and surrendered to the fairies by energetically lying down in the bed of leaves they had prepared for me.

Immediately I was whisked away. I felt as if I were wind sweeping out of a rusty old barrel as my spirit released itself from the physical into the metaphysical. Just as the shadows of leaves and vines had danced on my mosquito netting during the visits from the ushpahuasa spirit doctor, now the leaves, vines, bushes, and trees seemed to rush past me. I was being whisked deep into the jungle, but I had no idea where. In one last bout of rational thought, I knew I had to get my physical body into bed before I was totally immersed in this other world. Somehow John managed it.

Once my physical self was safe in bed, the full spiritual immersion began. I simply gave myself over to whatever the fairies wanted of me. My friend the Queen of the Fairies was there, a presence hovering in the background of my awareness, assuring me she would be there to help me deal with whatever might happen. And so I allowed myself to be carried off into the scintillating darkness of the jungle. The feeling of total and utter surrender is indescribable. To have finally bypassed my ego and my need for control was exhausting to the core but utterly liberating. I just was. No body. No mind really. Just being. And in that beingness, I was able to be in contact, in intimate and unmasked contact, with the people in my life. For the next four hours, I was immersed in telepathic communication with just about everyone I know in North Carolina, and with some whom I barely know.

A grand intuitive procession began, with one person after another appearing to me, communicating with me, merging with me emotionally. And it went on all night long. A face or the entire person would appear before me, and the template of that person's soul, his or her energy self, was laid bare before me. Overlaid atop that was that person's psychological body, exposing his or her wounds, fears, strengths, hopes, dreams. It was as if I were peeling back layers of that person's aura, revealing his or her inner essence. The contact was emotionally and energetically exhausting, for we were totally unmasked to each other. I knew just what that person was about and he or she knew just what I was about, but there was no ego, no judgment, only acceptance, understanding, compassion, and in some cases love. I somehow understood things about each person, and it was as if some universal intelligence were downloading messages for me to deliver to each one. I was interacting with each person, asking that person questions and receiving answers, and the pace was dizzying—and unrelenting.

The psychic contacts varied from brief encounters to intense interactions, but all were throbbing with energetic and emotional information and connection. For example, I was ecstatic at the appearance of one of my closest friends. The energetic filaments of our friendship shimmered between us. As if following one of those filaments, I was taken inside her energy body, and there I could feel her compassion, joy, and creativity. These qualities were palpable, and I felt them as my own. But then I also began to feel her insecurities, frustrations, and disappointments. I asked her where she would like to go, where she would feel safe, for I sensed her need to rest, to withdraw almost. She pointed to a hole in the ground that I had not noticed. I shepherded her down into this hobbitlike hole, where she curled up into a ball. As I crawled down into the hole—which felt womblike—with her, I intuitively understood her deep inner fear that she will never live up to her mother's expectations of her, even though her mother has been dead for years. I understood aspects of her relationship to her husband and her children that revealed a karmic web of stunning complexity and yet awesome simplicity. Through this first psychic encounter, I felt the immensity of the challenge of being human and, at the same time, the grace-filled essence of each individual. I understood in a way I had not before that we are each unique in our essence and yet we are never alone or isolated, for we are all one at some fundamental, primordial level of being. This insight was not intellectual. It was physical in a way I cannot describe, and it was overwhelming, as if I were expending enormous amounts of psychic fuel in making the contact and sharing the essence of another person's being.

I had barely registered my friend's contact when Karla, my sister-in-law, appeared. As soon as the person visually appeared to me, the visceral and energetic connection became established. I intuited aspects of Karla's childhood that perhaps even she is not consciously aware of, and we were able to talk of her deepest feelings, fears, hopes. I hesitate to relate most of what I saw and felt with each person, out of respect for his or her privacy, but suffice it to say that whatever was revealed to me seemed to come from that person's core, surfacing from the depths of his or her being like an air bubble released to the surface. As I intuited the aspects of Karla's childhood that were lingering as emotional and physical blocks in her adulthood, I wondered if she was aware of our contact. I thought of my friend the Fairy Queen. Was she aware that she was here with me, hovering in the background and cheerleading me on? All of these people would be home, fast asleep. Were their dream bodies aware of our meeting?

I was pulled back to Karla, who was looking down into the hobbit hole where I had been offering consolation and support to my dear friend, who has curled up there. "May I come down there with you?" Karla asked in a little-girl voice. We invited her in, and she crawled into the now crowded hole and we snuggled together. The space was suffused with emotion, as I felt the love that vibrated among us as well as the more subtle energies of the inner wounds that we were sharing. Soon I sensed another friend up above us. I could see her, sitting on a low wall, her head in her hands as she sank down in exhaustion. I knew she was in the midst of completing a challenging business project, and I felt her weariness. She also felt anger at having had to make so many decisions by herself, and under impossible time constraints. I felt the anger rise in her and explode through the crown chakra of her energy body. And then it was gone. Instantly evaporated. I felt joy rising as she acknowledged her accomplishments. She glowed with self-love as she leaped up and began dancing around, thrusting her hips out and punching her hands up into the air in a kind of victory dance. She sang out, at the top of her lungs, "I'm so great! I'm wonderful! I'm beautiful! I'm great! I'm great!" I was overcome with her joy and marveled at her dance, her unrestrained exuberance, her unselfconscious claiming of her gifts and vibrant exclamations of her worth. Her joy sparked in flickers of light from her auric field, and her power was a wind that swept toward the hobbit hole.

I immediately poked at my friend and sister-in-law, challenging them to go up and join this other woman in her celebration of self. They seemed lethargic and weak. I prodded them again. "Go!" I coaxed them. "Now is your chance to claim your joy and power as well." Reluctantly they crawled from the hobbit hole and joined the woman in her dance, but their efforts were at first pathetic. They were tentative, moving like rag dolls, their arms drooping at their sides and their legs barely moving. Their songs were barely audible. "I'm great" they croaked, self-doubt tingeing every word. "I'm . . . wonderful." It took many long moments before they felt the spirit rise within them and they began to sing and dance with confidence. I left the three of them there, dancing in the glowing darkness of the jungle, celebrating the power of self. "I'm great! So wonderful! So beautiful!"

The scenes shifted smoothly, as one person after another emerged into my field of inner vision. At one moment I was drinking a glass of wine with a friend, and she and I were renewing a friendship that had been strained almost to the breaking point. We finally saw behind the mask of the problem, able to discern the real issues and feelings instead of only those we were willing to show each other superficially. She and I and another person involved in the falling out discussed it, without animosity, and came to understand our own contributions to the problem. We let it go, knowing its power was no longer claiming us. Then the next moment, without warning, a different person would coalesce into being before me and we would share our truest selves with each other. As the parade continued, I understood my past-life relationships with many of these people and how our karma was entwined in this life. I understood in a more visceral way than I had before that no relationship is accidental. Everything has meaning, and every event and interaction has purpose.

The meetings continued in a whirlwind, so energetically intense that I could hardly keep up. The effect of making these connections was exhausting, and I could feel myself becoming depleted. But still they came. At one point a man I hardly knew appeared, and his message seemed especially important: he had one more chance to throw off the burden of his family history and belief patterns or he would be stuck living the same life as his parents. I could see his emotional roots as the roots of a giant tree, but the earth around them was compacted and cementlike. Soon those roots would be so firmly encased, he would have almost no possibility of freeing them. At the same time, I was shown his potential and the professional and personal heights to which he could rise if he would only become more of his own person and not be restricted by his family patterns. He was so entrenched by his need to be socially acceptable that there was no joyous spontaneity in his life, and he was losing the lifeblood of his spirit. I knew at that moment that I was going to have to go home and tell this man what I was being shown, but I could not imagine how I was going to do that. I hardly knew him.

The parade continued, hour after hour, one person after another swirling into my awareness, actually present for me energetically, our identification with each other staggering in its intensity. The energetic burden of this contact was taxing to the point of overwhelm, and I remember moaning out loud at one point. I knew John was in the hammock, and I remember weakly calling out, "John. I can't keep this up. It's too intense. I don't know how I will survive it." I was not being melodramatic. I was truly being stretched to my energetic limits. When I reached the point where I felt nearly drained, I inwardly pleaded, "Stop! No more! I just can't do this anymore." Like the old Warner Brothers Looney Tunes cartoons, I saw the big black circle appear, closing like the eye of a camera, and some cosmic narrator chiming, "That's all folks!" But just as the eye of the circle was about to close, another acquaintance popped through it and forced it back open, and the parade of intuitive connections and communications resumed.

At some point, also, I realized I had not "tapped into" John. His energy body suddenly appeared before me. He and I were kneeling, facing each other, and we held our hands up and touched palm to palm. We remained in that posture during my whole review of our life together. I saw how fated our meeting was, the spiritual agreements we had made to assist each other's growth, the meaning of challenges we had faced as individuals and as a couple over our twenty-five years of marriage. The unfolding culminated in my understanding that John really had not found his calling yet and that the next three years were to be crucial to his aligning with his soul's purpose. My mission was to support him unfailingly as he felt his way toward his heart's work.

By the time dawn arrived, the communications were winding down. I was utterly depleted. I have undertaken many strenuous trips to Peru, pushing myself to my physical and even emotional limits, yet I had never felt so drained as I did that morning. I feel frustrated now trying to describe this night, trying to convey in a way that readers will under-stand how a string of intuitive communications could challenge me to within an inch of my stamina. But it did. My ego surrender had been momentous for me in and of itself, but surviving that night seemed to me to be an astonishing accomplishment. I remember whispering to John, barely coherent and almost too tired to talk, "I can't believe it. I just can't believe I got through it."

But what was I to do with all this information? There had been dozens of connections and messages. As I lay in the hammock most of the day Monday, that question rarely left my mind. I understood that this information was mine as well as theirs. I owned many of the feelings and insights, and they gave me pause as I reviewed my own life's journey and spiritual growth. But most of what I saw, heard, and felt that night was extremely personal to the people who had been revealed to me. It would be awkward enough to relate the messages I had received to my close friends, but it would be much more difficult to divulge the information to people I knew only socially. Would I even dare?

It turns out that I did dare. In fact, even though I had not been ayahuasca dreaming during these contacts, I felt obligated to the Mother of All Plants to do so. To my relief, every person was receptive. Most were able to acknowledge the accuracy of my intuitive observations, confirming information I otherwise would have had no way of knowing. Some were brought to tears, realizing their deepest wounds were known to some universal energy or being who cared enough to send them a message about how to heal. Others just listened without comment.

Overall, I was given a lesson in humility and trust, which would stand me in good stead as I found myself being asked to give intuitive readings over the next year. I have always been intuitive and had occasionally done readings, but now it seemed that using this gift was to become a larger part of my life. Surprisingly, to me at least, long-dormant abilities as a medium were revived as well, and I have been able to bring through information from a person's departed loved ones. I find this aspect of the work especially challenging but deeply satisfying, for there is nothing more gratifying than to hear a grieving person say that he or she has at last found a measure of peace. I attribute this new path directly to my opening through ayahuasca, the Mother of the Voice in the Ear. At some level, it was she who guided me through the crisis of ego surrender and, in doing so, freed me to enhance these neglected abilities and to embrace kinder ways of engaging the world and a much deeper appreciation of the mystery—and the glory—of being human.

❧ 12 ❧

Saying So Long But Never Good-bye

Koan: How does one express the inexpressible?
Answer: "Thank you!"

—JIM DEKORNE, *PSYCHEDELIC SHAMANISM*

Monday was a blur, and I did nothing but swing in my hammock and marvel at the night I had endured. John came to check on me, and I spent an hour or more relating my experience to him. When Jack came by on his daily rounds, I could not even do that. All I could tell him was that I had finally had my breakthrough, and I would never be the same. I truly felt changed. Ayahuasca had shown me many strange and wonderful things, places, and dimensions. She had taken me to realms beyond my wildest imaginings. Now she had somehow facilitated this unmasking of myself and others. This connection with the people in my life, energy to energy, in love and understanding, was more profound than any of my actual ayahuasca experiences, except perhaps the heart opening that don Emilio had facilitated within me. Ushpahuasa, too, must have been an enabling factor in the unfolding of this intuitive dance, for it is a plant medicine known for softening the emotional center and stoking the heart's fire.

I understood now that dreaming with ayahuasca, and generally working with plant teachers, is not an "experience"—not a series of discrete journeys—but rather is something much more fluid. It is art, or at least it is artistic. It is not a series of still lifes, not even a mosaic or a collage. It is not so discrete or disconnected an experience. It is more like finger painting, where you smear one color into the next, and you cannot paint the subject you call your "life" without also getting paint on yourself. Your own fingerprints are indelibly a part of the picture. As I had so often in the past, I remembered the words of César Calvo, from his book *The Three Halves of Ino Moxo,* when he wrote that with ayahuasca "if you deserve it, you can pass from dreams to reality, without leaving the dream."[1]

I understood that everything that has happened to me is connected, and there is some intelligence behind "it" all. For instance, the alien dream episodes had opened me to being more attentive to sound, when I suspect that my normal approach to the jungle would have been much more visual and intellectual. The message that I am, and we all are, studying through a field of love was fully realized in this last break-through experience, but I do not believe I would have been able to sur-render had not ayahuasca first tested the limits of my fears. This entire trip made sense at an energetic level, but it was also beyond all real explanation.

Monday night was another ayahuasca night, since we were doing back-to-back sessions. I was still so wrung out that I thought about not even going to the maloca, but I did. I decided not to drink, and Jack asked me to explain to the group why. I briefly described my experience of the night before, with Jack translating for don Luis and don Emilio. They nodded their heads, but neither commented. I was not the only one not drinking. Michelle decided not to either, and John decided to take a half dose. Michelle had come a long way since her first few days of discon-nection and discontent. She had bonded with the jungle, and although she was still eating next to nothing, her sessions had been going well, taking her deep into her interior and clearing blocks and old resistances. She and I talked almost every day, comparing notes and generally commiserating. She was more eager to get home than I was, however. By now I was thoroughly in tune with the jungle and wondered how I would feel leaving it for the "real" world.

This was the first time I had sat for a session and not participated. It was pleasant, and the icaros still pulled me out of myself—or deeper inward, as the case may be. I wondered a time or two if I had made a mistake by not drinking, since I felt I had finally bypassed, if not conquered, my fear. I wondered how the experience would be different now that I had surrendered once. Would I be able to again? Or would I find that my fears went deeper than I suspected, and that as the vine helped me dig deeper into myself I might find still more intractable layers of "stuff" I had to dislodge or dissolve within myself? I couldn't answer those questions then, and as of the writing of this book I have not journeyed again with ayahuasca, so I cannot answer them now. Mostly, during that last session, I let the icaros wash through me and I listened to the night sounds of the jungle. I also talked silently with the Mother of All Plants, thanking her for her gifts to us, acknowledging her power and the mystery of self she can reveal to us if we are only open to receiving, and marveling at the magnificence of the opportunity I had been given to experience this at all. It was a night of giving thanks.

Tuesday was our "down" day, a day of recovery. It was a day to physically and mentally prepare to leave the jungle, to return to the "real" world. Our morning meal was the first indication that we were in rapid transition: a bowl of watery soup, with bits of vegetables and flavored with salt and a trace of other spices. To call it delicious is understatement. The first mouthful was startling, as if my taste buds had been shocked back to life. Every subsequent mouthful was sheer sensory pleasure.

We pretty much kept to ourselves during the day. That evening we were to meet as a group at the kitchen camp for a feast—a real meal, the first one in ten days. Jack had called it a celebration, and he asked each of us to prepare something to share with the group—a dance, song, poem, or a reading from a book. At first I thought I might read a passage from César Calvo's *The Three Halves of Ino Moxo*, a sumptuously written book that deals in part with ayahuasca. In its magico-realism, its breathtakingly imagistic prose and mind-warping time shifts, this book is one of the finest renderings of the mysteries of the vine that I have read. This was my third reading, but now that I had experienced the vine myself I felt that I actually understood it. There were passages I would have liked to share with others in the group, but I decided, being a writer myself, that I would see what I could produce from out of my own inner experience. Two poems tumbled out of me, almost writing themselves.

When we met, the cooks were hard at work and the aromas that filled the kitchen camp were literally mouthwatering. We ate plate after plate of chicken and rice, a delicately flavored chicken soup, a salad of tomato and avocado drizzled with lemon juice, and slice after slice of bread. We laughed and talked and recounted adventures I have not detailed in this book, such as the four-foot anteater that climbed the tree next to Michelle's tambo in the middle of the night, scaring her and me half to death. Of Andrew roaring like a lion during one of our sessions. Of Steve's penchant for stripping naked or wearing nothing but a button-down shirt and standing like a swaying statue during sessions. Of Heni's and Patrick's prodigious capacity to purge. It was painful just listening to them, and there were nights I thought one or the other of them was actually going to toss up stomach lining. We talked of my haunted tambo.

After dinner the fun began—our offerings for the evening's entertainment. I don't remember what everyone did, but there were a few highlights that stand out for me. Heni recited from memory four or five short, hilarious poems a friend of hers had composed. Jeff, the lanky, rather quiet farmer, shocked us by standing and singing a Broadway tune. He was not very good, but we respected the guts it took to belt out the song without the voice to carry it off. Jack translated for don Luis as he recited two poems he had written, and we were all struck with their beauty. He is quite a gifted poet. Michelle read a long passage from Carl Jung that struck to the heart of both psychological and mystical experience. John played don Luis's Native American flute. I read my poems. I started with the serious poem, which for me epitomized my ultimate identification with the jungle and my varied ayahuasca journeys.

Green Magic

Away! Into the other world.
Thick liquid smells.
Carpet of sound.
Gorgeous green monotony.
River like coffee with cream.
Above—a living hood draws itself over me.
Beneath—decay alive with ants
turning death into life's fuel.
Almost!
Almost I can taste it.

A lupuna trunk,
peeling red paper,
housing a dwarf as testy
as the fire ants.
Fairy lights!
Schacapa rattle singing.
Blue! Brilliant blue.
Cerulean blue in flight—
the morphos dance on breezes
precious and few.

I am born anew—
with song!
Syllables trembling in the dark,
twisting into the pinks, blues, greens, yellows
of memory and desire.

A shimmering silver fear
that dark cannot dress.
The glimmering gold of ego.
Clasping!
Clasping!
Closing the lock
on my transcendental self.
Until syllables as keys
set free an unknown me,
and in the gasping of surrender
I unspin myself.

I couldn't leave the jungle without making an offering to the ubiquitous plantain, and my second poem exactly expressed my feelings.

Ode to a Plantain (Or, Funerary Song for a Fruit I Detest)

Like a dry, yellowed smile
you're the pretense of food.
Jealous cousin of the sweet banana,
you nourish with a gag.
Even boiled your moisture
is a tease.
So, please,
if the jungle ever suffers
a contagious blight,
please plantain,
give up the ghost
without a fight.
And leave this garden
of earthly delights
to fruits that better satisfy
human appetite.

Many of the group identified with my sentiment and appreciated its not so tongue-in-cheek humor. Don Luis was not among them. He loves plantains, and the next day, when we were back in Pucallpa, he actually ordered them in a restaurant.

We did not linger too long after our fun, as we had to be packed and ready to go by six the next morning. I slept fitfully that night, partly with anticipation of returning to the "normal" world and partly from regret that I would soon be leaving this one. I truly knew my leaving the jungle was more a "so long" than a "good-bye." It's not that I thought I would be back, but more that I knew that once the jungle had gotten into the girl, the girl would never truly leave the jungle.

The hike out was uneventful. We hiked to a different area of the riverbank than we had come in on, and a rather worn dugout canoe waited there for us. We had to walk out onto a slippery log to board, and once we were all in the canoe, it was unstable and tipsy. Twice I thought we were going to overturn, but the boatmen were skilled and kept us afloat. They motored us a short distance to what appeared to be a very small village with a very nice boat dock. I did not remember passing it on the way in, and it turned out that it is not really a village at all but a grouping of houses for the men who patrol don Luis's land when he is not there. (Despite the remoteness of don Luis's camp, there were two armed men patrolling during our stay, on the lookout for any dangers, from animals to the mahogany poachers who are notorious for sneaking into camps where Westerners might be and stealing whatever they can find.) At the dock, several men loaded another mahogany canoe with empty water containers and leftover supplies from our camp, and we transferred to a much newer and sturdier canoe ourselves. After a long and mostly silent river trip, we transferred to cars, and we arrived back in Pucallpa in early afternoon.

Our remaining few days in Peru were delightful. We visited a Shipibo village, where the children danced for us, performing the *citaraku,* the dance of the black ant, and other dances that told stories of village life. At one point they even pulled us into their dance, whose hopping steps combined with the intense heat left us breathless and sweating. The villagers had also displayed all kinds of their crafts around the village courtyard, and we shopped for a while, buying Shipibo pots and weavings with their classic geometric patterns. On the return boat ride from the Shipibo village, we spotted pink river dolphins, who rose out of the water playfully and then sped off with agile grace.

Back in Pucallpa, we visited the studio-school of Pablo Amaringo, a former ayahuasquero who is now an internationally known painter. His canvases are explosions of color and form, reproducing his many ayahuasca visions. Pablo was there, and he greeted us and talked briefly about his work as we approached in groups of two or three. His students' work was displayed on two walls of the small showroom, and some of them were there to talk of their technique and training. John and I purchased two student works, watercolors of the jungle, one showing the Amazon cast in morning light and the other in the purple shades of dusk. On the other two walls of the showroom hung Pablo's magnificent works. He brought several other, smaller paintings down from his studio to show us, and Andrew and Michelle purchased one.

Before we knew it, two more days had passed and we were headed to the airport. Security was tight, and the officials checked our documents carefully and dug with more than normal care through our bags of smelly clothes, reminding me that we were back in the "real" world and that it was now a post–September 11 world. I could not identify with this world. The aura of the jungle still enveloped me, and I moved as if in a dream. Nothing bothered me, and although I usually walk fast and talk fast and like to get things done, I now moved like a slow stream, flowing at a more natural pace, more or less meandering through the world.

It took weeks before I felt at all connected with the everyday world again, and still longer for me to get back into its groove. Curiously, as real as the jungle still was to me upon my return home, as friends came by to see John and me, I talked about the jungle trip and ayahuasca as if it had been a two-week dream. But privately I thought about it differently, and certainly felt it differently. To this day, that time in the home of the Mother of All Plants remains with me like a quiet hum in my ears. Sometimes, when I am lying in bed in the dark, I can hear my blood swooshing through my body. It is a distinctive sound I hear only in one ear. But the jungle is like that—a lifeblood pumping through my veins and audible when I am quiet. Ayahuasca is another story, which tells a different tale. While it too is a part of me, infused at some deep DNA level within my being, it has not become my friend, as I feel the jungle—or at least the jungle's ambiance—has. Ayahuasca is a maestro, and I can only befriend it as I would a beloved but intimidating teacher: with respect, with a bit of wariness, with the understanding that I will never be the recipient of all it has to offer, but feeling honored, or lucky, to have been under its tutelage at all.

13

A Summing Up

The sun is the master of yagé [ayahuasca] and that's why
yagé has no end, because it's the patron of everything.
That's why it has a ray of light for everyone, a ray of light
like the sun which means the visions, whether they're good
or bad, but it has a ray of light for everybody.

—Don Hilario Peña, Columbian healer,
in *Ayahuasca Reader*

I promised I would come full circle and discuss what I make of all this: of the diet retreat, of the jungle, of the Vine of the Soul. Richard Evans Schultes and his coauthors write in *Plants of the Gods,* "The possibility of changing the wavelength setting on the 'ego-receiver,' and, with this, to produce changes in the awareness of reality, constitutes the real significance of hallucinogens. This ability to create new and different images of the world is why hallucinogenic plants were, and still are, regarded as sacred."[1]

Perhaps my most important lesson while working with ayahuasca was understanding that it is indeed a sacred undertaking. While it is definitely a psychological experience, capable of scrubbing away any detritus that obscures the content of at least portions of our unconscious, it also allows the clear light of a distinct, and I daresay divine, Otherness to shine through. Huston Smith, the eminent scholar of world religions and a psychonaut himself, describes how for most of us our inner divinity is as "a lantern . . . coated with dust and dirt, and finally caked to the point where the light within it is totally concealed."[2] As Mother Ayahuasca so pointedly made clear to me, just about any-thing—from meditation to prayer to tai chi—can be used to cleanse our inner and outer lenses. For me, ayahuasca was a heavy-duty solvent, dissolving resistances that might have taken much longer to discover, never mind overcome, using other means.

The territory such opinions lead us into is quite slippery, and the questions we must put to ourselves as we attempt to keep our footing only make our path even slicker. As Smith asks, "What part do chemi-cals, replacing angels as divine intermediaries, play in it?"[3] The "it" to which Smith refers is the potential change in our inner lives and, ulti-mately, one hopes, in our outer lives as well. The answers are multiple, applying to different layers of mind and self. Smith continues, "The drugs do not knock this consciousness [our rational, observing self] out, but while they leave it operative they also activate areas of the brain that normally lie below its threshold."[4] One of these multiple layers is the transpersonal, that place within ourselves from where we loose the bounds of the physical and free ourselves to the unbounded, infinite, and eternal. Professor Benny Shanon expands on this point by explain-ing his own transformation. "Personally, if I were to pick one single effect of Ayahuasca that had the most important impact on my life . . . I would say that before my encounter with the brew I was an atheist . . . and when I returned back home after my long journey in South America, I no longer was one. Likewise, a significant number of inform-ants I have interviewed indicated that the main lesson they received from Ayahuasca was religious or spiritual."[5]

Ayahuasca, like many other entheogens, and spiritual and energy practices, not only can grant us freer access to what may be hidden within us but also may be a doorway itself to other realms, dimensions, nonphysical modes of being, and connections to the vast network of Life. What we do with that access is up to us, and this is where I believe the real controversy arises. I again defer to Smith to further this line of inquiry: "The conclusion to which the evidence seems currently to point is that it is indeed possible for chemicals to enhance religious life, but only when they are set within the context of faith (conviction that what they disclose is true) and discipline (exercise of the will toward fulfilling what the disclosures ask of us)."[6] I could not agree more. No matter how you view ayahuasca—as sacred plant teacher or chemical messenger—it teaches us through the lens of our own beliefs. If we are curiosity seekers only, the vine will provide much to amuse and provoke us, but all we will come away with is an accumulation of good stories. If we are psychologically oriented, we can lie upon this green chemical couch to access our wounds, expose our repressions, encounter our resistances, and so make progress toward living a more emotionally authentic and personally satisfying life. However, if we approach ayahuasca as the Vine of the Soul, as a sentient being in its own right, one possessed of both power and light, then it becomes a teacher to us as we journey along a spiritual path.

Even this point is complicated, however, by other concerns and questions, such as, Is the spiritual experience alone enough to effect change? In the collection of essays *Entheogens and the Future of Religion*, multiple authors answer this question, all reaching much the same conclusion: The "'spiritual experience' alone, even repeated, is not the basis of becoming a better and more useful person. Rather, psychedelic insights tempered and put into practice using ethical and moral considerations appears the best way to harness the power of psychedelic drugs."[7] I agree.

In my own case, I had many opportunities to experience ayahuasca before I ever agreed to partake of it. Why did I delay my experience for so long? Because I sensed, or rather admitted, that I was not ready, even though I was tempted. My path—which includes the palimpsest of my Catholic upbringing, intellectual explorations of consciousness research, forays into the worldviews and spiritual practices of native North American and Eastern cultures, and immersion in the Andean spiritual arts—has taught me that a spiritual experience is best considered not as an *effect* but as a *cause*. In other words, such experiences—whether metaphysical, transcendental, even paranormal—are neither goals we aim to achieve nor destinations we seek to arrive at. They are, rather, gifts we learn to accept—and rather humbly at that. Supernatural or transformational experiences are not, as so many believe, indications of our worthiness. If we get caught in this snare of ego, then we accumulate these experiences like trophies to display upon our metaphysical mantles.*

Instead, we must be humbled by them, reading them for clues as to our *readiness* for living as sacred beings, for becoming serious explorers of the vastness of our own personal potentials and for applying our insights in our everyday lives. If we are not ready for such exploration, we tend to wear such an experience like a badge of shamanic or spiritual honor. If, however, we are ready, then the experience can be a catalyst for examining what has been unexamined within us, for awakening to our full potential, for finding the courage to change and even to heal, and certainly for learning to walk in the world in a more hopeful and loving way.

But inner experiences such as we can have with ayahuasca can become the cause of such change only if we can incorporate their messages and influences into our everyday lives. We have to first know— and then do. And sometimes we have to do even if we are not sure we know. An ayahuasca experience is simply part of a continuum of learning, each one a page in the Book of Self we are authoring. I am emphasizing this admittedly ambiguous distinction between effect and cause because I believe the nuance is crucial for understanding how we move from simply having an experience to living what we have experienced. We can take the easy route and make a checklist of our experiences, rather like putting together a metaphysical résumé, or we can undertake the challenge of alchemically allowing them to transmute our way of

---

* Roger Walsh has a similar opinion: "For those people who are graced with the mystical experience—whether induced spontaneously, contemplatively, or chemically—the crucial question is what to do with it. It can be allowed to fade; it can be ignored or even dismissed, or perhaps clung to as a psychological or spiritual trophy. Or it can be consciously used as a source of inspiration and guidance to direct one's life along more beneficial directions." (Roger Walsh, "Mysticism, Contemplative and Chemical," in *Zig Zag Zen*, 31).

being. The simplest way to make this distinction is to understand that an effect delineates and divides, whereas a cause joins and connects. To my mind, connection is the aim of any metaphysical exploration, psychedelic or otherwise.

My experiences with ayahuasca, I see clearly in hindsight and saw dimly while undergoing them, were the pages of myself that I was writing. To push the boundaries of this metaphor, Mother Ayahuasca was the ink in the pen of Self, helping me write a more coherent life narrative. But *I* am the storyteller, not she, and only I can script the story that I choose to tell.

As much as I believe what I just wrote, I also have to flip that opinion on its head, for another of the insights I gained from my jungle ayahuasca experiences is that our personal stories and histories are chimeras. For instance, because of my dream-vision, with its suggestion of a suppressed childhood memory, and Phil's and others' opinions that memory retrieval was one of the reasons I was drawn to working with ayahuasca, I had an expectation that ayahuasca and ushpahausa would help me remember. But they did not. I don't believe now there ever was a traumatic, personal memory waiting to be retrieved. Instead, I see that the lesson was about my need to release my identification with a personal past in order to view myself as more than my story. Ayahuasca plunged me into the world of paradox, where self and Other were not clearly delineated and where meanings were turned inside out. During my first ayahuasca experience, I was not drawn down into the basement of my childhood home, but propelled outward into the cosmos to gain a larger, more archetypal perspective of one stream of history (or her-story, as was the case in that particular vision). From this vantage, it became clearer to me that the personal past becomes subsumed into the larger voice of the collective, which itself is an echo—the remnant of the voice, not the voice itself. And when ayahuasca took me to realms beyond the human, I could no longer even understand the story, and that terrified me. The fear, I see now, was engendered both by the shattering of my self-image and the struggle to reconcile self and Other.

When I contemplate those otherworldly journeys with ayahuasca, I cannot deny that I was being shown, or even taken to, a different reality than my own—and I mean that quite literally, for I believe that the other dimensions and even some of the spirits are physically real. But I was also aware that I was creating my experience according to the "set" of my own mind and psyche, and according to the measure of my personal capacity for understanding, cognitively and spiritually. I realize now, a year after experiencing it, that the ground of being I touched through the impersonal "machines of life" of my first journey—that detached, impartial, non-human-feeling creative energy that so terrified me—may actually be the force of unconditional love. It is a kind of energy so beyond our human conception of love that it felt and appeared alien to me. If, as the man in my dream-vision told me, I am studying through the field of love, then this is the awesome ground of universal love from which the stream of the more human understanding and expression of love springs. But still, at that moment of touching the ineffable, I had to own the fear. Just as in other ayahuasca journeys I had to own the ego, the control issues, and the cockroaches. But I also had to own the fairies, the gorgeously dancing insects, the great expanse of the cosmos, the light that shown in my own heart. I had to own them all, and I had to learn not to judge them. Ugly, beautiful, wounding, healing, weak, strong, frightening, illuminating: in the end, it was the dissolving of the boundaries of such labels—a lesson I have had to receive repeatedly through various spiritual practices—that allowed me finally to surrender to myself and so to gather myself together. Once I could impartially own what was both within me and without me, I could not help but be changed—and made more whole than I was before. And so my experiences merge into who I am and are not simply things I have done.

So, ayahuasca has helped me see with new eyes, listen with new ears, and understand with a new respect for what is possible. During this year of processing my jungle ayahuasca experiences, I have also asked new questions of myself about myself. For me, at least, despite glimpsing my wholeness while in an altered state, it is difficult to consistently live the wholeness of myself in the here and now, and so I struggle still with self-compartmentalization. The following list includes, but by no means exhausts, the areas of self I have been exploring in relation to what I was shown by Mother Ayahuasca: What aspect(s) of myself was I valorizing then and am I now showing myself? Why am I showing myself this part of myself? How is this part connected to all the other parts of myself? How is this part a blessing? How have I seen it as an obstacle or wound? What am I telling myself that I think about myself? That I feel about myself? That I believe about myself? What am I still ignoring or denying about myself? What am I ready to acknowledge and/or heal? How is this life I am living connected to and contributing to the larger whole? The questions go on and on. I understand that any answers to these questions will be provisional; they will keep changing as I continue along my spiritual path. As I mature, I will see that what I thought was an answer was not, or at least was not complete. I will then, if I am to be faithful to my claim to want to live as a sacred human being, have to integrate the new answer into my life, and that will be the impetus of new change and, I hope, new growth.

I can attest that this process of deep change is neither easy nor necessarily pleasant. As a teacher of the spiritual arts, one of the points I make in my lectures and workshops is that to commit to walking as a sacred being is the toughest commitment you can make to yourself—and to others. It is not about putting on rose-colored glasses, expecting your life to suddenly change for the better. Many spiritual teachers tell us that we create, or cocreate, our reality, and most of us expect to create a reality that showers us with love, abundance, and fulfillment. But what so many teachers fail to warn us of is that in all probability before the dawn we will experience the dark. In my experience, and in that of so many of my friends and students, sincerely undertaking a spiritual practice and attempting to live it often precipitates a descent into chaos—that place where "things fall apart; the centre cannot hold." When we are serious about claiming our divinity, we are usually first shown the depths of our humanness. We each have to own our shadow and not polarize it by onerously labeling what we find there or deflating ourselves through harsh self-judgment. Then we usually have to wallow around in that inner darkness for a while.

To undertake this process, we must have courage—the courage to claim ourselves as who we really are. That phrase is not just so much psychobabble. It can resonate quite painfully through our lives when we make a commitment to gathering the disparate aspects of ourselves together. As we make choices that seem counter to common sense as our larger society sees it, we often find ourselves alone and feeling unfairly judged. Some of the issues we must objectively consider are whether the relationships we are in are healthy, whether the place we live is the place we should be and indeed want to be, and whether the way we serve/work is personally fulfilling and overall adding benefit to our families, communities, and the world at large. Asking tough questions of ourselves and making changes in order to live an authentic life can mean abandoning everything that feels safe and familiar. But the result is that we finally begin to realize that the perceived obstacles in our lives are really opportunities. They are the lessons we give ourselves and that are so useful for our spiritual growth. To be clear-seeing, we have to first find the light that casts the shadows, and not reject or ignore those shadows. This is a process of self-liberation, and it is a process that frightens established authority. To my mind, one of the reasons society at large fears psychedelics is because of the loss of control they may engender. This loss of control, however, is not of one's sanity, ethics, or morals but of one's slavish conformity to consensus reality. Few things threaten a parent, priest, or politician more than a child's, parishioner's, or constituent's expanded capacity for independent thinking.*

---

* In a *Village Voice* article titled "The State of the Stone" (which I discovered while searching the Academic Search Elite online database), reporter Richard Gehr paraphrases researchers and psychonauts such as Jonathan Ott, who coined the term *entheogen,* and Terence McKenna as asserting that "humans have lost their connection to land and roots . . . and psychedelics are the most effective way to regain this link. Psychedelics take us deeper into ourselves and our environment. Nothing in organized religion quite matches the power of a cosmic wave of electric bliss—or the sudden appearance of your darkest shadow. These compounds have a revolutionary capacity to obliterate bonds of control. Thus the fear and loathing with which they are regarded by the state. (Psychedelics rarely harm users, except those unfortunates who've ignored or, worse, never had the opportunity, thanks to head-hiding programs like DARE, to learn about the respect they should be accorded.)" *Village Voice* 41, no. 45 (November 5, 1996).

I view the sacramental use of ayahuasca—and the responsible use of other entheogens—as one of many possible paths to such self-liberation, although it is fraught with ambiguity. This is where personal ethics come into play. Indigenous ayahuasqueros will tell you that the path to knowledge is forked—there cannot be light without darkness. For instance, on the shamanic path, according to one's intentions, one may work as a shaman or a sorcerer. The energies with which they work are the same. Energy is just energy—it has no moral category. Still, in the face of such ambiguity, we must not hesitate. My most instructive journeys were not the blissful ones but the terrifying ones, for there I came face-to-face with my fears, psychic wounds, self-doubts—with how I did not love myself and so was fragmenting my Self. I saw how I could honor these darker parts of myself as teachers.

For me, experiencing ayahuasca was voluntarily abandoning all that was safe and familiar. But heading out to the territory of the unknown helped me to enlarge not only the scope of what is possible for me but also what is possible for our world. Some segments of our society would see ayahuasca only as a hallucinogenic drug, and so label it a green demon. But I see it as green magic. While journeying with ayahuasca, it is difficult to discern the illusionary from the real, and perhaps at heart there is no difference, but to my mind, just being open to asking the question frees us to the wonders of being.

I concur with this assessment. The societal anxiety raised by the use of psychoactive substances, and certainly by their use as entheogens, is exacerbated and perpetuated by the media's erroneous and hyperbolic reporting (now and during decades past) about the "dangers" of psychedelics. Much of the latest research has shown that earlier reports of chromosomal damage and youths flinging themselves from windows or ending up in mental institutions are fallacious. Used responsibly, and even therapeutically, psychedelics are quite safe and can provide significant personal benefit. Media, government, and our society at large simply refuse to distinguish between abuse of psychedelics and the sacramental use of such substances. For these reasons and others, we are unwilling to have a serious and considered discussion about the possible beneficial uses of psychedelics. For more on this subject, see the excellent volume of essays *Entheogens and the Future of Religion*, edited by Robert Forte.

As Professor Benny Shannon reminds us, "drinking Ayahuasca is not a game. It should not be taken lightly, it should not be played with in an irresponsible manner. . . . If not used with prudence, the brew can exact a price, even a heavy one. One should partake of it only when one is in a good state of mind, prepared both physically and psychologically, under the guidance of a competent person whom one trusts."[8] It was because I intuited this about ayahuasca that I chose to partake of it only under these circumstances, and it was under these conditions that I journeyed to the Amazon to study with ayahuasca in the "old way." Indeed, part of what most profoundly changed me was meeting Mother Ayahuasca on her home turf. I approached the diet retreat in the jungle as a sacred responsibility, a self-purification process that was both physical and energetic. This retreat helped me be receptive to the self that appears separate and to the Self that is never separate in a way that experiencing ayahuasca here in the States, over the course of an evening, could not.

The isolation in the jungle was a test at many levels, and a test I could not study for in advance—but that in itself was part of its efficacy. The jungle was sensory in ways I could not have imagined, an opening not only of my ears but also of my heart. The alien in my dream-vision asked me if I was ready finally to hear the sounds. That question originally threw me into panic. But it turns out I was ready after all, and the music of the jungle turned out to be the song of myself. My relationship with the jungle was reciprocal: I learned to relax—even to immerse myself—in its mystery and it insinuated itself in me, changing forever the cadence of my inner rhythms. Senses also merged and heightened through the songs of the plants. The ayahuasqueros' icaros were alchemical, turning sounds into a visual language of color and pattern and, ultimately, into feelings and knowings. Like tongues of fire, the icaros both anointed me and forged within me finer ways of seeing, feeling, and understanding. For these reasons and more, I believe that the traditional ayahuasca ceremony, with its sometimes demanding requirements, is a useful way to "dream" yourself to life. While I understand that the opportunity to undertake such a retreat may not be realistic for most people, I do think that we should try to reproduce the ritual tradition as closely as we can if we are using ayahuasca on a regular or long-term basis.*

There is no end to a "summing up" of spiritual experience, for, as in mathematics, there is always one more quantity that can be added to the previous sum. In this chapter I have summarized some of what I now feel and understand about ayahuasca, from my limited experience. Ask me in another year and no doubt I will have come to new understandings, insights, conclusions. The gathering of self is not an endeavor that is worked quickly or to a specified end. It is ongoing, as all things of the spirit must be. And so I have been able to offer only a provisional summing up, and one that might not be altogether philosophically satisfying.

The bottom line is that the Mother of the Voice in the Ear offered me a new perspective about how I fragment myself and how I can go about gathering myself back together. She provided another perspective from which to view myself as part of the greater whole. The intensity of the experiences, and the speed at which they opened my inner eyes, was far greater than in any other spiritual practice I have undertaken. The Vine of the Soul shows us ourselves and each other with such clarity that it is hard to deny or forget the lessons over the course of time.

---

* I believe that the approach to using ayahuasca and the conditions under which it is used should be modeled as closely as possible after the ancient ayahuasca ritual. I understand how difficult this is, especially for the clinical use of this and other psychoactive substances. Dr. Rick Strassman's clinical studies provide a good example of what can happen when set and setting are sacrificed in the name of scientific procedure. See his book *DMT: The Spirit Molecule.* My own reservations about the protocol Strassman used in his clinical trials and my general opinions about the conclusions he reached are eloquently elucidated by Timothy White, the editor of *Shaman's Drum.* I agree with almost everything White has to say about Strassman's protocol, especially White's critique of the sterile setting within which the research was carried out, the high doses some of the participants were given, and the short time frames over which they were administered. It is no surprise that most of the participants in that study did not easily integrate their experiences into their everyday lives. See Timothy White, "In Quest of Endogenous Doorways to Spirit: A Review of *DMT: The Spirit Molecule* by Rick Strassman, M.D.," *Shaman's Drum* 62 (2002), 63–68.

It is that experience of connection—among the seemingly disparate aspects of myself and between myself and others—that was most useful to me.

Jack said ayahuasca is a group experience. At first I could not understand that, for it is such an intensely personal journey. But when we go in, we also go out. And no matter which direction we go, ayahuasca reveals, as do most religions and sacraments, that we are not separate. The pronoun of the ayahuasca journey is not *me* but *we*. We are all wounded, we are all healed. We are all lost, we are all found. We are all damned, we are all saved. We are all separate, we are all one. By helping us heal as individuals, by gathering together the varied aspects of the self, ayahuasca shows us how one person's healing contributes to the healing of us all, how our self is really part of a larger Self. When don Emilio's breath illuminated my heart, I saw and felt the heart that beats in the one collective body. When the fairies whisked me into the jungle, I was joined by many of the people in my life, and we were one mind, communicating with itself. Their gifts and wounds were mine as well. Ayahuasca showed me that we are all one and the same, yet glorious in our individuality. I know this will sound like shopworn metaphysics to some readers, but it is true to my experience, and that is all I promised to offer in this book.

I opened this book with Wallace Stevens, and I will close with him, for his poetry, which can sometimes be so heady, reveals my heart. When all is said and done, ayahuasca, for me, accomplishes its magic when within the dreamer:

> *Something imagined . . . has been washed away.*
> *A clearness has returned. It stands restored.*
> *It is not an empty clearness, a bottomless sight.*
> *It is a visibility of thought,*
> *In which hundreds of eyes, in one mind, see at once.*[9]

Notes

Introduction

1. Wallace Stevens, *The Palm at the End of the Mind: Selected Poems and a Play*, ed. Holly Stevens (New York: Random House, Vintage Books, 1972), 545.

2. Ibid., "Description without Place," part 6, 275–76.

3. See Rick Strassman, M.D., *DMT: The Spirit Molecule: A Doctor's Revolutionary Research into the Biology of Near-Death and Mystical Experiences* (Rochester, Vt.: Park Street Press, 2001).

Chapter 1

1. Wade Davis, *One River: Explorations and Discoveries in the Amazon Rain Forest* (New York: Simon & Schuster, 1996), 153.

2. Ibid., 194.

Chapter 2

1. Davis, *One River*, 37–38.

2. Ram Dass, foreword to Daniel Goleman, *The Meditative Mind: The Varieties of Meditative Experience* (New York: Jeremy P. Tarcher, 1988), xi.

3. Respectively, see "Jaguar-Becoming" by William Torres C., 107–12, and "A Visit to the Second Heaven: A Siona Narrative of the *Yagé* Experience" by E. Jean Matteson Langdon, 21–30, both in *Ayahuasca Reader: Encounters with the Amazon's Sacred Vine*, eds. Luis Eduardo Luna and Steven F. White (Santa Fe: Synergetic Press, 2000).

4. César Calvo, *The Three Halves of Ino Moxo: Teachings of the Wizard of the Upper Amazon*, trans. Kenneth A. Symington (Rochester, Vt.: Inner Traditions, 1995), 177.

5. Carol Cumes and Rómulo Lizárraga Valencia, *Pachamama's Children: Earth Mother and Her Children of the Andes of Peru* (St. Paul, Minn.: Lewellyn, 1995), 23.

6. See Jeremy Narby, *The Cosmic Serpent: DNA and the Origins of Knowledge* (New York: Jeremy P. Tarcher, 1999).

7. Quoted in Goleman, *Meditative Mind*, 159–60.

8. Benny Shanon, *Antipodes of the Mind: Charting the Phenomenology of the Ayahuasca Experience* (Oxford: Oxford University Press, 2002), 317.

9. Ibid., 396.

10. Ibid., 401.

11. Ibid., 374.

12. My primary sources for this discussion include Paul Devereux, *The Long Trip: A Prehistory of Psychedelia* (New York: Penguin Putnam, 1997); various essays in Ralph Metzner, ed., *Ayahuasca: Human Consciousness and the Spirits of Nature* (New York: Thunder's Mouth Press, 1999); Richard Evans Schultes and Robert F. Raffauf, *Vine of the Soul: Medicine Men, Their Plants and Rituals in the Colombian Amazonia* (Oracle, Ariz.: Synergetic Press, 1992); and Dennis McKenna, J. C. Callaway, and Charles S. Grob, "The Scientific Investigation of Ayahuasca: A Review of Past and Current Research" (online:www.csh.umn.edu/Education/CSpH_5401/AyahuascaHR.htm).

13. J. C. Callaway, "Phytochemistry and Neuropharmacology of Ayahuasca," in *Ayahuasca: Human Consciousness and the Spirits of Nature*, ed. Ralph Metzner (New York: Thunder's Mouth Press, 1999), 256.

14. Ibid., 253.

15. Narby, *Cosmic Serpent*, 117.

16. Ibid., 157.

17. Paul Devereux, *The Long Trip: A Prehistory of Psychedelia* (New York: Penguin Putnam, 1997), 242.

Chapter 4

1. Terence McKenna, *The Archaic Revival: Speculations on Psychedelic Mushrooms, the Amazon, Virtual Reality, UFOs, Evolution, Shamanism, the Rebirth of the Goddess, and the End of History* (New York: HarperCollins, 1991), 69.

2. Shanon, *Antipodes of the Mind*, 324–28.

3. Ibid., 328. Brackets in the original.

4. Ibid., 358.

Chapter 6

1. Tom Robbins, *Fierce Invalids Home from Hot Climates* (New York: Bantam Books, 2000), 43.

Chapter 8

1. Calvo, *Three Halves,* 6.

Chapter 12

1. Calvo, *Three Halves,* 6.

Chapter 13

1. Richard Evans Schultes, Albert Hofmann, and Christian Rätsch, *Plants of the Gods: Their Sacred, Healing, and Hallucinogenic Powers* (rev. and expanded ed., Rochester, Vt.: Healing Arts Press, 2001), 188.

2. Huston Smith, *Cleansing the Doors of Perception: The Religious Significance of Entheogenic Plants and Chemicals* (New York: Jeremy P. Tarcher, 2000), 156.

3. Ibid., 15.

4. Ibid., 29.

5. Shanon, *Antipodes of the Mind,* 260.

6. Smith, *Cleansing the Doors of Perception,* 31.

7. Rick J. Strassman, "Biomedical Research with Psychedelics: Current Models and Future Prospects," in *Entheogens and the Future of Religion,* ed. Robert Forte (San Francisco: Council on Spiritual Practices, 1997), 159.

8. Shanon, *Antipodes of the Mind,* 330.

9. Stevens, "An Ordinary Evening in New Haven," in *The Palm,* 350–51.

Bibliography

Badiner, Allan Hunt, ed. *Zig Zag Zen: Buddhism and Psychedelics*. San Francisco: Chronicle Books, 2002.

Callaway, J. C. "Phytochemistry and Neuropharmacology of Ayahuasca." In *Ayahuasca: Human Consciousness and the Spirits of Nature,* edited by Ralph Metzner. New York: Thunder's Mouth Press, 1999.

Calvo, César. *The Three Halves of Ino Moxo: Teachings of the Wizard of the Upper Amazon,* translated by Kenneth A. Symington. Rochester, Vt.: Inner Traditions, 1995. (First published in Spanish as *Las tres mitades de Ino Moxo*. Iquitos, Peru: Proceso Editores, 1981.)

Cumes, Carol, and Rómulo Lizárraga Valencia. *Pachamama's Children: Earth Mother and Her Children of the Andes of Peru*. St. Paul, Minn.: Llewellyn, 1995. (Republished by Llewellyn as *Journey to Machu Picchu: Spiritual Wisdom from the Andes*, 1998.)

Davis, Wade. *One River: Explorations and Discoveries in the Amazon Rain Forest*. New York: Simon & Schuster, 1996.

DeKorne, Jim. *Psychedelic Shamanism: The Cultivation, Preparation, and Shamanic Use of Psychotropic Plants.* Port Townsend, Wash.: Breakout Productions, 1994.

Devereux, Paul. *The Long Trip: A Prehistory of Psychedelia*. New York: Penguin Putnam, 1997.

Forte, Robert, ed. *Entheogens and the Future of Religion*. San Francisco: Council on Spiritual Practices, 1997.

Gehr, Richard. "The State of the Stone: A Psychedelic Reformation Is Underway: A Report from the Edge." *Village Voice* 41, no. 45 (November 11, 1996): 33–36. (Available online through Academic Research Elite database.)

Goleman, Daniel. *The Meditative Mind: The Varieties of Meditative Experience*. New York: Jeremy P. Tarcher, 1988.

Hayes, Charles, ed. *Tripping: An Anthology of True-Life Psychedelic Adventures*. New York: Penguin Books, 2000.

"Herbal Drugs of Abuse: Ayahuasca Vine (or 'Yage')." Online from Northern Illinois University: Student Affairs, Counseling and Student Development Center, 2001, at www.stuaff.niu.edu/csdc/herbaldrugs.htm.

Langdon, E. Jean Matteson. "A Visit to the Second Heaven: A Siona Narrative of the *Yagé* Experience." In *Ayahuasca Reader: Encounters with the Amazon's Sacred Vine*, edited by Luis Eduardo Luna and Steven F. White. Santa Fe: Synergetic Press, 2000.

Luna, Luis Eduardo, and Steven F. White, eds. *Ayahuasca Reader: Encounters with the Amazon's Sacred Vine*. Sante Fe: Synergetic Press, 2000.

Mabit, Jacques, Rosa Grove, and Joaquin Vega. "Takawasi: The Use of Amazonian Shamanism to Rehabilitate Drug Addicts." In *Yearbook of Cross-Cultural Medicine and Psychotherapy*, edited by Michael Winkleman and Walter Andritzky, 1995.

McKenna, Dennis, J. C. Callaway, and Charles S. Grob. "The Scientific Investigation of Ayahuasca: A Review of Past and Current Research." Online at www.csh.umn.edu/Education/CSpH_5401/AyahuascaHR.htm.

McKenna, Terence. *The Archaic Revival: Speculations on Psychedelic Mushrooms, the Amazon, Virtual Reality, UFOs, Evolution, Shamanism, the Rebirth of the Goddess, and the End of History*. New York: HarperCollins, 1991.

Metzner, Ralph, ed. *Ayahuasca: Human Consciousness and the Spirits of Nature*. New York: Thunder's Mouth Press, 1999.

Meier, Brigid. "Relative Truth." In *Zig Zag Zen: Buddhism and Psychedelics*, edited by Allan Hunt Badiner. San Francisco: Chronicle Books, 2002.

Narby, Jeremy. *The Cosmic Serpent: DNA and the Origins of Knowledge*. New York: Jeremy P. Tarcher, 1999.

Narby, Jeremy, and Francis Huxley, eds. *Shamans Through Time: Five Hundred Years on the Path to Knowledge*. New York: Jeremy P. Tarcher, 2001.

Pinchbeck, Daniel. *Breaking Open the Head: A Psychedelic Journey into the Heart of Contemporary Shamanism*. New York: Broadway Books, 2002.

Polari de Alverga, Alex. *Forest of Visions: Ayahuasca, Amazonian Spirituality, and the Santo Daime Tradition*, edited by Steven White, translated by Rosana Workman. Rochester, Vt.: Park Street Press, 1999.

"Research/Clinical News: Secrets of Two Medicinal Plants May Help Psychiatric Researchers." *Psychiatric News,* August 21, 1998. (Online version at www.psych.org/pnews/98-08-21/two.html.)

Robbins, Tom. *Fierce Invalids Home from Hot Climates.* New York: Bantam Books, 2000.

Schultes, Richard Evans, Albert Hofmann, and Christian Rätsch. *Plants of the Gods: Their Sacred, Healing, and Hallucinogenic Powers.* Revised and expanded edition. Rochester, Vt.: Healing Arts Press, 2001.

Schultes, Richard Evans, and Robert F. Raffauf. *Vine of the Soul: Medicine Men, Their Plants and Rituals in the Colombian Amazonia.* Oracle, Ariz.: Synergetic Press, 1992.

Shanon, Benny. *The Antipodes of the Mind: Charting the Phenomenology of the Ayahuasca Experience.* Oxford: Oxford University Press, 2002.

Smith, Huston. *Cleansing the Doors of Perception: The Religious Significance of Entheogenic Plants and Chemicals.* New York: Jeremy P. Tarcher, 2000.

Statnekov, Daniel. *Animated Earth.* Berkeley: North Atlantic Books, 1987.

Stevens, Wallace. *The Palm at the End of the Mind: Selected Poems and a Play,* edited by Holly Stevens. New York: Random House, Vintage Books, 1972.

Strassman, Rick J., M.D. "Biomedical Research with Psychedelics: Current Models and Future Prospects." In *Entheogens and the Future of Religion,* edited by Robert Forte. San Francisco: Council on Spiritual Practices, 1997.

———. *DMT: The Spirit Molecule: A Doctor's Revolutionary Research into the Biology of Near-Death and Mystical Experiences.* Rochester, Vt.: Park Street Press, 2001.

Topping, Donald M. "Making Friends with Cancer and Ayahuasca." *Shaman's Drum* 55 (2000): 33–39.

Torres C., William. "Jaguar-Becoming." In *Ayahuasca Reader: Encounters with the Amazon's Sacred Vine,* edited by Luis Eduardo Luna and Steven F. White. Santa Fe: Synergetic Press, 2000.

Walsh, Roger. "Mysticism, Contemplative and Chemical." In *Zig Zag Zen: Buddhism and Psychedelics,* edited by Allan Hunt Badiner. San Francisco: Chronicle Books, 2002.

White, Timothy. "In Quest of Endogenous Doorways to Spirit: A Review of *DMT: The Spirit Molecule* by Rick Strassman, M.D." *Shaman's Drum,* 62 (2002): 63–68.

BOOKS OF RELATED INTEREST

FOREST OF VISIONS
Ayahuasca, Amazonian Spirituality, and the Santo Daime Tradition
by Alex Polari de Alverga

PLANTS OF THE GODS
Their Sacred, Healing, and Hallucinogenic Powers
by Richard Evans Schultes, Albert Hofmann, and Christian Rätsch

DMT: THE SPIRIT MOLECULE
*A Doctor's Revolutionary Research into the Biology of
Near-Death and Mystical Experiences*
by Rick Strassman, M.D.

LSD, SPIRITUALITY, AND THE CREATIVE PROCESS
Based on the Groundbreaking Research of Oscar Janiger, M.D.
by Marlene Dobkin de Rios, Ph.D., and Oscar Janiger, M.D.

ECSTASY: THE COMPLETE GUIDE
A Comprehensive Look at the Risks and Benefits of MDMA
Edited by Julie Holland, M.D.

MAGIC MUSHROOMS IN RELIGION AND ALCHEMY
by Clark Heinrich

MOKSHA
*Aldous Huxley's Classic Writings on Psychedelics
and the Visionary Experience*
by Aldous Huxley
Edited by Michael Horowitz and Cynthia Palmer

TRANSFIGURATIONS
by Alex Grey

Inner Traditions • Bear & Company
P.O. Box 388
Rochester, VT 05767
1-800-246-8648
www.InnerTraditions.com

Or contact your local bookseller